ARM Assembly Language
- an Introduction

J. R. Gibson

Department of Electrical Engineering and Electronics
The University of Liverpool

ISBN 978-1-84753-696-9

Preface

Most students following electronics or computer science courses study at least one module that introduces programming using assembly language. Some academics suggest that assembly language should not be taught. However, while a high level language should be used for most applications, there are situations where it is necessary to prepare a small section of program in assembly language; also an introduction to assembly language assists in studying computer architecture.

When learning to use an assembly language it is essential to perform exercises using the language. As a consequence most courses are restricted to the study of assembly language for one particular type of central processing unit, CPU. This is not ideal; however introduction of assembly language programming in a general manner to large groups of students has rarely been very successful.

Over many years, using several CPU types, it was not often possible to suggest introductory books to accompany courses. Books exist for a small number of CPUs but, at the time of writing, no introductory assembly language text is available for the family of CPUs, cores, designed by ARM Holdings plc.

The existence of the ARM core is not well known to the general public although most people probably own at least one. They are the most widely used type of CPU incorporated as a component within electronic products. For example most cellphone handsets incorporate an ARM core and recently Apple Inc., have had commercial success with the iPod range of products that incorporate ARM cores. The use of the ARM processor is not obvious because it is embedded; the ARM system is an integral part of a product with the brand name of the product manufacturer appearing on the complete system. Because of their wide use as system components ARM processors are increasingly being adopted as the CPU studied by students following electronic engineering courses.

In addition to the problem that an assembly language is unique to a particular type of CPU there are differences in the detailed form of assembly language for a specific CPU when the software used to convert assembly language into the CPU codes is from different suppliers. There are even some differences between versions of the software from the same supplier. Here the main text adopts the form of the ARM package ADS rather than the newer RealView. This is because the RealView development tools accept all the ADS forms of the assembly language but the reverse is not true. In addition the widely used GNU software, while having many differences, accepts many ADS features but does not support the RealView alternatives. A very brief outline of the GNU requirements is in Appendix F while indications of the extra features, usually minor, of the RealView assembler are indicated as they occur.

When studying any type of computer programming practice is essential; this requires development software and target systems. Many are available for ARM; each has its own unique features. As far as possible this text is general; examples should run on many systems but are specifically targeted at those from ARM or their subsidiary Keil Elektronik GmbH. Examples are easily converted for use with other systems using the instructions and examples provided by the system manufacturer. If no hardware target is available the evaluation package from Keil Elektonik GmbH is recommended, it includes an excellent simulator. An appendix describes how to use this package for assembly language.

It is stressed that this is an introductory book; it does not attempt to cover the material to the level required by a professional engineer developing a product that incorporates an ARM core; such material is already provided by books and technical documentation produced by ARM. This book is for students studying assembly language programming and assumes no previous knowledge of the topic. Also this is not a technical manual, nor is it a reference document defining the precise behaviour of ARM processors; such material is readily available elsewhere.

My thanks to ARM Holdings plc., for permission to reproduce copyright material. In some cases this has been simplified; any mistakes in the reproduced material are my fault. Anyone using an ARM device in a commercial application must not use this book as the definitive source describing ARM cores, their behaviour and use. Such information must always be obtained from documents published by ARM Holdings plc.; the user must also check that the documents used are the latest versions.

Although not written for the skilled professional the book provides a quick start guide for experienced programmers using ARM systems for the first time. The RISC structure of the 32-bit ARM differs significantly from many 8-bit and 16-bit embedded CPUs widely used in products that do not demand the computing capability or low power consumption of ARM cores. The different structure of ARM requires some changes in approach by anyone familiar with other microcontrollers. Differences are stressed as they are encountered, both to assist those familiar with other CPU types and to indicate to those who use ARM for their initial studies the features to expect if they later use another type of CPU.

The largest use of programmed computer systems is in embedded systems. The approach adopted here is biased towards programming such systems, a task often undertaken by electronic engineers rather than by computer programmers. Assembly language programming is presented as a design task that must be undertaken in a disciplined manner; engineering software must be as reliable as hardware in critical situations. As far as possible the text is general in nature introducing the reader to the usual way of performing a task in assembly language for any CPU. However the language details are specific to the ARM core and at times techniques are also be specific to ARM.

Only the minimum details of ARM hardware necessary for assembly language programming are provided as excellent detailed descriptions are provided in the well established book by S. Furber. Other reading suggestions are provided as *'References and Further Reading'*; these suggest sources of material on topics not examined in detail.

As usual there will be typographical errors in a large document such as this and there may be errors of a factual nature. There will also be differences of opinion as to how the subject material should be approached. I will be pleased to receive details of errors, either typographical or of fact, and will attempt to maintain a list of such errors. For those who disagree with the approach used I can only state that this approach to teaching the subject has been effective in introducing assembly language programming to many students who now use assembly language as an essential element in their professional careers.

I have attempted to include an adequate number of examples but have restricted the number to avoid breaking the text to too great an extent. Similarly I have ignored advanced topics; too much material tends to discourage students and those who quickly grasp the concepts are capable of studying more advanced general texts and the many data sheets supplied by ARM.

I will produce a compressed file of the text of many of the example programs and reported errors. This will be provided as an email attachment to anyone who requests it; an early version of the programs is available. Please send requests for the file and details of any errors found to   jrgjrg@liverpool.ac.uk

J.R. Gibson
Liverpool
July 2007

Contents

1 Processor Systems

Many consumer products incorporate electronic systems which users configure to perform the tasks they require. Users readily accept that they must *'program'* the systems; that is they must define the required sequence of actions. Any automatic machine that performs a sequence of actions to execute a complex task may be referred to as a processor or a **processor system**. If the sequence of tasks is defined by a list of encoded instructions the system is a programmed one and the list of instructions is a **program**.

Programmed systems evolved over many years; early examples include clocks that strike the hours and music players. Some of the first systems that allowed programs to be changed were looms for weaving patterned cloth introduced in France about two and fifty hundred years ago. Each instruction code was a pattern of holes in a row across a card defining the loom setting for one pass of thread, the weft, across the width of the cloth. After each pass the card automatically advanced to the next row; the sequence of rows of holes formed the program. By changing the program cards different patterns were produced.

1.1 Electronic processor systems

Today the names processor and processor system describe digital electronic systems whose actions are determined by programs held in high speed memory. The systems are **stored program digital computers**. The program is a list of patterns called operation codes, **opcodes**, instruction codes or code numbers. Each opcode causes the processor to perform a simple action; actions are performed in the order of codes in the list. Possible actions and relationships between codes and actions are unique for each processor type.

Other names for these systems include computers, processors, microprocessors, microcontrollers and digital signal processors. All are similar; the names indicate construction features or an area of application for which special features have been included. Even the smallest programmed electronic system has a very large number of components, operates at high speed, uses little power, is very small, and costs very little. Most systems are complex and programs to perform many of the tasks to which they are applied are also large and complex.

The design and construction of processor systems, the **hardware**, is the task of electronic engineers. Development of methods of preparing programs, research into behaviour of programmed systems and related topics are the concern of the computer scientist. However preparation of programs, the **software**, is undertaken by people with many different qualifications. Detailed knowledge and understanding of the application is often as important as knowledge of the hardware system and programming methods.

A stored program digital computer is an unusual product as, by itself, it does not perform any particular function. It only performs a task when it executes a program, the software; different programs cause it to perform different tasks. Hence it is a universal machine that can perform any task for which a program can be devised provided that suitable systems are connected to implement input and output. Software is one component of a complete system to perform a task; it must be produced with as much care as any other manufactured item. Success in producing a product that contains software depends as much on the quality of the software as on the capability and quality of the hardware. Hardware and software are of equal importance in creating products that incorporate processor systems.

1.2 Program preparation

Even a simple program has a large number of instruction codes listed in the order in which the instructions are to be performed. The most common method of program preparation is with an artificial computer language, a **high level language**. The programmer usually requires little, or no, knowledge of the processor system and many high level language programs run correctly on several types of processor. The high level language text is converted by a program, a **compiler**, into the sequence of code numbers required by the hardware system being used. It is the compiler, not the high level language program, which is unique for a particular type of processor system.

Many high level languages are available; for example C, C++, Pascal, Fortran and Java. One reason for so many is that each is best for a particular type of application. A second reason is that high level languages are still evolving; new languages enable programs to be prepared more rapidly and more reliably. Whenever possible use a high level language to create a program. However some situations require direct preparation of the code sequence, a **machine code** program. Typical reasons are critical requirements of input or output hardware, or because compiler produced code runs too slowly or requires too much memory.

There are many reasons why compiler generated code may run more slowly or require more memory than directly prepared code. For example the compiler generates code for all possible situations whereas a programmer preparing code directly may know that some combinations of circumstances cannot occur. If a program prepared using a high level language is too slow or requires more memory than the hardware can support the system should be replaced by a faster or larger one. However this is not always possible or, if the system is part of a low cost mass produced product, a larger system is not economic.

Hence there are situations where all, or part of, a program is prepared directly instead of in a high level language. Such a program could be written as a sequence of code numbers; this method was used for early computers. The task is onerous, it is impossible to produce programs with many instructions, and there is a high risk of errors. Various aids, tools, are available to assist in direct code generation to reduce the effort required and the risk of errors. The main tool is an **assembler** which allows programs to be prepared as a list of text statements in a low level language, an **assembly language**. Each statement corresponds to a single processor instruction code using easily remembered names for the instructions, or parts of instructions. The assembler converts the list of statements into the corresponding binary code sequence. Program development using an assembly language is the subject of this book.

Unlike a high level language, an assembly language is directly related to the instruction codes of the processor used. A different assembly language is required for each type of processor, or family of closely related processors. Although many general techniques of the use of assembly language are similar the detailed implementation is unique for each processor type and it is necessary to know some internal details of the CPU to prepare assembly language programs. The language described here is for systems using the ARM *'core'* designed by ARM Holdings plc., as the **central processing unit**, **CPU**. The ARM core belongs to a class of CPUs known as **R**educed **I**nstruction **S**et **C**omputers, **RISC** machines.

The ARM core features needed to program using assembly language are described in Chapter 3; detailed hardware descriptions are given by S.Furber[1][1]. The ARM core is intended for use as an element of integrated circuits in electronic products. For example the majority of cellphone handsets contain at least one ARM core. Processor systems built into products and programmed to perform the fixed task are

---

[1] The 'References and Further Reading' section lists all books and articles to which reference is made. It also suggests further reading and sources of technical data. References in the text are shown as [number in reference list].

embedded systems. As well as being the most widely used CPU in embedded systems ARM cores are used in small general purpose computers; such systems are particularly useful for programming exercises.

The ARM family of CPUs are continually evolving; more advanced versions are produced regularly and the CPUs are upwardly compatible so that nearly all programs that run on early versions will also run on later ones. Most descriptions here apply to all current ARM versions; if it is necessary use a specific version ARM7TDMI (architecture version v4T) is chosen as, at the time of writing, this is widely used and low cost systems are available for exercises when studying program development.

1.3 General form of processor systems

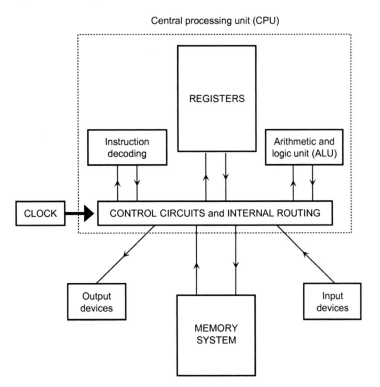

Figure 1.1 Schematic outline of a simple processor system

A simple processor system consists of a small number of interconnected units. A typical small system is outlined in Figure 1.1; the figure is schematic and it does not show the actual interconnection of components. Many systems are much larger and more complex with multiple units implementing each function. Except for some high performance systems program preparation is not greatly affected by hardware complexity.

The core component is the central processing unit, CPU, or processor which includes control circuits, registers, instruction decoding circuits, and an arithmetic and logic unit, ALU. An oscillator, clock, drives the system through the sequence necessary to follow the instructions of a program. Once power is connected, or a reset switch is operated, the control circuits automatically fetch the instruction codes of a program in the correct sequence from the memory. After each fetch the control system uses the code number obtained to determine which action it represents and then performs the action.

The memory holds the program, data values, temporary working quantities, and other items required by programs as they run. In large systems the memory may hold several programs simultaneously; one program is a master program, an **operating system**, and controls when each of the other programs runs. Simple memory systems have two types of component; one has permanently fixed contents which cannot be changed, it is a read only memory, **ROM**. The second type is read and write memory which is known as **RAM**, an acronym for **r**andom **a**ccess **m**emory; the acronym does not fully describe read and write memory but is the accepted term[1]. The type of ROM that holds a program is also a random access memory, it is read only random access. Hence using RAM to describe random access read and write memory is not ideal.

The main memory of a processor system consists of a large number of storage units, **memory words**. All the units contain the same number of storage elements or cells; that is all memory words are the same size and store one item of information. The size of the memory unit, the number of storage elements it contains, is often called its **word length** or **memory word length.** It is sometimes necessary to specifically indicate memory word length to distinguish it from the word length used inside the CPU as, for some designs of CPU, the two differ. In particular many systems, including ARM, use several memory words to store one CPU word of information. For all systems each memory word is identified by a number called its **address** which defines its **location** in the memory. Memory addresses are usually expressed as binary numbers, they form a contiguous sequence starting at zero and extending to some maximum value. Those readers who are not familiar with binary, octal and hexadecimal numbers should read the brief introduction to number systems in Appendix C before reading further. Large processor systems have complex memory systems with several types of memory device; details of these are not of concern here.

Address (binary)	Contents (example)							
0 0 · · · 0 0 0 0	1	0	0	0	1	1	1	0
0 0 · · 0 0 0 1	0	1	0	0	0	1	0	0
0 0 · · · 0 0 1 0	1	0	1	0	1	0	1	1
0 0 · · · 0 0 1 1	0	0	0	0	0	0	0	0
0 0 · · · 0 1 0 0	0	0	1	1	1	0	1	0
⋮	⋮	⋮	⋮	⋮	⋮	⋮	⋮	⋮
1 1 · · · 1 0 1 1	1	1	1	1	1	1	1	1
1 1 · · · 1 1 0 0	0	1	0	0	0	0	1	0
1 1 · · · 1 1 0 1	0	0	1	1	1	1	1	0
1 1 · · · 1 1 1 0	1	0	0	1	1	0	0	1
1 1 · · · 1 1 1 1	0	0	1	1	1	0	1	0

Figure 1.2 Example of memory organization (arbitrary contents)

The organisation of a memory is illustrated by Figure 1.2 which is for a memory with each word having eight storage elements; the contents shown in each word have been chosen arbitrarily and have no particular significance. Memory addresses have a fixed number of digits and always start at zero rather than at one. Numbering from zero, **all digits 0**, is usual for sequences of numbers in digital electronic systems. Hence for a system with a thousand words (1024 would be more common) the addresses will start at 0 and be in a sequence that includes all values up to and including 999 (or 0 up to 1023 when there are 1024 words).

---

[1] Random access means the time to store or retrieve an item is the same no matter where it is. The contents of other memory types are in a fixed order; the further an item is from the start the longer it takes to store or retrieve it.

All processor systems must have input and output (IO) devices; the input devices allow the data or input signals required by the program to be input. In many cases one input device also provides the means to input programs. The output devices provide a method of obtaining the results of the program when it runs. IO devices are selected for each processor application; consequently the form of IO systems varies greatly from one system to another.

The CPU, memory and IO devices are assembled in a systematic manner; most systems have a three bus structure to connect memory, input and output devices to the CPU as outlined in Figure 1.3. A **bus** is a group of several connecting lines; all lines in the bus perform a similar task. The bus structure allows additional memory, or input, or output modules to be easily added. The three busses are:-

Address bus: Signals on this bus indicate which memory or input or output device is to be used in a transfer to or from the CPU.

Data bus: Signals on this bus define the data value being transferred to or from the CPU.

Control bus: The signals on the bus lines are more varied than on the other busses. They indicate the type of transfer being performed and the time at which it occurs.

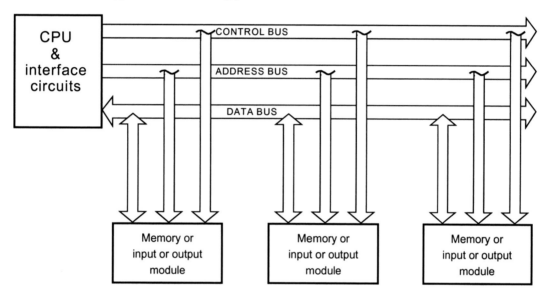

Figure 1.3 Outline of processor system bus structure

The range of processor systems is very large. Control units in modern domestic equipment such as washing machines include a small processor, a microcontroller. These have a relatively simple CPU and their memory is divided into two parts. There is a ROM with the program permanently fixed in it and a very small RAM to hold working values. The inputs include switches used to indicate which action the machine is to perform; for example the type of wash cycle, required temperature, etc. Other inputs are sensors to indicate water temperature, water level, and so on. The outputs are control indicator lights to show the user actions in progress and switching devices to turn on heaters, pumps, motors and valves.

A typical personal computer, PC, is more complex with a powerful CPU and a relatively large main memory. Most of the memory is RAM but there is a small ROM containing a program automatically run at power on to start the system. There are slower back-up memories consisting of hard disc systems, compact discs, DVDs, etc. The most common output device is a visual display unit, VDU; many systems also have a printer to provide a permanent copy of the output. Standard input is by a keyboard and a mouse; in addition special purpose devices such as scanners, joysticks, etc., may be present. Generally PCs also have input and output systems that allow the computer to communicate with other computers.

1.4 Processor operation

Most, but not all, processor systems have a von Neumann structure and operate according to the von Neumann sequence or cycle. The name originates because a team that included the mathematician John von Neumann prepared a report for the US military in 1946 [2]; this recommended the general structure that should be adopted when building an *'electronic computing instrument'*. The report suggested a structure close to the basic form followed by most modern processor systems. Of necessity the limitations of available technology in 1946 led to suggested system sizes and capabilities that are very small compared with those of modern systems, for example the maximum size of memory suggested was about 40000 words.

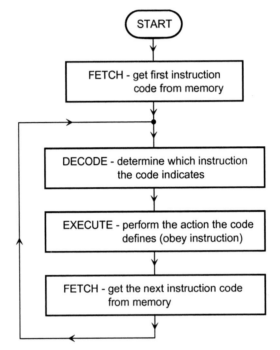

Figure 1.4 The von Neumann cycle

The hardware structure in the von Neumann report contains the elements outlined in Section 1.3 and Figure 1.1 although some names differ. The report suggests the operating sequence common to most modern systems. A program consists of a sequence of code numbers; each code number corresponds to a particular CPU action. The complete set of possible codes is known as the **instruction set** of the CPU. The code numbers for the actions to be performed by a program are placed in successive locations in memory in the order in which the actions are to be performed. The system operates by a simple **fetch, decode** and **execute** cycle, loop, illustrated by Figure 1.4; this is often called the von Neumann cycle as, although used by earlier systems, the cycle was first clearly described in the report.

1.5 Transfers to and from the CPU

When a program is running fetch operations obtain the instruction codes from the memory. Similar memory retrieval actions are necessary to obtain data and other working values from memory. The action of obtaining a value from a memory location is called a memory **read** or a **read access**. In some situations reading from memory is called a **load** operation or **loading**.

Running programs must be able to put working items, numbers and other quantities, into memory so that they can be retrieved later when required. The action of putting a value into memory is a memory **write** or a **write access**; also referred to as a **store** operation or **storing** the value.

In addition to memory read and write operations processor systems must obtain values from input devices and send results to output devices. A processor system performs four types of data transfer; all operate to or from the CPU and are memory read, memory write, input and output. The mechanisms to perform data input and data output are similar to those for memory read and memory write respectively. Many systems are constructed such that the circuits that perform similar processes are the same. That is input operations are performed as if they are memory reads and output actions are performed as memory writes; systems with this form have **memory mapped IO**. ARM cores operate with memory mapped IO.

1.6 Numbers and codes

Modern programmed electronic systems are built using electronic logic devices; these are constructed such that inputs and outputs can only take either of two conditions, usually voltage levels. When a voltage is below a specified value it is defined to represent one of the conditions, no matter how far below the value it is; when the voltage is above a significantly higher value it represents the other condition. There is a distinct gap between the two voltage levels and circuits are designed such that when the voltage changes it passes through the region between the two levels extremely quickly. The two voltage conditions, **states**, are given names to distinguish them. Often the names zero, 0, and one, 1, are chosen; other names such as low and high, down and up, false and true are also in common use. Circuits that use only two levels are called logic circuits or switching circuits. Very large numbers can be manufactured and interconnected simultaneously on the surface of a small piece of semiconductor material, an integrated circuit, at very low cost. Generally logic circuits are used to implement the functions of Boolean algebra. Although a detailed understanding of Boolean algebra is not essential some knowledge of the subject is necessary to perform some common programming tasks; the introductory chapters of the logic circuit design texts listed as further reading are adequate for most requirements.

Each unit, word, of the memory system consists of the same number of small logic circuits or units which are **bistable** logic circuits. A bistable has an output that is in either the 0 or the 1 state; once the output has been forced into a particular state it remains in this state until changed by some action that deliberately forces it into the other state. Therefore a bistable is a memory or storage element; it remembers the most recent condition it was forced to take and may be used to hold one **binary digit**, a **bit**. The name bit is interchangeably used to represent both a binary digit and a memory element to store one binary digit. Groups of eight binary digits are used so frequently that they are referred to as **bytes**; again the name may refer to eight binary digits or a circuit module containing eight memory elements.

The number of bistables in one memory unit, that is the number holding a word at one address, is the memory word size or memory word length. The contents of a memory word can be denoted by the logic levels representing the bistable output states. If 0 and 1 indicate the two states then the contents of a word can be written as a pattern; for example at some time the contents of a memory with eight bistables might be 00101001. If this pattern represents a number it has only two digit symbols, 0 and 1. Numbers which can only have digits 0 and 1 are **binary numbers**; numbers in base two. In everyday use the base ten is adopted and many people assume that all numbers are base ten ones; most, but not all, electronic systems that manipulate numbers operate use base two. Appendix C is a brief introduction to numbers, bases and related topics; it should be studied by readers unfamiliar with these topics before reading further.

Binary numbers require many digits even for small values; for example one thousand requires ten binary digits but only four decimal digits. It is easy to convert binary numbers to hexadecimal, base sixteen, ones which use many fewer digits than the binary equivalent. Therefore binary numbers are often replaced by the equivalent hexadecimal number. It is assumed that the reader can manipulate numbers in bases two, ten and sixteen; for example one thousand decimal is 1111101000 binary and is 3e8 hexadecimal. The base of a number is not always obvious; 1000 could be the binary number with value eight; it could be the decimal number with value one thousand, or the hexadecimal number with the decimal value four thousand and ninety six. Throughout this book any numbers with only the digits 0 and 1 are binary numbers unless it is clearly stated that they are in another base. All hexadecimal numbers are preceded by 0x, for example 0x3e8; all other numbers without any indication of base are decimal. If it is necessary to indicate the base of a number, other than hexadecimal, an obvious suffix notation is used.

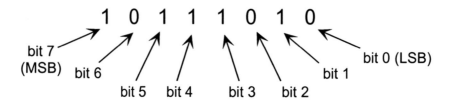

Figure 1.5 Example of bit numbering (arbitrary 8-bit data value)

Sometimes it is necessary to refer to an individual bit in a memory location or binary number. In any number system the digit at the extreme left of the number is the **most significant digit**; for binary numbers it is the **most significant bit, MSB**. The digit at the extreme right is the **least significant digit**, for binary numbers it is the **least significant bit, LSB**. When referring to bits elsewhere in a binary number they are identified by a decimal number indicating their position. Conventionally the bit on the extreme right, the LSB, is bit 0; the bit immediately to the left of bit 0 is bit 1, the next bit is bit 2 and so on as in Figure 1.5.

Conventionally when numbers are printed or written initial, left most, digits are not shown if they are 0; this is suppression of leading zeros. However an electronic system uses a fixed number of storage elements of to hold numbers, hence the number of digits is fixed. When describing digital electronic systems it is usual to write all the digits; that is leading zeros are printed to make it obvious that they are present in the system.

The majority of processor systems are designed from the viewpoint of binary numbers although the **processor system does not operate using binary numbers**. A processor system uses electrical signals that the user may choose to interpret as binary numbers. Binary numbers with N digits, N-bit numbers, can only have 2^N different possible values. If the N digits are regarded as representing positive unsigned integer numbers then they represent the values 0 to 2^{N-1}. For example a 4-bit number can only have the sixteen values shown in Table 1.1; these may be chosen to represent the integer values from zero to fifteen. Earlier it was stated that a memory of a thousand words would be unusual; it would typically have 1024 words. This is because the number, address, that defines a memory word used is a binary number. Addresses have a fixed number of bits, M, and hence have 2^M different possible values from all bits 0 to all bits 1; that is from zero to 2^M-1. To simplify circuit design memory modules are built with words at all possible addresses, hence a memory unit with individual words identified by a ten bit address would have exactly $2^{10}=1024$ words.

It is **very important** to recognise that a processor does not consider a value held in memory, or elsewhere, to be a binary number. The memory contains a pattern that can be read, retrieved, as a set of electrical signals; the programmer may choose to use the pattern to represent a positive binary integer, usually called an **unsigned integer**. Equally the programmer may choose to use the pattern to represent other forms of number or alternative quantities such as codes representing letters, punctuation marks, or part of an image. Some of the patterns in the memory will represent the instruction codes for the program itself. It is the programmer who determines how the program interprets the patterns in the memory system.

Binary number	Decimal equivalent	Hexadecimal equivalent	Value
0000	0	0	zero
0001	1	1	one
0010	2	2	two
0011	3	3	three
0100	4	4	four
0101	5	5	five
0110	6	6	six
0111	7	7	seven
1000	8	8	eight
1001	9	9	nine
1010	10	a or A	ten
1011	11	b or B	eleven
1100	12	c or C	twelve
1101	13	d or D	thirteen
1110	14	e or E	fourteen
1111	15	f or F	fifteen

Table 1.1 Values of all 4-bit numbers

1.7 Program development

The processor hardware performs any tasks for which programs can be prepared. Preparation of a program, the software required to make the processor perform some required function, is a complex task as most applications require programs with a large number of instructions which are executed at high speed, often hundreds of millions of instructions every second.

As a product software is unusual; it is an abstract concept, it is not a physical item. The final program produced for some task is a set of instructions; at the lowest level it is a sequence of code numbers unique to the processor, each different code corresponds to a different possible action by the processor. Software is developed or engineered; it is not manufactured in the way that an aircraft, a telephone or other machine is manufactured. Similarities exist between software development and hardware product design but there are major differences in production. Good design of both software and hardware is essential for a high quality product; hardware also requires high quality manufacturing. Another difference is that software production costs are almost entirely those of design engineering whereas a large part of hardware production costs are those of the manufacturing process. Hardware has the feature that it wears out and components break whereas software does not wear out.

A major requirement of any program development is management of the problem of designing a system with many components. The large number of instructions in the program must be arranged so that the program is reliable; that is it must always behave exactly as specified and should be easily modified when enhancements are required. **Software engineering** has developed as a discipline to provide a framework for the process of program development; it is a relatively new discipline and is developing rapidly. Before considering assembly language programming a very brief introduction is given to some concerns of software development; this also outlines the approach to designing programs adopted in the following chapters. Any reader who will be actively involved in software development and is not familiar with the discipline of software engineering should study several of the standard books on the subject suggested as further reading.

1.8 Problems

1.1   If the addresses used by a CPU are binary numbers with sixteen digits how many different words of memory can be connected to the processor?

1.2   Repeat problem 1.1 for each case of addresses with twenty, twenty four and thirty two binary digits.

1.3   Perform the following conversions.

a)   Binary number 10110110 into both decimal and hexadecimal forms.

b)   Hexadecimal number 0xe38c into both binary and decimal forms.

c)   Decimal number 283 into both binary and hexadecimal forms.

1.4   Express the numeric value one hundred in each of the following bases

a)   base two   b) base three   c) base five   d) base eight

e)   base nine   f) base twelve   g) base sixteen

1.5   The ASCII codes that are often used to represent letters and other symbols are given in Appendix B in both decimal and hexadecimal forms. There is a close relationship between the codes for upper case (capital) letters and the codes for lower case (small) letters. Clearly state this relationship.

1.6   A computer stores the following sequence of 8-bit values in the order shown. It is a message using ASCII codes, Appendix B, to represent each character of the message. What is the message?

01001000   01100101   01101100   01101100   01101111   00100000

01110111   01101111   01110010   01101100   01100100

2 Software Engineering

To perform any task a processor system requires a program; preparation of a program is a complex design process for which a disciplined approach is essential. There are many well publicised examples of badly managed software development projects; the consequent high costs are well documented. A report by the Royal Academy of Engineering and the British Computer Society [3] describes the problems and makes recommendations for management of complex projects. A report prepared for the U.S. Department of Commerce [4] estimates that inadequate software testing alone costs the U.S. economy over $50 billion a year and that adequate testing could reduce this figure by over $20 billion.

Formal software engineering methods have evolved that provide constraints that reduce the probability that programs do not meet specifications. If a high level language is used the language provides some constraints; using assembly language constraints must be self-imposed by the programmer. For critical applications software must meet defined standards and be extensively tested and validated using software quality assurance tools, **SQA tools**, before its use is permitted.

Controlling the development of programs is a major software engineering topic; many methods have been devised although none is ideal. Many readers will not have used an assembly language so example programs are small allowing the use of a restricted approach to program design. The bibliography lists a few texts that examine software engineering in more detail [5, 6, 7].

As only small programs are examined the very important topics associated with manipulation of large data sets **are not considered**. Programs that manipulate large amounts of data often combine the data and the operations on it; they should be prepared in a high level language which has good support for manipulating data structures. Most assembly language program tasks are relatively small and use small amounts of data; often they perform hardware control functions which may be considered separately from the construction of the data system. This separate treatment is adopted here; the main consideration is the program control function and examples only use small amounts of data. Such separation is only appropriate when the amount of data is small.

2.1 Program specification

Supply of a product or service for payment is a commercial transaction and contract law in most countries imposes a *'fit for purpose'* requirement on the provider. A product or service for many customers will be fully specified in the sales literature. If a customer needs software for their own unique application a *'tailor made'* program is required and both parties must develop the specification. Production of a specification that is interpreted identically by all parties to a transaction is very difficult; software is extremely complex and its specification is particularly difficult.

A specification must define the program actions for every situation but, because most programs are complex, many actions are not included in the initial statement of requirements. For example a program built into many general purpose computers obtains a multiple digit number from users; users press keys with each press supplying a code number indicating the key pressed. The program obtains codes until one, usually called *'Enter'* or *'Return'*, indicates end of input. After all input the codes are converted into individual digit values then combined into the single value. The initial requirement for this program might state *'a multiple digit number is to be obtained by the user pressing keys on the keyboard'*. This ignores many possibilities; for example a user may press a non-digit key on the keyboard.

The first task when creating a program is to analyse the original requirement and develop a detailed specification for all situations. Producing this is determination of the **requirements**; sometimes called **system engineering** or **system analysis**. A digital electronic processor system is deterministic; when it executes a program the behaviour can be predicted exactly although most programs are so complex that such predictions cannot readily be made. The processor behaviour is defined by the program so the actions in all possible situations are an inherent property of the program; hence all the required actions must be known before the program is prepared.

To develop a detailed specification for the number input example requires definitions of what happens when a key is pressed that does not correspond to an allowed digit, how the end of input is indicated, any correction method, *etc*. The problem of producing program specifications has been widely studied; a reliable method is the *'black-box'* function which requires definition of the required responses to every possible sequence of inputs. This appears to require an almost infinite specification; fortunately real systems have a cyclical nature and recursive definitions are possible. Methods are advanced topics; typical found under titles such as Cleanroom Software Engineering (CSE) and Analytical Software Design (ASD).

An essential feature of program development is production of **good documentation** at all stages; it is not written after the program is completed. The first document is an agreed requirements document; this is prepared before any design work is done. It may be modified later if faults are found, or improvements become obvious as development proceeds. After any revision all the design work already completed must be examined and, when necessary, performed again to ensure that the new requirements are met.

2.2 Design processes for complex systems

Most published examples and exercises illustrating programming in assembly language are small programs whose design is straightforward whereas most real applications require large complex programs. A common approach to the design of any complex system is a **top down** one; this is well suited to software development using assembly language. The overall system is divided into sub-sections (modules, units, tasks); if necessary a sub-section is divided into smaller ones which may themselves be divided again. Division continues until modules are sufficiently small to be designed and tested in a reliable manner.

Top down design is used in most large engineering and commercial projects. For example designers of an automobile divide it into units such as body shell, engine, transmission, electrical system, *etc*. A unit such as transmission is divided this into gearbox, transmission shafts, etc. Division continues until the components are small enough for detailed instructions to be prepared for their manufacture. It is **not sufficient** to design the components; there must be specifications for the assembly of components, and test procedures must be devised which ensure that individual components and assemblies of components meet specifications.

After determining the detailed requirements for a program the next step is to break the complete program into modules. Modules are broken into smaller modules and division continues until units are of manageable size. Each module is completely specified and the manner in which modules interact is fully defined. The division process is largely intuitive and is assisted by experience. There is never one solution to a design problem; there are good and poor solutions, often several of each.

One method of illustrating the relationship of modules is a **hierarchy chart**. The essential feature is that modules are assigned levels in the chart. A module may use any module that is at any level below its own but cannot use a module at a level that is the same or higher. Failure to follow this rule produces circular references that cannot be resolved. A first example of a simple hierarchy chart is later, Figure 2.5.

From the top down structure detailed specifications are prepared for all modules; the structure of each module is designed and methods of testing modules and assemblies of modules are devised. **Designs must be testable**; testing is considered early in the process as extensive testing is essential in software development. The program code is only prepared when the full design of a module is complete; coding occurs very late in software development; the sequence is specify, analyse, design, code, test, integrate and test again. Generally descriptions of programs in assembly language use examples with obvious clear requirements; as a result the analysis and design processes are straightforward and the difficulties in real situations are not apparent.

During each stage of the development faults in the initial requirements may be discovered and better methods of performing the task may be apparent. Designers must be prepared to discard the work completed and start the design process again. All designers find this **extremely difficult**; the ability to discard work and start again is an attribute of all good designers and programmers. A typical sequence of software design steps and the need to return to earlier steps in a design process is outlined in Figure 2.1.

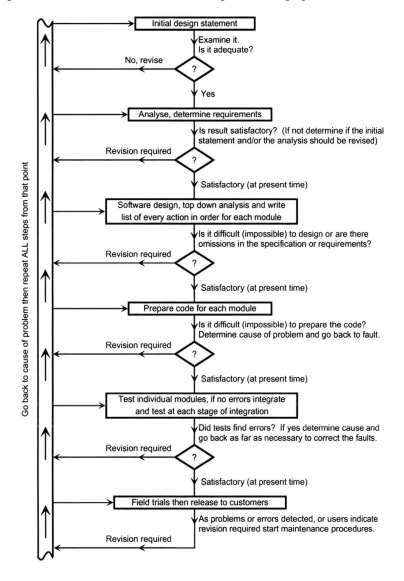

Figure 2.1 Outline of the software design process

2.3 Defining the operation of programs and modules

All programs can be defined as systems that perform the operations

- o   Obtain the input data.
- o   Process the data (perform operations on it).
- o   Output the processed data (results).

in this order. This definition applies to a complete program and to every module of a program.

There are two components of any program or module; the **control** or **processing** sequence and the data. Good design requires that the control actions are performed in a well organised manner and the data has a well defined **data structure**. Complex data systems are best implemented using high level languages therefore this introduction to assembly language uses only very simple data structures. The area of most concern in assembly language programs is usually the creation of a control structure that is clear and easily understood so that program faults are unlikely. A well designed structure also allows mistakes that do occur to be found quickly and, if the requirements change, revision is easily made.

The control structures for all possible computer programs can be constructed from three basic elements. Well structured programs are built using only the three elements; these are **sequences** of actions, **selection** (conditional actions) and **repetition** (loops). Actions may be called processes or tasks; each action may be any of the three basic types, or a combination of several, or a lower level module which itself is built from the three elements. Lower level modules may use even lower level modules and so on.

A **sequence** is the execution of one action after another in a fixed order; these are an inherent feature of programmed machines. **Selection** is the process of choosing one sequence of actions from a set of several sequences; the set may include the option of doing nothing. **Repetition** is repeated execution of a sequence of actions; the repetition may be forever or may end if some condition is met.

2.4 Graphical representation of program control structures

An important item of documentation is a graphical representation of control sequences. Early attempts used simple flowcharts as they provide a good visual description of program behaviour, especially when performing engineering control tasks. However, if simple flowcharts are used as program specifications their unstructured form often leads to poorly constructed programs with obscure faults. If required, simple flowcharts are produced after a program has been developed; they show the exact behaviour and are produced automatically by some SQA tools.

Many attempts have been made to devise flowgraphs that assist and constrain designers to produce programs with good structures. There is no ideal form; the Nassi-Schneiderman chart, **NS chart**, is used here. It is easy to read but a little harder to draw than some alternatives. Readers who prefer alternative graphs that support well structured programming can easily convert NS charts into the form they know. There are minor differences in NS charts drawn by different authors. The main chart features are:-

- •   The whole chart is a rectangular box; therefore it is the same width at all points.
- •   Chart elements are boxes inside the main box.
- •   Flow is always from a box to one immediately below except for loop structures which are clearly identified by indentation.
- •   Charts can only contain the three elements of well structured programs.
- •   Loop structures repeat a set of actions by going from the last action of a sequence back to the first until an exit condition is met. This is the only case of upward chart movement.

- Alternative actions are shown side by side separated by vertical lines. They indicate parallel paths, only one path is followed during one passage through that part of the chart; movement sideways across the vertical lines is not allowed.

If a program is prepared to behave exactly as described by an NS chart the chart construction rules ensure that the program has a good structural form. The most important rules that the program must follow are:-

- A program or program module must start at the single entry point at the top of the chart.
- A program or program module must exit from the bottom of the chart.
- No entry is allowed except at the top and no exit is allowed except at the bottom.
- GOTO, EXIT, JUMP, BREAK and similar flow controls DO NOT EXIST.
- Either END or RETURN (not both) can only occur once in a chart and whichever one is used is the last item in a chart.

2.4.1 Sequences

Sequences are an inherent property of programmed machines and the chart form consists of the actions written in boxes one after another in the order in which they are to be executed. A simple program to perform the function *'add two numbers'* could have a top level module that behaves as Figure 2.2.

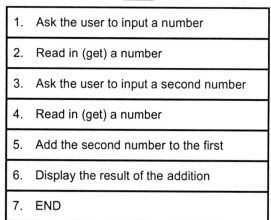

Figure 2.2 Example NS chart for a sequence of actions

It is advised that each chart should have a name, as in Figure 2.2, that matches names identifying modules in hierarchy charts and elsewhere. Each statement is numbered; although not essential it assists in referring to elements of the chart. 'END' is the last entry in this top level chart; some authors omit this as the bottom of the chart is the end. Charts for lower level modules should use RETURN instead of END showing that after completing module actions the program continues by returning to a higher level module.

2.4.2 Selection

There are several forms of selection; all start from the most simple form, that is the choice of an action or no action defined by **IF** *condition is true* **THEN** *perform action*. It is implied that if the condition is false then no action is performed. A requirement to perform one of two alternative actions could be written in sequence as

> **IF** *condition is true* **THEN** *perform action 1*
>
> **IF** *INVERSE condition is true* **THEN** *perform action 2*

This sequence has an inherently hazardous feature; it is only correct **provided action 1 does not change the condition.** To avoid this problem always use the extended form

IF condition is true **THEN** perform action 1
ELSE (OTHERWISE) perform action 2

Good structures always uses the 'IF-ELSE' version; *'do nothing'* is indicated as one of the actions when the simple form 'IF *condition true* THEN *perform action'* is required. The actions inside conditional structures may be sequences of many structure elements; they may include further conditions allowing selection from many possibilities. For multiple choices most structure forms also define a **case** selection, also known as a **switch**. Case structures are complex and implementation in assembly language varies greatly with CPU type; implementation for ARM is described in Chapter 12 after the required features of the instruction set have been introduced.

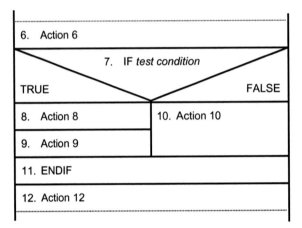

Figure 2.3 Example: partial NS chart for an 'IF-ELSE' selection

NS charts for selection by an 'IF' condition always use the form that includes an 'ELSE' component, Figure 2.3 illustrates the structure for part of a module. It is assumed that after *'action 6'* some condition has been generated that can only be true or false; any condition that can only take either of two allowed values is a Boolean value. The Boolean value is examined and the actions that are required after this differ according to the value. The chart clearly shows that the program performs some actions leading to a Boolean value; following actions are selected using the Boolean value then the program continues with further actions that do not depend on the value.

The chart in Figure 2.3 is incomplete so it has not been given a name. Minor variations are use of T and F for TRUE and FALSE; also ENDIF may be omitted because the end of the vertical line indicates the end of the alternative actions. For an 'IF' without an 'ELSE' one branch will have no entry, for clarity the chart always indicates two branches and *'Do nothing'* or a similar statement is written in the branch for which there is no entry.

2.4.3 Repetition

Repetition or loop structures are the mechanism for repeatedly performing a sequence of actions is until some condition is satisfied. When the condition is met the program stops performing the loop actions and moves on to the next sequence of actions. There are two possible forms of loop structure usually known as WHILE and REPEAT. Figure 2.4 shows examples of their representation by NS charts. Again there are minor differences in the detailed forms used by other authors.

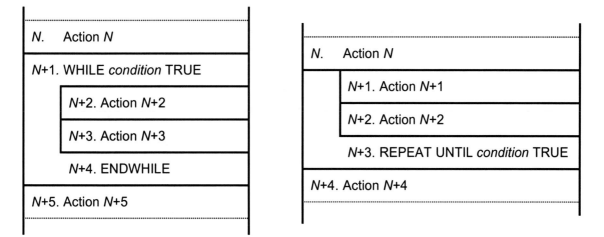

Figure 2.4 Example: partial NS charts for WHILE and REPEAT loops

The WHILE form of loop is regarded as the better one although in assembly language it is often easier to create the REPEAT version. WHILE is better because a programmer could create a situation such that the test condition is not true on entry to the loop and the actions inside the loop should never be executed. If the repeat form is used the actions inside the loop are always performed at least once because the test follows the loop actions.

The FOR loop provided in many high level languages is not included as a structure element. It is a restricted version of the WHILE loop so is not necessary. It is avoided because many high level languages implement it in a manner that allows the programmer to create difficult to find program faults.

2.5 Data

Most programs use several different types of data item and it is convenient to classify types of data as simple or compound. Simple types are those for a single item such as a number represented in a specific form; for example an unsigned integer, a signed integer, a code for a printed character such as a letter or a similar quantity. Compound types are constructed from well organised assemblies of simple types and may contain other compound types.

Table 2.1 lists some common data types with an indication of some uses. Large programs require elaborate data structures so specification and description is complex. For small programs with very little data simple text statements in the documentation may be adequate. If the amount of data is small but too much for text statements a table listing each data item, its type and purpose is adequate. Text statements or tables describing data should be produced for all programs. They should indicate which data belongs to the whole program, **global data**, and which belongs only to a module, **local data**. It is also important to include documentation defining the data items transferred between modules and the transfer mechanism.

Although the simple data types are clearly defined more information is required as the hardware limits the number of bits, and hence the range of values, represented in any form. The number of bits used for each data type should be stated. Most ARM programs use 32-bits for signed and unsigned integers and 8-bits for characters; other sizes are used if required. If data items of the same type use different numbers of bits each is given a different name; for example if a program uses integers with two different numbers of bits they may be called short integer and long integer, or just short and long. The ARM floating point implementation, not examined here, uses a 64-bit format to the IEEE 754-1985 [8] standard.

Data	Type	Comments
Unsigned integer	Simple	Used for counting, indicating position in a list, memory address, etc.
Signed integer	Simple	General purpose integer only arithmetic
Character	Simple	General purpose codes for letters of the alphabet, numeric digits, punctuation, etc.
Fixed point	Simple	Infrequent use; used for fixed precision fractions.
Floating point	Simple	Known as real, float, etc. The general form of number used in many calculations (not financial ones).
Array	Compound	A well organised collection of a number, usually fixed, of items of one of the simple types
String	Compound	An array of a variable number of characters; it includes an indication the number of characters
Record or structure	Compound	A collection of a number of quantities of several types, including other compound types.

Table 2.1 A few common data types

2.6 The software design process - a requirements document example

Using the design sequence outlined earlier the first step is to determine the requirements; the program's behaviour is defined for all possible situations. If during development the requirements are found to be incomplete, or have poor features, or are difficult to implement, it is necessary to return to this step and start again. For example if NS charts are used to specify structures and a chart is difficult to draw either the design has poor features or the top down division process has not been followed to a sufficient extent.

A previous example was the small program built into many systems to input a multiple digit number using a keyboard. Because it is used often this is frequently in permanently fixed memory, ROM, and can be used by all programs removing the need to create a module for this task for every new program. Examination will probably show that the initial requirement was a simple statement such as *'the program accepts a sequence of key presses and converts these to the single numeric value they indicate.'* Although clear, many features are not present in this statement. Some of the features that must be considered are:-

- There is no way a user can be prevented pressing keys that do not represent numeric digits, behaviour when a user presses such keys must be part of the detailed specification.
- Does a user receive indication that a key press has been detected immediately?
- The user may press a large number of keys; what is the limit and how is it implemented?
- How does the user indicate that all digits have been input?
- Is the number allowed to be signed?
- Is the number decimal only, could it be in another base?
- Is there a delete or backspace mechanism? If there is how is it used?
- How are incorrect inputs handled?

In an industrial environment a design team would suggest detailed implementation decisions and refer to the originators of the requirements for approval. Assume that after review the following requirements statement is adopted; it meets black-box testing requirements of specifying all possible input situations with the resulting outputs.

"The user presses keys to represent the digits of a multiple digit decimal number; input is ended by pressing the *'Enter'* key. Each time a key is pressed a code number for the key is obtained and the corresponding character is displayed. For simplicity no limit is placed on the number of digits (a real program requires a limit). Numbers are restricted to unsigned decimal integers; the digits are obtained by pressing keys labelled 0 to 9 and the largest allowed number is 999999999. There is no backspace mechanism, user errors are only indicated after *'Enter'* is pressed. In error cases a simple *'invalid input'* message is output after the enter key is detected and the program using the module must specify the behaviour after a user error. It is assumed that the built in programs include a module **Char_In** which waits until a key is pressed then returns the code number indicating the character embossed on the key. The system also has a module **Char_Out** that takes a code number and causes the corresponding character (letter, digit, etc.) to appear on the display. The construction of the processor system is such that the key corresponding to a digit does not produce a code number with the digit value. The input and output code values used by **Char_In** and **Char_Out** will be the same and are the ASCII codes (Appendix B)."

2.7 Development of a top down design

The requirements document fully specifies the program task; the next step is to examine possible methods of performing the task. For complex tasks it is necessary to develop several designs and perform enough work for each to allow the best approach to be determined. It is also good practice to examine how others have solved similar problems; only devise new methods if significantly better designs can be produced.

For the number input example the usual method is to create a general purpose input module for all types of user input, not only input of one type. An area of memory, a **buffer**, is reserved and holds the input codes. Codes are obtained, the character represented is displayed and the codes are stored in the buffer in order of receipt. The only checks made during input are to detect the end of input code and to implement any editing methods supported. In practice the buffer has a finite size; this is ignored here although several methods of limiting input are easily implemented. This general purpose input module can be used for input of many quantities, not only numbers. A feature of good software is that **program modules should be general purpose and re-used whenever possible**. Because production of reliable software is very difficult using a module many times increases its use and hence the chance that faults will be discovered and corrected.

Most programs that perform number input only check the input codes after the whole input sequence is complete. The first check of input of unsigned integers is to ensure that the keys pressed only represent the digits 0 to 9. If the check finds no errors the individual digit values are determined from the key codes and combined to form the input number. Features of real hardware are such that it is necessary to check to see if the number exceeds the maximum value allowed at each step in the combination process. If an incorrect user input is detected this is indicated **after all the checks** are completed.

An important feature of this design is that it only performs one task at a time. First the codes are input and stored; there is no attempt to check them except to find the terminating code. After all the codes are input they are first checked, then converted, then the total numeric value is determined. Whenever possible a program module should not perform two or more tasks simultaneously. The requirements of multiple tasks often conflict and this leads to complex structures. The more complex a program or module, the higher the chance of faults and the more difficult it is to test it. When possible perform simple tasks in succession rather than together as a single complex task. For any design a simple solution is always best; it is easier to prepare and test, it is more likely to meet the specification and the design effort is usually less. As E.W. Djikstra [9] the eminent computer scientist stated *"Simplicity is prerequisite for reliability."*

Once the general method by which the design will perform the required function has been decided the top-down design process is started. A simple method is to write a list of actions to be performed in the order in which they must take place. Each action should be a significant task and the total list, even for a complex program, should easily fit onto one page of a moderate size notebook. Typically the list should be less than thirty actions; if it exceeds fifty the tasks selected are not large enough. This first list describes the actions of the top-level, main, module; a list for one design for the number input example is Table 2.2.

Step	Action
1.	Get key codes from the input; store in the buffer as they are received. Test each code after receipt and stop getting more when *'Enter'* is input. Display (reflect) the characters corresponding to the key codes as they are input (one decision required is should *'Enter'* be reflected or not).
2.	Check that all the codes that were input only represent digits 0 to 9; set an indicator to show the test result as true or false.
3.	If the digit check indicated only digit key codes found convert the key codes into the single number they represent.
4.	Check that the number does not exceed the maximum (if not included in step 3); set an indicator if the test indicates that the number was too large.
5.	If either of the checks indicates an error indicate this.

Table 2.2 List of actions for the input of a number

When the list is complete examine each entry to determine if it describes a simple task that can be implemented using a few lines of program; that is decide if a lower level module is necessary. If a task is not simple it should become a module. This requires programming experience and is difficult for the beginner. Even an expert programmer may make the wrong decision and in such situations it is necessary to return to this point and modify the design. Most of the steps Table 2.2, while not complex, will require separate modules. The processes of obtaining a key code and displaying a character will be complex. They are the modules that have been named *Char_In* and *Char_Out*; they are unique for each different hardware system so cannot be determined here. Programmers must be prepared to return and modify all design decisions, including this initial list, if later work suggests that they were not the best ones possible.

Give each task in the list that requires a lower level module a name, return to the list and include the names in the list. The first task in the example is of moderate size and the module to implement it has been called *Buff_In*; the next is *Check*, the following one is *Combine*. The test that the number was in the allowed range is simple; it probably will not require a separate module or will be part of *Combine*. The final task is different; it is to output some text. A sequence of characters representing text is a **string** so this is string output. Most programs that interact with users require string output so a general purpose string output module is useful, call it *Str_Out*. Table 2.2 is revised and becomes Table 2.3.

Step	Action
1.	Get key codes from the input; store in the buffer as they are received. Test each code after receipt and stop getting more when *'Enter'* is input. Display (reflect) the characters corresponding to the key codes as they are input (one decision required is should *'Enter'* be reflected or not). ***Buff_In***
2.	Check that all the codes that were input only represent digits 0 to 9; set an indicator to show the test result as true or false. ***Check***
3.	If the digit check indicated only digit key codes found convert the key codes into the single number they represent. ***Combine***
4.	Check that the number does not exceed the maximum (if not included in step 3); set an indicator if the test indicates that the number was too large.
5.	If either of the checks indicates an error indicate this. ***Str_Out***

Table 2.3 Revised list of actions to input a number.

The process of creating a list of actions is repeated to produce lists of actions for each module in the top level list; if necessary, lower level modules are created for tasks that are complex. The process continues until lists of actions contain no lower level modules.

To illustrate this process consider ***Str_Out***; creation of the lists for the other modules is left as exercises. A string is a sequence of code numbers, one for each character, in order in successive memory locations; it must also have a feature indicating the string size. Strings are not easy data structures to manipulate because different strings have different sizes. There are several solutions to the variable size problem; a simple one is to reserve one character code as a marker and place this after the last character of the string; the reserved character is called a **terminator**. Table 2.4 outlines one possible list of actions for ***Str_Out***; it is assumed that the module receives the value from the higher level module that requires string output that indicates the start address of the memory area holding string.

Step	Action
1.	Set a pointer to the address of the start of the memory area holding the string; the address is transferred from the higher level module that uses this module.
2.	Start a *'While'* loop performing steps 3, 4 and 5 as long as the value of the code at the pointer position is not the string terminator.
3.	Obtain the code at the pointer position, check for the terminator and exit the while loop if it is the terminator.
4.	Send the code obtained to a lower level module which drives the display to show the character represented by the code ***Char_Out***.
5.	Advance the pointer position so it points to the next character code in the list.

Table 2.4 List of actions to perform string output

In the list for string output a lower level module was required that causes a single character to be shown on the display; this is the module ***Char_Out*** suggested in the detailed requirements. The form of the module ***Char_Out*** will depend on the hardware being used.

The process of developing a list of actions for the top level, then further lists for each module required by the top level, then lists for modules required by this second set of lists continues until the list produced for a module is so simple it does not require lower level modules. Assuming ***Char_In*** and ***Char_Out*** do not require lower level lists the hierarchy chart for the number input module is Figure 2.5.

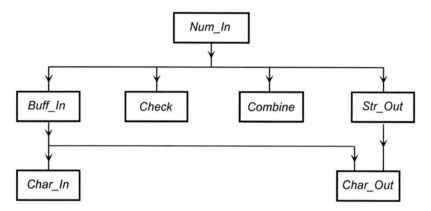

Figure 2.5 Hierarchy chart for the number input module Num_In

It will not always be obvious early in the design process, especially to the inexperienced programmer, when modules are so simple that they do not require the use of lower level modules. The programmer must be prepared to return to earlier stages, revise the design and repeat all work from the revision point when initial design choices are not the best possible. Figures 2.6 and 2.7 are first versions of the NS charts corresponding to the actions required by Tables 2.3 and 2.4 respectively.

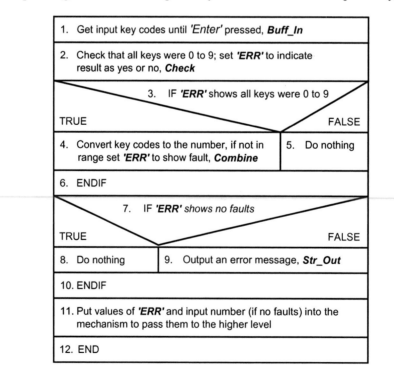

Figure 2.6 First version of the NS chart for the number input module, Num_In

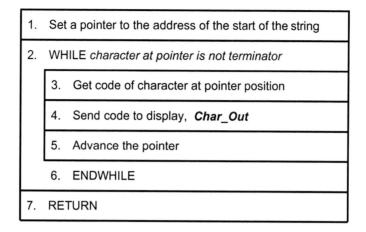

| 1. Set a pointer to the address of the start of the string |
| 2. WHILE *character at pointer is not terminator* |
| 3. Get code of character at pointer position |
| 4. Send code to display, ***Char_Out*** |
| 5. Advance the pointer |
| 6. ENDWHILE |
| 7. RETURN |

Figure 2.7 First version of the NS chart for module *Str_Out*

In Figure 2.6 the program has been simplified by including the check for the number size inside the same conditional branch as **Combine**; this small change shows that design is an iterative process. **Check** must provide an error indicator, the data item **'ERR'**, whose value indicates *'error'* or *'no error'*. The test for out of range also sets **'ERR'** to show an error and the test in statement 7 is simplified to *'if no error was found'*. Note how **'ERR'** is set to indicate no error at the start of **Num_In** and the only actions when checking for errors set **'ERR'** if an error is found; the error indicator must not be cleared by each individual test.

2.8 Testing

Thorough testing of programs is essential; it must be shown that there is a very high probability that a program has no faults, *'bugs'*, and always behaves as required by the specification. At the present time it is impossible to prove that any program, except a trivial one, will behave as specified. As Djikstra [9] states *"Program testing can be used to show the presence of bugs, but never to show their absence!"* Another statement by the same author is *"How are you going to prove that your program functions as required? Not by testing."*

Software engineering has not reached the point of providing a proof that a program meets its specification. Only rigorous testing provides a reasonable level of confidence that a program performs as specified. When software is part of a system with safety implications there are additional requirements; national laws often require the international standard IEC61508 [10] to be followed. Although written for software developers in a special area the review for the UK National Physical Laboratory [11] is a good introduction to software testing, testing requirements, meeting standards and it suggests further reading.

Devising adequate tests for software is difficult as it is impossible to check every possible situation. For example if two 32-bit numbers are combined by some rule there will be 2^{64} possible cases, checking them all is impossible; even the fastest CPU would not perform all cases within its lifetime. Tests must use a sub-set of all possible cases that is sufficient to convince others that the program will always function correctly.

Testing should be considered during the design process as features that will simplify testing should be included whenever possible. The range of test situations is as large as the range of applications of processor systems so general rules cannot be given. The main purpose of testing is to find faults and it is essential to include situations known to cause problems in the testing process. A simple case is devising tests of modules or programs that perform calculations. For example if a module combines two integer numbers *A* and *B* to produce a single integer result then a minimum set of test values for each of *A* and *B* should be selected as suggested in Table 2.5. All possible combinations of all the selected test values should be used in testing, that is eighty one cases for the values suggested.

1.	Slightly less than smallest allowed value
2.	Smallest allowed value
3.	Just above smallest allowed value
4.	A mid-range negative value
5.	Zero
6.	A mid-range positive value
7.	Just below largest allowed value
8.	Largest allowed value
9.	Slightly more than largest allowed value

Table 2.5 Suggested test values of a signed integer

Table 2.5 is a minimum set of values, when using mid-range values those chosen for *A* and *B* should be different. Preferably several mid-range values should be used and tests should include cases using both the same and different values for *A* and *B*. It is not always possible to have test values outside the allowed range; for example if all 32-bits of a word of an ARM system represent integers all possible 32-bit values are allowed numbers.

For more complicated situations adequate testing is often difficult. For the number input example it is straightforward to devise tests for a reasonable selection of cases for users pressing keys for a valid number. However the number of cases where users can perform incorrect actions is almost infinite. Devising tests that fully check for all possibilities is difficult but essential for programs to be used in commercial applications.

It is essential to test all combinations of routes through branches, loops and evaluation of conditions. This is assisted by use of SQA tools although they are often unavailable for assembly language programs; they perform many functions. One function is to detect features which cause problems or lead to a high risk of problems. For example they find any part of a program that can never be executed; as it is included it must have a purpose and if it cannot be executed there must be a fault. A more complex task of SQA tools is to monitor testing; they check that during testing every path through a program is executed; such tests are required for approval for use in safety critical situations. When preparing programs in assembly language the programmer must devise similar tests.

2.9 Summary

Reliable creation of software is a large and complex task; formal procedures must be imposed to control the process. Only a brief introduction at an elementary level has been given and it only applies to small programs with very little data. Any reader who becomes involved in major software projects and is not familiar with software engineering should study software engineering methods in detail.

This book is an introduction to preparation of assembly language programs and mostly concerns production of program code. The simple design methods that have been described are followed when creating examples used to illustrate assembly language features.

2.10 Problems

2.1   Prepare lists of actions for modules **Buff_In**, **Check** and **Combine** in Table 2.3. *Hint.* The list in the buffer requires an end marker; consider how the end of input is indicated when selecting it.

2.2   Prepare NS charts for each of **Buff_In**, **Check** and **Combine** in Table 2.3.

2.3   Modify the plan for **Buff_In** to restrict the maximum number of keys a user may press. A simple method is that after the maximum number keys are ignored except the key indicating end of input.

2.4   Develop a hierarchy chart for a program that requires the user to input two unsigned integers with values from 0 to 999999999 and then outputs the sum of the numbers.

2.5   Each digit of a multiple digit 7-segment display is connected to appear to be a single memory location to which 8-bit values can be written. The memory locations are in order with the least significant digit the first. Assume a module exists that takes any value 0 to 9 and converts it into the 8-bit value to show the equivalent digit on a 7-segment display.
Design a program that outputs a 32-bit number as the equivalent decimal value on the display which has as many digits as necessary.

3 The ARM Processor

To develop programs in a low level language it is necessary to select the type of CPU and know some features of the internal organisation. The CPU family selected here is that designed by ARM Holdings plc., and the internal information required is provided by the **programmer's model**, Figure 3.1. In the few cases where a CPU version must be specified ARM7TDMI is selected. Any system that includes an ARM core will also have some memory and the input and output, IO, systems required for the task.

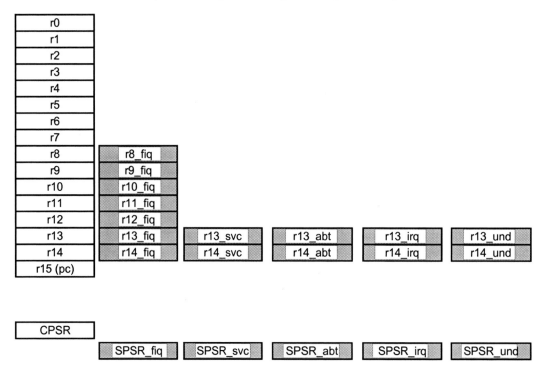

Figure 3.1 ARM Programmers' Model

3.1 The CPU architecture

A complete system incorporating an ARM CPU, memory devices and the IO devices is built as outlined in Chapter 1. The assembly language programmer must know where temporary values are held in the CPU and the operations that can be performed using them. A major feature of any CPU is the block of registers whose contents the programmer can manipulate. **Registers** are similar to words of memory as each holds a fixed size binary pattern representing numbers, codes for letters, etc.. They are used for values that are required immediately. Some registers are reserved for special tasks set by the CPU designer; the others are general purpose and are often called **scratch pad** registers. The action of an instruction, an **operation**, is to transfer values to and from the registers; often the values are modified during the transfer.

Figure 3.2 is a simplified outline of the internal organisation of the ARM7; it shows the paths on which data moves in the CPU and the connections for data transfer between the CPU and memory. All ARM registers are 32-bit ones, the CPU is said to have a 32-bit word length. The registers available to programmers are shown in the Programmers' Model, Figure 3.1. For initial studies the bank of sixteen registers r0 to r15 and the current program status register, CPSR, are the important ones and are shown without shading in Figure 3.1. The shaded registers are only used by more complex CPU operating modes which are not required for simple programming tasks.

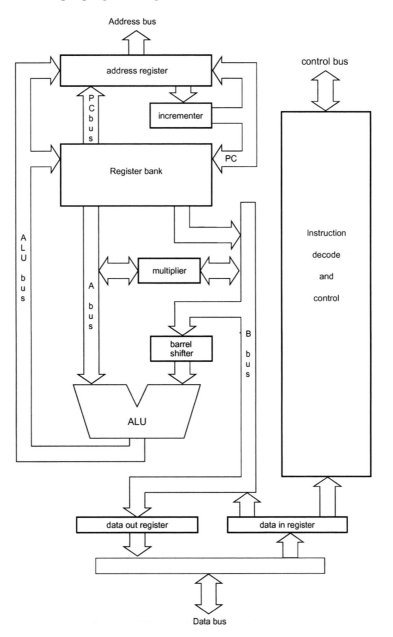

Figure 3.2 Simplified outline of the internal ARM7TDMI structure

When the CPU executes instructions it transfers values to and from registers. The programmer uses registers r0 to r11 as general purpose ones; that is r0 to r11 hold 32-bit values for any purpose the programmer chooses during execution of the program. Registers r13, r14 and r15 perform special functions and should only be used for these. ARM suggest additional restrictions in register use when a program consists of several modules. For advanced tasks r12 is used for a special purpose that is not examined. Although r12 may be used as a general purpose register when not used for the special purpose the risk of creating program faults is reduced if it is only used for the special function.

Register r15 is the most important CPU register and its alternative name is **program counter, pc**, because it holds the address of the next instruction to be fetched for execution. The program counter is automatically advanced after each instruction is fetched. Although it is possible, programs should not alter the value of the program counter as if it as a general purpose register; also programs should not directly use the contents of r15. There are exceptions to these rules but they are special well defined cases.

Registers with special uses have alternative names; as indicated r15 is the program counter, pc. Either r15 or pc may be used as the register name but pc is preferred as it indicates the register's function; that is use pc rather than r15 to improve documentation. The von Neumann cycle, Section 1.4, described operation as a fetch-decode-execute cycle. To perform the fetch the CPU uses the address held in the program counter. The von Neumann cycle for an ARM processor is more fully described by Figure 3.3.

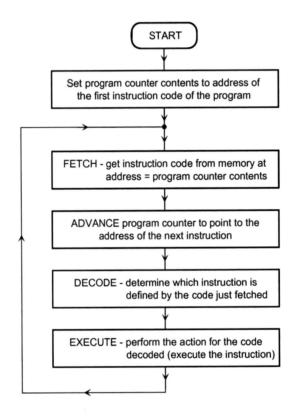

Figure 3.3 Detailed von Neumann cycle sequence

Here, and previously, the problem of *'How does it start?'* has been ignored. Processor systems include a reset circuit which forces the system into a known condition at power on and when a reset switch is pressed; the reset process forces the program counter to a specified value. Most programs are developed using tools that handle the start up process during testing, this allows the exact start up details to be ignored initially.

3.2 Memory for ARM systems

Almost all ARM features are 32-bit; registers hold 32-bit values, instruction codes are 32-bit numbers, addresses are 32-bits, and most calculations are performed using 32-bit values to produce 32-bit results. As 32-bit values are used for addresses then 2^{32} memory locations can be used. 2^{32} is 4,294,967,296 which is a very large number that is usually written as 4G where G indicates giga. In the S.I. system giga represents

10^9; in digital electronics it is used for 2^{30} which is about 7% larger. Very few applications will require the maximum amount of memory; the amount used depends on the application; very small systems have a few thousand words and large ones several million words.

Usually the manipulation of data by ARM programs uses 32-bit quantities, words. However the memory organization is such that every 8-bits, each byte, has a different address with 32-bit word values stored at four consecutive addresses. This rarely concerns the programmer provided sequences of 32-bit values are placed in memory **starting at addresses that are divisible by four;** that is the two LSBs of the address of the first byte are both zero. If only 32-bit values are used the CPU and development tools will automatically keep everything in order. For example every instruction is 32-bits; when an assembler or compiler produces code it automatically puts the first byte of the first instruction at an address divisible by four. As all instruction codes are four bytes the following codes are all correctly positioned. When the CPU fetches an instruction it fetches all 32-bits and adds four to the program counter. That is *'ADVANCE program counter to point to the address of the next instruction'* in the von Neumann cycle of Figure 3.3 is more precisely *'Add four to the program counter'.*

The feature, **byte addressing**, where each group of eight bits has a different address has many advantages and is used by many types of CPU. For some advanced tasks programmers must know how the memory is organised; this requires the answer to the question is *'How are 32-bit values arranged as four bytes in the memory?'* ARM allows the hardware designer to select either of two methods; the method is usually fixed when the CPU is built and cannot be changed by the programmer but systems can be built that allow selection by the programmer. The two methods are termed *'little-endian'* and *'big-endian'*.

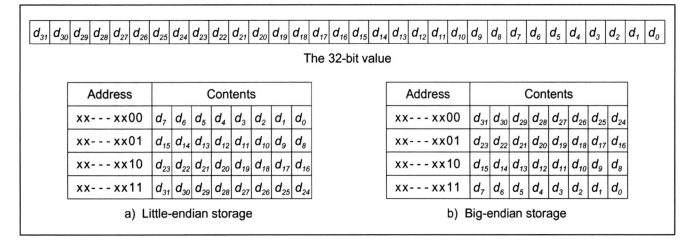

Figure 3.4 Little-endian and big-endian memory organisation

For little-endian systems the least significant 8-bits of the 32-bit quantity are at the lowest address of the four used with the LSB in the LSB position of the memory byte. The next 8-bits are in the memory at the next address, the third 8-bits are in the next location and the most significant 8-bits are in the last address, Figure 3.4a. Big-endian systems have the most significant 8-bits of the 32-bit quantity at the lowest address with the most significant bit, MSB, in the MSB position of the memory byte; the next most significant 8-bits are at the next address, and so on; Figure 3.4b. CPU designers argue about the best arrangement but the choice has little effect on system performance. Little-endian form will be assumed in the small number of cases for which it is necessary to know the details of number storage.

IO devices are connected to an ARM core as if they are memory components; ARM systems have memory mapped IO. Input devices behave as a memory that can only be read from and output devices as a memory that can only be written to. Many IO devices are 8-bit ones so the ability to address individual bytes is important for IO operations. A low level programmer often needs to know the addresses of IO devices and special restrictions on their use. Also systems rarely have memory at all addresses; the addresses used and the types of memory, ROM or RAM, at each address must be known when building complete programs.

Most tools do not require the addresses of the memory units connected to the CPU as part of the assembly language program. The code is produced in two stages, although a single stage is adequate for simple programs. Development tools are designed for creating large complex software divided into modules with each developed separately. The assembler processes each source module separately producing intermediate output for each one. A further tool, a **linker,** combines the intermediate modules into a single structure and determines the correct addresses. This two stage approach supports:-

- Modular design of software.
- Many programmers working on a large software project simultaneously, each responsible for different modules.
- Development of mixed language programs; some modules in assembly language and others in one, or more, high level languages.
- Provision of library facilities so that commonly required modules can be developed once then used by many different software projects.
- Simple modification of programs so they run on slightly different hardware.

In simple situations the programmer is not aware of the two stage process; it is only when more complicated tasks are met that a detailed understanding of the development tool capability and operation may be necessary.

3.3 Instruction execution

As every ARM instruction is a 32-bit code number there are 4,294,967,296 possible instruction codes, some are not used but a very large number are used. The processor follows the von Neumann cycle with the contents of the program counter, register r15 or pc, used to indicate the memory addresses of instructions. The control circuits in the CPU use the address in the program counter and fetch, read, the contents of the memory at this address. Once the contents are in the CPU the value in the program counter is advanced by adding four to it. The 32-bit value fetched is decoded to determine which instruction it represents. The processor then performs the actions to execute the instruction; the actions are fully defined by the code number.

ARM is a RISC processor with a **pipelined operation**; while one instruction is being executed the one to be executed next is being decoded and the one after that is being fetched as in Figure 3.5. The operation is more complicated than the von Neumann cycle of Figure 3.3; the exact sequence in which instructions are executed is identical but the rate at which they are executed is much higher. A pipelined CPU simultaneously performs fetch, decode and execute operations and when an instruction is executed the program counter value is not always that expected. As Figure 3.5 does not apply to all instructions the value is not easy to predict; for example some instructions require two time periods for execution. Figure 3.5 is for ARM7; later versions are more complicated. Furber [1] describes the operation of the various forms of pipeline with reasons for the changes. The pipeline is one reason why the assembly language programmer should avoid changing the contents of the program counter, or even use the value it holds, except in certain well defined situations.

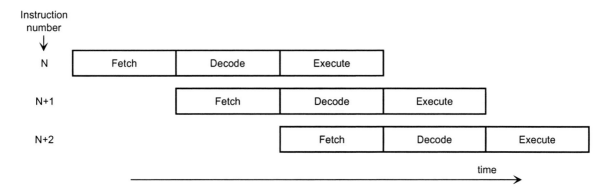

Figure 3.5 Operation of ARM7 pipeline for simple instructions

The pipelined structure of the ARM processor with most instructions executed in the same time that it takes to fetch or decode them means that the ARM instruction set can only have instructions that can be executed very quickly. Consequently only instructions which are simple to execute are possible; only a small number of different instructions meet the requirement of fast execution hence CPUs designed with this form have only a small number of instructions. This is the origin of the name reduced instruction set computer, RISC; the primary design aim is fast instruction execution rather than the use of a small instruction set.

3.4 Development tools

ARM processors are supported by powerful development tool packages from ARM Holdings plc., and by alternatives from other suppliers. One alternative set is that from the Free Software Foundation, usually called the GNU software tools, Appendix F. In general development tools are complex large computer packages that perform many functions. They are intended for development of complete software systems for large commercial applications and the large number of features included makes using them difficult for the beginner. Except in Appendix F it is assumed that either the ADS or RealView assembler from ARM is used; features only available in RealView are not used so that examples work with either version. There are differences in the syntax, text rules, for assembly language programs when packages from different suppliers are used; the main differences using the GNU tools instead of ARM tools are outlined in Appendix F.

Evaluation versions of the ARM tools are available; one form is a CD from ARM restricted to use for sixty days. The other is downloaded from the internet site of Keil Elektonik GmbH which became an ARM subsidiary in 2005. The Keil version allows download of both the RealView and GNU assemblers. Most versions have no time limit but the maximum program size using the evaluation version of the RealView tools is 16kbytes of code; this is adequate for initial studies of assembly language.

Any development package that includes some simple set-up instructions, an assembler and support for testing programs may be used provided any syntax differences are known and understood. Most packages run on standard desktop computers and are available for machines running either the Windows or Unix/Linux operating systems. The assembler in the packages is called a **cross-assembler** because it runs on one type of CPU, the one in the desktop computer, but produces code for another type of CPU, in this case the ARM core.

Having designed a program structure and composed the assembly language program the text is input to a **source file** using a text editor; usually one is included in the development system. A word processor **must not** be used to create source files although many text editors allow text to be cut and pasted from a word processor package. Once the source file is complete the assembler is used to produce the binary code which is tested to ensure that it performs as specified. Thorough testing covering all possible situations is an essential part of software development. First tests are often performed using a simulator provided with the development system. A simulator is a program that runs on the same computer as the development tools and imitates the actions of the target CPU running the code produced. Simulators include aids that allow the user to inspect the register contents as the program runs. Both the ARM and Keil evaluation packages include powerful simulators with provision for simulating input from, and output to, external devices by the ARM program.

Most development tools provide simple methods of loading programs into hardware target systems that contain a real CPU and monitoring their execution when running on this CPU. Several low cost simple development targets are available for ARM systems.

3.5 Summary – what the programmer needs to know

The programmer should consider the ARM CPU as operating on a bank of sixteen registers, r0 to r15. For most programs r0 to r11 are general purpose and may be used however the programmer chooses; r13, r14 and r15 should be reserved for their special functions that will be introduced as required. r12 may be used as a general purpose register by simple programs but is reserved for special use in advanced programs.

System memory is a block of 32-bit storage units at contiguous memory addresses in a range set by all possible 32-bit numbers; individual addresses apply to 8-bit values. The 8-bit values are grouped so that values from four adjacent addresses starting at the address with the two least significant bits zero form the 32-bit word value.

This brief outline description provides enough detail of the CPU structure to begin studying the process of preparing ARM programs in assembly language. As programming can only be learned by performing exercises development software and testing tools are required. Evaluation packages are adequate for exercises but are too restricted for developing commercial applications. A good knowledge of how to use the development package chosen must be acquired.

3.6 Problems

3.1   Produce a table or diagram showing the values in each memory location of an ARM system starting at address 0x00008000 and ending at address 0x0000800f with the following values stored as 32-bit values in order using little-endian form.

0x0023e45a, 0x90d270c1, 0x04ef130a, 0xff016b38

3.2   Repeat problem 3.1 but use big-endian form.

3.3   Which ARM registers are available for general use and which have special functions?

4 Starting to Use Assembly Language

Assembly language programmers must acquire some knowledge of internal CPU structure, have detailed knowledge of the instruction set, and know how to use the development tools. As it is not possible to instantly acquire detailed knowledge of all these the approach adopted to the study of program preparation using assembly language is incremental. Any attempt to create complex programs before all the topics are fully understood leads to development of poor techniques that become habitual and are difficult to correct.

4.1 Methodology

Details of the ARM CPU and its instruction set are introduced in small stages; examples and exercises are organised so that the reader only requires concepts and information already introduced. Exercises at the end of each chapter should be performed as soon as the relevant topics have been studied as development of the use of assembly language requires practice.

Even expert programmers do not attempt to learn all details of a new CPU on first use. When they start to prepare assembly language for an unfamiliar CPU they read summary documents that list all the instructions and the actions they perform. Using experience gained using other CPU types they note the very small number of instructions that will probably be used frequently and learned by repeated use. Note is also made of where details of less frequently used instructions are in the manuals; when a program requires these the manuals are examined to find full instruction details. The approach here is similar; the most frequently used ARM instructions are described first, further instructions are introduced as required. Because this approach is used readers should follow topics in the order in which they are introduced.

4.2 Instruction action

The CPU details required by an assembly language programmer are shown by the Programmers' Model; that for ARM is repeated as Figure 4.1. For simple programs all the shaded registers and the CPSR register may be ignored; only r0 to r15 are required and each one holds a 32-bit quantity. When preparing a program the register names may be written[1] in lower case as r0, r1, r2, etc.; or in upper case as R0, R1, R2, etc.; the choice is not important but for clarity only use one form. Lower case is adopted here for actual register names r0 to r15; upper case forms such as Rm and Rn indicate that the programmer must select any one of the sixteen registers. Definitions of instructions indicate that a programmer must choose any register by printing <Rn>. The *'less than'* and *'greater than'* characters stress that the programmer must make a selection. In a program <Rn> or Rn must be replaced by one of the actual registers r0 to r15; the one used is chosen by the programmer. The characters < and > **are not typed**; they emphasise that the programmer must make a choice.

Some registers have alternative names that indicate a special function; for example r15 is also called pc and any of the allowed names pc, PC, r15 and R15 may be used. To produce clear documentation

---

[1] The process of preparing a program for input to an assembler is usually called writing the program although the input process is one of input, by typing, into a text editor program; a word processor program must not be used.

that makes programs easy to understand the form, such as pc, indicating the special function of a register should be used. Although pc or PC may be used many assemblers do not allow the mixed case forms Pc and pC; use of these produces obscure error messages.

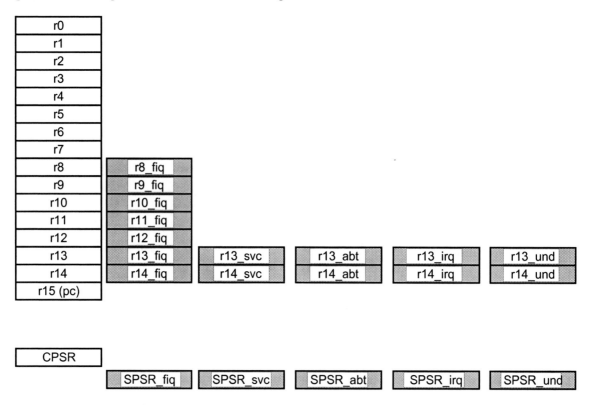

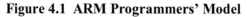

Figure 4.1 ARM Programmers' Model

To prepare assembly language programs regard the processor as a system that can perform, **execute**, a sequence of simple actions, **operations**, on data values, **operands**, stored in either the registers or memory. Execution of most instructions changes the contents of one or more registers. For ARM only registers r0 to r11 should be used to hold general purpose program values. All the other registers, especially r15, should be reserved for the special functions that are introduced as they are required.

Although it has a pipelined structure an ARM processor follows the conventional fetch-decode-execute von Neumann cycle of Figure 3.3. The instruction fetch obtains a 32-bit binary pattern from the memory location at the address that is the program counter contents. Most, **but not all**, of the 2^{32} possible patterns represent valid instructions. In assembly language each large group of similar instructions is given a simple common name, a **mnemonic name**; this reduces the number of different things the programmer must know. Mnemonics are chosen to indicate actions of instructions in an easily remembered manner.

An assembly language program consists of the instruction mnemonics written in the order in which the instructions must be executed to perform the required task. The assembler converts the list of mnemonics into the corresponding sequence of instruction code numbers. Many other features are included in assembly languages to assist in program preparation.

This book is for those who have never used any form of assembly language; it may also assist those who have previously used assembly language for other CPU types when they first meet an ARM system. A programmer who has previously programmed a Complex Instruction Set Computer, **CISC**, in assembly language will find some features of ARM unusual because of its RISC structure. Most CISC instructions perform a single, often complex, operation in a well defined way but may obtain the values, operands, in many different ways. An ARM instruction can perform several very simple operations simultaneously with operands obtained in one of a small number of simple ways.

As it is a RISC processor the ARM instruction set is small, even so **DO NOT** attempt to learn it. Instead note where the necessary information is in the following chapters and in the ARM Architecture Reference Manual [12]. Because the ARM instruction set is small much of it is quickly remembered with repeated use. The ARM feature of instructions being able to perform several operations at once means that an instruction is built from several components; compound instructions are created by the programmer. This can be confusing when first met and the problem is overcome by introducing the assembly language in a slightly different manner from that used for a CISC processor. As not all of the components of instructions have to be used assembly language instructions are introduced by techniques for doing single things rather than by complete description of the full instruction; that is components of instructions are introduced one at a time.

4.3 A first instruction, ADD

An assembly language allows each processor operation, action, to be described by its mnemonic name. For example the mnemonic **ADD** represents many of the instructions that perform addition. Either letter case may be used when typing a mnemonic; here upper case is used to emphasize the mnemonics. Anyone familiar with the C language or Unix operating system may prefer lower case. An unusual feature of the ARM assemblers in the ADS and RealView development packages is that mixed case is not allowed. That is **ADD** and **add** are allowed but **Add**, **AdD** and other mixed case combinations are not allowed. This feature is not present in assemblers from other suppliers; many regard upper and lower case as identical, they are case insensitive.

To perform operations such as ADD the processor acts on some numeric values, operands, and produces a result. The general form of addition is $C = A + B$; that is a quantity A is combined with a second quantity B using the rules for arithmetic addition to produce a sum C. ADD requires three operands; two input or **source operands** to provide the values A and B, and one output or **destination operand** denoted as C here.

When ARM performs arithmetic operations it can only use registers to provide source operands and to hold destination operands. Therefore the ADD instruction takes the contents of any one of the registers r0 to r15 and adds it to the contents of any register, again any of r0 to r15; the result is put into any register r0 to r15. As previously stated, although it is allowed, registers r13, r14 and r15 should not be used for general operations. If their contents are used as input operands detailed behaviour of advanced features must be understood to ensure the intended result is obtained. If one is used as the output operand the effect on the behaviour of the program will be extremely complex and in some cases behaviour cannot easily be predicted.

The complete assembly language instruction is the mnemonic plus the operands allowed for that instruction; the simple form introduced for the addition instruction may be written as

```
ADD   <Rd>, <Rn>, <Rm>
```

When a program is written each operand indicated by <Rd>, <Rn> and <Rm> is replaced by the required register name, r0 to r15. There must be **at least one space** between ADD and the register name used in place of <Rd>; spaces either side of the commas are optional. Punctuation marks, such as the commas, in a list of operands are usually called **separators**. The order of the registers confuses some beginners because the register order seems to be written in the reverse order of their use. It is written so that the registers appear in the order of quantities in the equation $C = A + B$. That is the instruction adds the contents of Rm to the contents of Rn and puts the result in Rd. The instruction should be regarded as:-

'the contents of Rd become equal to the sum of the contents of Rn with the contents of Rm'

Hence to add the contents of r5 to those of r11 and put the result in r3 the instruction used is

```
ADD   r3, r11, r5
```

The addition is performed assuming the two registers hold unsigned, that is positive only, integer values. The addition circuit of the CPU regards the two 32-bit patterns in the registers as unsigned binary integers and produces their 32-bit sum. Figure 4.2 is a simple illustration of the addition process for two arbitrarily selected values, more complicated cases are described later.

```
0 1 1 0 0 1 0 1 0 0 1 0 1 0 1 1 1 1 0 0 0 1 0 1 0 0 1 1 0 1 0 1   addend in Rn
0 1 0 0 0 1 1 1 1 0 0 0 0 1 0 0 1 0 1 0 0 0 1 0 0 0 1 0 1 0 0   augend in Rm
1 0 1 0 1 1 0 0 1 1 1 0 1 1 1 0 0 0 0 1 0 1 1 0 0 1 0 0 1 0 0 1   sum to Rd
```

Figure 4.2 An example of the addition of two 32-bit values

The same register can appear in more than one operand position; the following are some of many versions allowed with more than one operand the same

```
ADD   r3, r5, r5
ADD   r3, r5, r3
ADD   r3, r3, r3
```

An important feature of all instruction definitions is that they **only state what the instruction does**. Descriptions do not state what instructions do not do; so many things are not done that the description of each instruction would be a large book if this information were included. If something is not indicated as happening in an instruction description it does not happen. For example the complete ARM specification of ADD   r3, r12, r5 does not indicate any change in the contents of r12 and r5; the contents are **not changed**, the operation makes a copy of the values in the registers and uses these. Similarly the description states nothing about the original contents of r3; the **original contents of r3 are lost**, they are overwritten.

4.4 Instruction definition

In documents defining the CPU behaviour ADD is the instruction mnemonic and the various Rd, Rn and Rm quantities are the operands. The complete definitions for all the ARM instructions are given in the ARM Architecture Reference Manual [12]; this specifies every detail of every action performed when the instruction is executed. To determine the exact behaviour of any instruction always refer to this manual. In ARM documents the ADD instruction is written in a general form as

```
ADD{<cond>}{S}   <Rd>, <Rn>, <shifter_operand>
```

In section 4.3 a number of elements of this were ignored and will be introduced later; it is only necessary at this point to describe why the instruction is written this way. When curly brackets { } appear in the definition of an ARM instruction they indicate that the particular item is optional. The item inside the curly brackets can be included or omitted as required by the programmer. The curly brackets are not typed when the item is included, just the item itself is typed. Unfortunately there is **one exception to this**

rule which will be met much later. For example when the {S} item, described later, is used the instruction mnemonic becomes ADDS. At present ignore the items {<cond>} and {S} as these are optional and are not required for simple addition.

The use of the symbols < and > with some text between them indicates one of several different items must be placed at this position. As for curly brackets the symbols < and > are not typed. However unlike curly brackets there must always be something here; the programmer chooses which of several allowed quantities is used. A choice of nothing where the < and > symbols appear is not allowed **except** when the < and > are also inside curly brackets as for {<cond>}. Thus <shifter_operand> indicates that something is essential here; many items are allowed and a detailed description of all quantities that may be used for <shifter_operand> is left until the necessary prerequisite topics have been examined. One allowed quantity for <shifter_operand> is any register indicated by <Rm>. Whenever <Rd>, <Rn> or <Rm> appears as an operand any of the sixteen registers r0 to r15 may be used.

By using this text form a large number of different ADD instructions have been represented by a single general form. Even the reduced form ADD   <Rd>,   <Rn>,   <Rm>   corresponds to 4096 different instructions each with a different binary code. The assembly language allows all 4096 instructions to be written in the same easily remembered manner; the assembler determines the actual binary codes when it processes the program.

4.5 Another instruction and more operands

Before the ADD instruction can be used it is necessary to have some values in the registers whose contents are to be added. The most simple instruction for putting values somewhere is the instruction **MOV**. This is **move** and, as the mnemonic indicates, it moves something from one place to another although this is not an exact description. The choice of MOV (move) for the name of this type of instruction is used in the instruction sets of many CPUs but is poor; copy would be a better name because MOV makes a copy of some value and puts the copy in a destination. Again there is a general form

MOV{<cond>}{S}   <Rd>, <shifter_operand>

which should be read as   *'the contents of Rd become equal to the value of <shifter_operand>'*

MOV has only two operands, there is no operand <Rn>; this instruction copies something from one place to another. For example MOV   r4, r11 copies the contents of r11 into r4. It is important to **note the direction**; the action is copy **from r11 to r4**. After execution of this instruction both registers have the same contents equal to the original value in r11; the original value in r4 is lost.

So far no method has been described to put a number chosen by the programmer into a register. One very simple quantity that may be used whenever <shifter_operand> appears in a definition is a number. This is called an **immediate operand** because the numeric value is built into the instruction and is used immediately when the instruction is fetched. All ARM instructions are exactly 32-bits and some of the 32-bits must be a code to indicate the operation to be performed; consequently only a small number of bits can be used as an immediate value.[1] In simple cases the immediate operand is any number from 0 to 255 decimal and must be written with the character # before the number to show that the operand must be the actual numeric value. There should be no spaces between the # character and the first digit of the number although some assemblers do allow spaces.

---

[1] Programmers who have used CISC processors may not have met the problem of immediate operands having a restricted range. Many CISC processors have a variable size instruction word and instruction codes may use as many memory locations as required. It is possible to include any size of immediate value as part of an instruction code.

An immediate operand can be used with any instruction wherever <shifter_operand> is shown in the mnemonic definition, for example

```
MOV   r4, #164
ADD   r2, r7, #97
```

`MOV   r4, #164` moves, copies, the binary pattern equivalent to the decimal value 164 into r4; the value is placed in all 32-bits so a large number of bits in the most significant, the left most, positions are cleared to 0. The instruction `ADD   r2, r7, #97` adds the decimal value 97 to a copy of the value in r7 and puts the result into r2. In ARM assembly language, as most programming languages, numbers are **always assumed to be decimal** unless they are written in a form that indicates that another base is being used. Mechanisms exist for providing numbers in bases other than ten when this assists in program preparation and documentation. For example hexadecimal numbers may be written in the form 0x*hhhh* or as &*hhhh* where *hhhh* is replaced by the required hexadecimal digit symbols, Appendix C provides a brief description of numbers in several bases.

The instructions that have been introduced enable the simple, but **incomplete,** first program to be written; this is Program 4.1.

```
MOV   r3, #25          ; load first value
MOV   r7, #204         ; load second value
ADD   r2, r3, r7       ; form the sum of the two values
```

Program 4.1 A simple incomplete program

Alternatively if the programmer does do not wish to retain one of the initial values in a register the same total value is obtained in r2 using Program 4.2.

```
MOV   r3, #25          ; load first value
ADD   r2, r3, #204     ; form the sum of the two values
```

Program 4.2 An alternative version of incomplete program 4.1

This first simple example illustrates that often many different programs will produce the same result. A problem when preparing computer programs in all languages is that a program may produce the required results for a limited range of tests but not in all possible cases. Extensive testing is always necessary to identify programs containing such faults.

4.6 Program comments

In both incomplete program examples, Programs 4.1 and 4.2, each mnemonic plus operands is followed by a semi-colon and some text. The text items are **comments** and are used to add explanation to the program. The comments are ignored when the assembler converts the assembly language into instruction codes.

- The semi-colon and everything following it on a line is ignored by the assembler when it generates the instruction codes.
- A comment **does not** state what an instruction does; the mnemonic and operands do this.
- The comment shows **why** the programmer put this particular instruction at this point.
- Comments are used to help the reader understand the program. They also provide detailed reminders to prevent the programmer creating errors when modifying the program.
- **Every line** of a program should have a comment.

- Comments are typed when the line is typed, they are not added later.
- Additional lines containing only comments are used to explain the program structure, etc.
- Every source file should have a comment header giving date written, revision history, author and the purpose the program or program module in the file.
- Each section of a program should have a comment heading describing the section (what it does, the transfer of data between this section and the rest of the program). Any other useful general information about the section of program should also be in this heading.

Good documentation is an essential part of good software design and always has generous use of complete, brief and relevant comments. Organisations that produce high quality commercial software often define standard rules for the form of comments and insist that all programmers follow them.

4.7 Completing and testing the first program

The most important part of program development is comprehensive testing; that is the programmer must run the program with as many different sets of data as possible and check that it produces the expected results. Testing requires that the programmer can examine intermediate values and program results; this requires some form of display. Assemblers are usually part of an **integrated development system**, a software package that runs on a personal computer, PC. Common development systems for ARM are ADS and RealView from ARM Holdings or the Keil μVision system which allows the user to select either the RealView or the GNU assembler. Most development systems provide an **integrated development environment, IDE**. The IDE operates with a window allowing the user to select each development task as it is required; the development system correctly combines each program development step with little user intervention. The development system usually includes either a simulator, or a link to a target board, or both; these allow the user to *look inside* the CPU and memory. The user can see what is in registers, memory locations and other hardware elements while a program runs. A program can be **stepped** to run one instruction then stop, run the next after a specified key on the PC keyboard is pressed, and so on. Each time it stops the registers and memory contents can be examined. Another feature is that **break points** may be set; these allow the program to be run at full speed until a particular instruction is reached. The program stops at the break point allowing register and memory contents to be examined; execution can continue after inspection or even after modification. For early studies of assembly language development systems avoid the need to learn how to perform input and output operations; such operations depend on hardware and are often complicated.

Commercial development systems are complex and each is different. Manuals explain how to install and use the system and provide examples of use. Most educational establishments select a single type of system and instructors configure them for initial exercises. For readers who do not have access to such systems the evaluation version of the Keil tools is suggested for initial work and Appendix E provides a brief description of installation and use.

To test an assembly language program it is converted into the binary code then run. The assembly language program is prepared as a text file, usually using the editor built into the development system. The file is an assembly language source file; for ARM systems the file may have any name but must have the extension **.s**. The source file is the input to the assembler program which produces the binary code as one output. Some extra information must be provided in the source file to assist in the code production and this varies slightly for each development system. Details are given here for typical systems from ARM Holdings and Keil; most examples are easily adapted for other systems.

4.7.1 Using systems from ARM Holdings

A complete example of a source file is Program 4.3 which will run on the simulator, the ARMulator, in development systems from ARM and on many ARM target boards, for example Evaluator-7T. The program has blank lines to separate components and is arranged in columns. Programs in all languages should be arranged so that they are clear and easily followed. In assembly language each field of the same type of quantity should be in the same column. Program 4.3 has all the instruction mnemonics in the same column, operands are another column, and other items appear in their own columns. The ARM assembler restricts use of the first position on a line, called column 1, to the type of items printed in italic form and described later. Alternatively column 1 may contain a semi-colon if a line consists entirely of comments.

```
; First complete example program in file Prog4_3.s
; Filenames should indicate program functions; here they refer to the text
; Date:-      1st July 2007
; Revision:-  (date and details added here each time a change is made)
; Author:-    J.R. Gibson
; Performs simple addition to illustrate two instructions, version for use
; with development systems from ARM Holdings

          AREA    Add_Test, CODE, READONLY  ; code module named Add_Test
          ENTRY                             ; indicate which instruction to run first

mystart   MOV     r3, #25         ; load first value
          MOV     r7, #204        ; load second value
          ADD     r2, r3, r7      ; form the sum of the two values
stop

; the next 3 lines are used by ARM systems (e.g.Armulator, Evaluator-7T) to
; automatically return to the IDE when the program finishes
          MOV     r0, #0x18
          LDR     r1, =0x20026
          SWI     0x123456
          END
```

Program 4.3 A first complete program for ARM development systems

After input to the editor Program 4.3 is assembled and run from the IDE using the ARMulator or a real target board. It is very short so it should be run in single step mode; that is using the facility of the development system to run one instruction, display the contents of all the registers, then run the next instruction and display the new register contents and so on. Some development tools set the initial register contents to zero while other systems set random values. Setting all registers to zero automatically is not the best method as this does not happen when a real processor is used without the development system; in such situations the registers will contain random values when power is first connected.

4.7.2 Using the Keil tools

Program 4.4 is a modified version of Program 4.3; the changes have been made so that it can be assembled and run using the Keil development system set to use the RealView assembler. The changes are minor;

they are not a function of ARM assembly language but implement the different mechanism used by Keil to combine various tasks of program development. Further details describing the set up and use of the Keil tools are in Appendix E. Note that very large changes are required if the Keil system is used with GNU assembler.

```
; First complete example program in file Prog4_4.s
; Filenames should indicate program functions; here they refer to the text
; Date:-       2nd July 2007
; Revision:- Prog4_3.s modified for use with the Keil development system
; Author:-     J.R. Gibson
; Performs simple addition to illustrate two instructions, version for use
; with development systems from Keil Elektronik GmbH

           AREA    Add_Test, CODE, READONLY  ; code module named Add_Test
           EXPORT Reset_Handler       ; indicate which instruction to run first

Reset_Handler

mystart    MOV    r3, #25           ; load first value
           MOV    r7, #204          ; load second value
           ADD    r2, r3, r7        ; form the sum of the two values
stop

; the next line causes the program to wait for the user to tell the IDE to
; stop the program running
           BAL    stop
           END
```

Program 4.4 A first complete program for the Keil development system

4.8 Directives, labels and other features of a complete program

Programs 4.3 and 4.4 have some items shown in bold or italic print. A normal source file would not use bold or italic print; in this book example programs use these forms for emphasis and to identify important features. Items in **bold print** are **assembler directives**, sometimes called pseudo operations. Directives do not generate any instruction codes; they determine how the assembler generates code or provide features making program preparation easier and less error prone. Directives are usually put in the same column as the instruction mnemonics.

Several directives are essential in assembly language programs; those required vary according to the development system being used. **AREA** indicates a section of program with additional optional items **CODE** and **READONLY** to indicate that the section contains instructions and that the code produced may be put into read only memory. *Add_Test* is the title for this program unit and was chosen by the program writer. As indicated in Chapter 2 most large programs are broken into modules that have to be combined, **linked**. The line with the AREA directive provides information that the assembler passes to the linker; when there are several modules this assists the linker in the task of putting the final program together.

The directive **ENTRY** in Program 4.3 sets the program starting point; it must only be present in one module of a multiple module program. This directive may appear unnecessary but it is possible to write programs that do not start at the first instruction in the list. Many ARM development tools have extra facilities to help in testing and use this entry point when the tool is instructed to run a program during development. The entry point is also used by the linker when separately developed modules are combined into a single program.

In Program 4.4 for Keil systems the entry point is set by two lines; **EXPORT** *Reset_Handler* is one and the other contains only *Reset_Handler*. Together the two lines perform the same task as the ENTRY directive required by ARM development systems but are a little more complicated; an explanation of the EXPORT directive is left until Chapter 14.

It is essential to have the ENTRY directive when using ARM systems and the two lines containing *Reset_Handler* for Keil systems; inclusion of both forms in a program does not cause problems; each system ignores the one that is not necessary.

END indicates that the program is complete, anything after this is ignored. This is essential as some types of error can suggest that more program lines than exist should be present; the END directive ensures that such errors are detected. Always type a new line after the END directive; some assemblers report an error if the END directive does not appear on a complete line with a new line code at the end.

Italic print is used in example programs to emphasise that these items are names chosen by the programmer; they are **user names**. User names do not generate code but they assist the assembler to generate code and improve the documentation. *Add_Test* provides a name for the section allowing it to be identified when the linker combines several separately developed components. *mystart* and *stop* are a particular type of user name called **labels**; here their only function is to identify points in the program. Labels **must** be positioned so the first letter of the label is in the first column of the line. A label may be the only item on a line, also lines with only a label and a comment are allowed. Placing only a label, or label and comment, on a line can assist in making a program easier to understand; that is in some cases it improves the documentation.

User names should be chosen to indicate their purpose; this assists in program documentation and helps to reduce mistakes. There are restrictions in the choice of names. Most assemblers prohibit the use of the mnemonics, directives and registers as user names; a very unusual feature of the ADS and RealView assemblers is that they do not. However any use of a mnemonic, directive or register name as a user name is confusing and likely to lead to program errors so should be avoided.

User names consist of letters, numeric digits and the underscore character. The full rules allow more choices but for simple programs always use a letter or underscore as the first character of a user name. User names are case sensitive for ARM assemblers but not for some from other providers; for example *Add_test* and *Add_Test* are different names. Avoid using two names that are similar; in particular do not use names that differ only in the case of some letters as the risk of program errors when similar names are used is very high. The length of names is not restricted for most ARM assemblers although the maximum length of a program line is often restricted to between 128 and 255 characters depending on development system constraints.

In many situations a user name corresponds to a numeric value and the name may be used in place of the value. When the name is a label its value is that of the address of the memory location which will hold the code of the next instruction after the label. The next instruction may be on the same line as the label, as is the case for *mystart* in Program 4.3; alternatively it may be several lines later as for the label *stop* which has the value of the address where the instruction `MOV   r0, #0x18` is placed.

User names should be short to save typing; however they should not be so short that they do not indicate their purpose. A common method adopted by many programmers is to include the underscore character in a name. For example if a program has many modules, sections or other divisions then a name of something defined within one module might have the form *xxx_mod* or *mod_xxx* where *xxx* is chosen to indicate what the name defines and *mod* is the name, or part of the name, of the module. Other common techniques include forms such as *mod_NN* where *NN* is a two digit number; usually *NN* values are used in a 05, 10, 15, 20 sequence and the values identify position in the module. These methods both help to locate a named item and also prevent the same name being used in different modules of a large program.

The two development systems require different program endings although that used for Keil systems will cause no problems if used with ARM systems; the only effect is the loss of a useful feature of the development system. A description of both end mechanisms is left until later; their primary function is to prevent a running program fetching random values in memory locations after the last program instruction and executing the values fetched as if they are required instruction codes.

All the elements of a line of an ARM assembly language program have been introduced. Each line is independent of all others and can be represented by the general format

      {*label*}   **{*instruction* or *directive* or *pseudo instruction*}**   **{*;comment*}**

This format consists of three fields and each field is optional. An assembly language line may have no fields; that is it is blank to assist in producing a clear layout. Alternatively a line may have any single field, any two fields or may have all three fields. Each field must be of the form described.

4.9 Typing the program, running the assembler, *etc.*

The IDE of a modern software development system links all the tools together and usually operates in a window similar to that of other desktop computer programs. The complete development of a program is a project; for large programs this includes information describing all the components and how they are combined into a single program. Many tasks are performed automatically using the IDE; the programmer only makes adjustments for advanced tasks. Assembly language source files are prepared using the editor which appears as a separate window in the main IDE window. For ARM systems assembly language source files must always have the extension **.s**. Once the text input is complete the command is given to run the assembler. If the assembler reports errors it is necessary to find the cause, correct the errors, and assemble the program again (and again and again....). The assembler only detects errors in the assembly language; for example incorrect spelling of a mnemonic, immediate values over 255, and many others. The assembler **cannot detect** errors when instructions are correctly typed but the program does not perform as required by the specification; this is the programmer's responsibility and detection of such errors requires extensive thorough testing procedures.

```
assembling Prog4_3.s...
Prog4_3.s(12) error A1150E:Bad symbol, not defined or external
Prog4_3.s(14) error A1163E:Unknown opcode AdD, expecting opcode or Macro
Prog4_3.s(15) error A1163E:Unknown opcode stop, expecting opcode or Macro
Target not created
```

Figure 4.3 Error message output from the ARM RealView assembler

Figure 4.3 shows the messages produced by the RealView assembler when three errors were introduced into Program 4.3. Figure 4.4 shows the less detailed messages from the ADS assembler.

Although the second produces more cryptic messages it does reproduce the source line where the error was detected and an eight digit hexadecimal number related to the memory address for the instruction code.

The first error is that there is no # character before the immediate numeric value 25. The second is because this assembler only accepts 'ADD' or 'add' as the mnemonic, not a mixed case form such as AdD; other assemblers may not indicate an error in this case. Finally the error on line 13 is not easily noticed; there is a single space before the label *stop* so it does not start in column 1. Because the label does not start in column 1 it is assumed to be a mnemonic or directive; as it is not one of these and is in mixed case it is indicated as an invalid mnemonic (opcode).

```
Error    : A1150E: Bad symbol
Prog4_3.s line 12
   12 00000000 mystart   MOV   r3, 25      ; load first value
Error    : A1163E: Unknown opcode
Prog4_3.s line 14
   14 00000004           AdD   r2, r3, r7  ; put the sum of two values
Error    : A1163E: Unknown opcode
Prog4_3.s line 15
   15 00000004  Stop
3 Errors, 0 Warnings
```

Figure 4.4 Error message output from the ARM ADS assembler

Assemblers from other suppliers will indicate errors but produce a different output. For example the GNU assembler allows mixed case mnemonics so does not indicate an error if they are used. It has a different syntax for labels, they do not have to start in the first column but they must end with a colon. Hence introducing the errors of omitting the # character and also omitting the colon after the label *Stop* produces the error messages in Figure 4.5.

```
Prog4_3.s Assembler messages
Prog4_3.s(12)  error register or shift expression expected -- 'mov r3,25'
Prog4_3.s(14)  error bad instruction 'stop'
```

Figure 4.5 Error message output from the GNU assembler

All assemblers output reasons for errors found; they may be code numbers with the cause of error determined using a look-up table, they may be reasons for errors which are often cryptic, or they may be numbers and reasons. Usually messages indicate the name of the source file and the number of the line on which the error was detected; it is important to realise that complicated errors may not be on the lines on which they are detected by the assembler.

Assemblers also produce warnings when a program contains something which may lead to a problem but the assembler cannot determine that it will. Warnings should not arise for simple programs but any that occur must be investigated. Some warnings indicate that the action of an instruction with the operands used is **unpredictable**. The terms unpredictable and **undefined** tend to be used interchangeably when referring to assembly language. In general they indicate that the behaviour of the program or CPU cannot be predicted. For example a few special ARM instructions restrict the combinations of registers which may be operands. If a combination that is not allowed is used a code may be produced but the CPU behaviour is not defined; behaviour may even vary depending on the values in the registers. There are also situations where program features imply that other information is elsewhere; if it is missing the assembler may indicate that something is undefined.

When there is a warning the program should be amended to remove it unless the programmer understands the cause and is certain it will not cause problems. When the program has no errors the assembler and linker produce a complete file of program instruction codes in the correct order, an **object code file**. Usually this is in a special format defined by the supplier of the development tools. The format is not important as the tools will have mechanisms for loading the program into target systems. Once loaded the program must be thoroughly tested to ensure that it behaves as specified. Development tools from ARM and Keil include simulators for initial testing; the final program must be tested on real hardware as there are always features a simulator cannot reproduce exactly.

Most assemblers also produce **list files**; this may require that a control setting is turned on in the IDE. The program documentation should always include a copy of the list file rather than the source file; the source file is part of the list file which also includes other useful information. For large programs the linker will produce a map file; this is useful for checking linker actions or problems when a program is built from a large number of separate modules. List and map files have not been included here because they are too large to fit onto the printed page of a book; when performing exercises requiring assembly of a program the reader should **always examine** the list files and note the information they provide.

4.10 Some more simple instructions

There are several other instructions closely related to the ADD and MOV instructions already introduced. A variant of MOV is **MVN**, move negate.

```
MVN{<cond>}{S}   <Rd>, <shifter_operand>
```

which is *'the contents of Rd become equal to the inverted (negated) value of <shifter_operand>'*. Every bit of the value <shifter_operand> is changed to the opposite value and put into the destination register, Rd. For example if `MVN  r9, r3` is executed when register r3 contains

1000 0101 1001 0011 0001 1110 1011 0100

then the value put into r9 is   0111 1010 0110 1100 1110 0001 0100 1011

As well as addition instructions the ARM processor has **subtraction** instructions, the main one is

```
SUB{<cond>}{S}   <Rd>, <Rn>, <shifter_operand>
```

read as *'the contents of Rd become equal to the contents of Rn minus the contents of <shifter_operand>'*

The instruction SUB performs subtraction; however unlike addition where `ADD  r3, r7, r2` produces exactly the same result as `ADD  r3, r2, r7` the instructions `SUB  r3, r7, r2` and `SUB  r3, r2, r7` produce different results. For subtraction **the order of the source operands is very important**. Features of <shifter_operand> examined later show that it is sometimes useful to be able to perform subtraction with the operands subtracted in the opposite order; to implement this there is an instruction RSB, reverse subtract.

```
RSB{<cond>}{S}   <Rd>, <Rn>, <shifter_operand>
```

read as *'the contents of Rd become equal to the contents of <shifter_operand> minus the contents of Rn'*

A feature of subtraction is that a number may be subtracted from one that is smaller. In such cases the minuend has an extra 1, a **borrow**, automatically put in the position to the left of the MSB and the subtraction performed with this adjusted 33-bit value. Figure 4.6 illustrates this process.

The programmer, not the CPU, chooses how the contents of registers represent numbers. However the CPU incorporates features that encourage certain choices. Addition and subtraction instructions operate with unsigned integers; all 32-bits represent a positive integer from 0 to 2^N-1. However, the programmer may decide that the values represent signed integers or any other quantity. ARM performs exactly the same operation for ADD and SUB regardless of the form of number representation used; it is how the programmer interprets results that is different. Further details are in section 5.7 and Appendix C.

Borrow

```
1│0 0 1 0 0 1 0 1 0 1 1 0 1 0 1 1 1 1 0 0 0 1 0 1 0 0 1 1 0 1 0 1   minuend
  0 1 0 1 0 1 1 1 0 1 0 0 0 0 1 0 0 1 0 1 0 0 0 1 0 0 0 1 0 1 0 0   subtrahend
  1 1 0 0 1 1 1 0 0 0 1 0 1 0 0 1 0 1 1 1 0 1 0 0 0 0 1 0 0 0 0 1   difference
```

Figure 4.6 Binary subtraction when the subtrahend is larger than the minuend

4.11 Pseudo instructions

Because ARM is a RISC processor there are limits on the capabilities of some instructions. One is that an immediate operand can only have a restricted range of values; this is particularly inconvenient when using the move instruction to put a fixed value in a register. To overcome such limitations the ARM assembler contains more features to assist the programmer than the assemblers for many CISC processors. One such feature is the provision of **pseudo instructions**; one such pseudo instruction is

```
LDR{<cond>}   <Rd>, =<immediate>
```

For the LDR pseudo instruction the operand <immediate> may be any 32-bit value; it is not restricted to the range 0 to 255. The operand is a number, a user name or other allowed quantity and must be preceded by an equals sign. LDR loads any 32-bit value into a register without the programmer having to determine the best method. When the assembler converts the pseudo instruction into an instruction code it selects the code for one of several possible instructions. The assembler always chooses the most efficient method of transferring the required value to the destination register.

There are two other uses of LDR which require that care is taken to use the correct syntax. The main alternative form of in Chapter 7 is a real instruction. The second operand of this instruction has square brackets around part of the operand so it is obvious when the real LDR instruction is being used. The LDR version that most frequently causes problems is a special version of the real instruction which does not have brackets or an equals sign before the second operand which must be a user name. The behaviour of this alternative version is described in Chapter 12. Because this alternative form exists the programmer must be careful to always type the equals sign for the pseudo mnemonic as omission will not always produce an error message.

All pseudo instructions except one generate a single instruction code but may cause additional numeric values to be stored elsewhere. Pseudo instructions cannot have the {S} field but most may have the {<cond>} field. Unless the {S} field is required always use LDR <Rd>, =<immediate> instead of MOV <Rd>, #<immediate>. The assembler uses MOV when it is possible to load the required value into the register with MOV; otherwise it uses the most efficient alternative.

A second pseudo instruction NOP, no operation, is the only one which **may not** have the {<cond>} field. It does nothing! An instruction code is placed in the code sequence so the CPU fetches, decodes and executes it; the only effect is that it wastes time. Most assemblers generate the code for MOV r0, r0; the CPU transfers the value from r0 through the arithmetic unit without change and puts it back into r0. This may seem pointless but it is useful, especially during program development. NOP instructions can be placed at critical points to slow execution. They also provide convenient points to set break points during testing and blocks of NOP instructions may be used temporarily instead of code sections causing problems during development.

```
; Revised form of simple addition in file Prog4_5.s
; Date:-   1st July 2007
; Author:- J.R. Gibson
; Revisions:- 3rd July 2007. Use of large immediate values
; Performs simple addition and illustrates the use of pseudo mnemonics

            AREA    Add_Test, CODE, READONLY  ; code module named Add_Test
            ENTRY                             ; indicate which instruction to run first
;           WARNING - insert lines with Reset_Handler for Keil systems
mystart     LDR     r3, =912345     ; load first value
            LDR     r7, =0x3f9836   ; load second value
            ADD     r2, r3, r7      ; form the sum of the two values
stop
            NOP                     ; NOPs added to assist in insertion. . .
            NOP                     ; . . .a break point

; For ARM systems the next 3 lines return control to the IDE, replace with
; line  BAL  stop for other systems
            MOV     r0, #0x18
            LDR     r1, =0x20026
            SWI     0x123456
            END
```

Program 4.5 Illustration of the use of pseudo instruction mnemonics

Program 4.5 is a revised version of Program 4.3 using the LDR pseudo mnemonic to load large values into registers; one value is decimal and the other is hexadecimal. The program includes a group of NOP instructions that have been added to assist in inserting a break point during testing.

4.12 Summary

The elements of preparing very simple assembly language programs for ARM processors have been outlined. The syntax rules described are for ADS and RealView assemblers. If an assembler is obtained from another source, for example the GNU tools from the Free Software Foundation, the manuals for that assembler must be studied to determine the syntax rules that must be followed. Brief details of the main syntax differences for the GNU tools assembler are in Appendix F.

The ARM instructions introduced in this chapter only allow very restricted program forms to be created; subsequent chapters build on the material introduced to create full programs. This book is not a complete programming manual for ARM processors. Such information is contained in the large number of datasheets produced by ARM and by the ARM Architecture Reference Manual [12]; these are written as manuals for the experienced programmer rather than as educational documents and are difficult to follow until the reader has some familiarity with the use of the assembly language.

4.13 Problems

For problems that require development of a program test the solutions with data values selected to cover the widest possible range of situations. For problems which require the development of only part of a program devise a test program with additional instructions to enable the partial program to be fully tested.

4.1 a) When ADD   r3, r5, r12 is executed what happens to the value that was in r3?

b) What is the effect (result) of executing ADD   r3, r5, r5 ?

c) What is the effect (result) of executing ADD   r3, r3, r3 ?

4.2 a) When MOV   r11, r2 is executed what happens to the value that was in r11?

b) What is the effect (result) of executing MOV   r4, #28 ?

c) What is the effect (result) of executing MOV   r3, r3 ?

4.3 Prepare a program to add together the numbers 127 decimal, 0xe45ad hexadecimal and 2_10101110010 binary (ARM assembly language uses prefix 2_ to indicate a number in base 2). Using a development system, assemble your program, repeatedly correct it and assemble again until there are no errors. Test that the program behaves correctly. What is the total obtained?

4.4 a) Assume that register r2 holds the value 0x0f45, what is the value in register r5 after the execution of the instruction SUB   r5, r2, #209 ?

b) Assume that register r2 holds the value 0x045, what is the value in register r5 after the execution of the instruction RSB   r5, r2, #209 ?

c) What problems arise when register r2 holds 0x0f45 and the instruction RSB   r5, r2, #209 is executed? What will be the value in register r5 after the execution of this instruction?

4.5 a) What is the value in register r8 after the execution of the instruction MVN r8, #0xf4 ?

b) Assume that register r3 holds the value 0x045 and r10 holds 0xffff; what is the value in register r3 after the execution of the instruction ADD   r3, r3, r10 ?

c) Describe the form of the value that will be in register r6 after the execution of the instruction ADD r6, r6, #1 ?

5 Breaking the Sequence

Examples in Chapter 4 illustrate that a simple assembly language program defines the order in which the CPU performs a sequence of actions. The program is a list specifying the order of instruction codes in memory; it is also the order, sequence, in which simple instructions are executed. Sequences are one of the three structure elements described in Chapter 2. Creation of the other structures, conditional actions and loops, requires the use of the decision making capabilities that are a feature of digital processor systems. Decisions are used to break the sequence of executing the instructions in the order in which they are listed in an assembly language program.

5.1 Branches

Normal CPU operation follows the von Neumann sequence, Figure 3.3, of fetch an instruction, advance the program counter, decode the instruction then execute it. The sequence is broken by a **branch instruction**. The execution of a branch instruction loads the program counter with a new value, this change causes the processor to **branch** to a new position in the program instead of performing the next instruction in sequence; branches may also be referred to as **jump to** or **goto**. The basic ARM branch instruction is **branch** and has the simple mnemonic name **B**. The mnemonic **BAL**, **branch always**, may also be used; the assembler generates the same code for both mnemonics.

For most types of CPU the determination of the new value to be loaded into the program counter when a branch instruction is executed is complicated. All ARM instruction codes are 32-bit values. Some bits of the instruction code must indicate which action the instruction performs hence for branch instructions only part of the instruction code can indicate the branch destination. ARM uses 24-bits of the 32-bit branch instruction code to represent a signed integer value. This value is called the **offset** and is added to the present value of the program counter to create the new value, the **branch destination**.

The branch offset is 24-bits; however all instruction codes are four bytes with the first byte at an address with the two LSBs zero so the offset used is the 24-bit value multiplied by four. A branch destination can only be at an address that has a value within a range approximately $\pm 2^{25}$, that is $\pm 33,554,432$, from the present instruction address. There are 2^{32} possible memory addresses for any ARM system therefore it is not possible to reach all allowed addresses by a branch instruction. This limitation is not a serious problem as most ARM programs have less than 2^{25} bytes of code; additionally most branches in well designed programs are within modules and require changes in the program counter of much less than the maximum offset. More advanced programming techniques provide methods to overcome the limitation that branch instructions do not allow all possible addresses as the destination.

There are several restrictions on branch offset values in addition to maximum size; for example if the offset value results in a new address below zero the program behaviour is unpredictable. If the assembly language program is written conventionally the additional restrictions are never encountered.

Programmers do not attempt to determine the offset value to be used with branch instruction as it is probable that errors will be made. Also the values required for most branch instructions in a program change every time minor modifications are made. The offset calculation for a pipelined CPU, such as ARM, is more difficult than for a simple system as the value of the program counter at the time of execution is not the same as it was when the instruction was fetched. To avoid all problems and the risk of mistakes the assembler determines the offset value automatically as part of the process of generating the instruction codes. The complete branch instruction definition is

$$B\{<cond>\} \quad <label>$$

where <label> is any user label in the program. This is a **very important use of labels** and is the main reason that assembly language programs have labels. The branch instruction does not have the optional field {S} and the field <label> is essential as the destination of the branch must be specified.

For example Program 4.3, which executed a simple addition, can be modified to repeatedly add one to the contents of a register. Program 5.1 is a new program illustrating this simple loop.

```
; Simple loop for ever example in file Prog5_1.s
; Date:-      4th July 2007
; Revisions:- none
; Author:-    J.R. Gibson
; Performs simple addition in a loop to illustrate the branch instruction


        AREA   Add_loop, CODE, READONLY   ; the only code module
        ENTRY
;              WARNING - insert lines with Reset_Handler for Keil systems
mystart MOV    r3, #0               ; load initial value
        MOV    r7, #1               ; load value loop increment amount
loop                   ; ** loop entry point
        ADD    r3, r3, r7           ; repeatedly increment value in r3
        B      loop                 ; loop for ever
; nothing more needed - this program can never get out of the loop
        END
```

Program 5.1 A simple looping program

This program runs forever and has no output so it can only be tested by single stepping. It is not particularly useful but, if the processor is connected to operate some automatic equipment and ADD is replaced by instructions to implement the required control function, this loop form is essential.

5.2 Flags, tests and conditional branches

Creation of *conditional statements* and *loops which exit* requires that the CPU instruction set supports some form of **condition testing**. ARM has powerful condition testing features; their form is slightly more complicated than that used by many other CPUs.

A first requirement when constructing tests for the conditional selection and loop structures described in Chapter 2 is a method of obtaining true and false values; that is there must be condition **indicators that can be tested**. One function of the Current Program Status Register, CPSR, is to provide the indicators. The contents of the CPSR register include a small number of elements, single bits or status bits, which indicate what has happened as a consequence of executing instructions; CPSR shows the **current status** of the system. Four bits in the CPSR are particularly important, these are bits N, Z, C and V. ARM literature usually calls these the **status bits**, for some other types of CPU they are called **indicator bits**, and programmers usually call them **flags**. The flags indicate features that are the consequence of executing an instruction. When ARM executes most instructions it automatically generates four signals that can be true or false and correspond to the CPSR bits N, Z, C and V.

An unusual feature of ARM is that the four signals that indicate properties of the result of executing an instruction are only copied into the corresponding CPSR bits N, Z, C and V **when the programmer deliberately indicates that they should be copied**. Except for the branch instruction, the definitions of all of the instructions introduced so far include the optional item {S} that has been ignored. The optional field {S} controls the action *'set flags'*. If the letter S is added to an instruction mnemonic the signals indicating result features are copied to the CPSR status bits; if the letter S is omitted the instruction does not change the values of the CPSR bits. For example the option to *'set flags'* used with

```
ADD{<cond>}{S} <Rd>, <Rn>, <shifter_operand>
```

leads to two versions of ADD which are **ADD** and **ADDS**. The only difference between these is that

- execution of ADD **does not modify** the values any of the N, Z, C and V bits in CPSR
- execution of ADDS **does modify** the values of all of the N, Z, C and V bits in CPSR

In Chapter 4 the problem of cases where the result of an operation, such as ADD, exceeds the size of the register where the result will be placed were ignored. There are many such cases, for example suppose at the time when the instruction ADD r3, r2, r5 is executed the binary values in the registers are

```
1100 1111 0000 1110 1100 0101 0011 0101  in register r2
0011 0111 0100 0010 0100 0001 0001 0100  in register r5.
```

To execute the ADD instruction the processor performs the normal operation of addition which is illustrated in Figure 5.1.

```
  1 1 0 0 1 1 1 1 0 0 0 0 1 1 1 0 1 1 0 0 0 1 0 1 0 0 1 1 0 1 0 1   addend in r2
  0 0 1 1 0 1 1 1 0 1 0 0 0 0 1 0 0 1 0 0 0 0 0 1 0 0 0 1 0 1 0 0   augend in r5
[1] 0 0 0 0 0 1 1 0 0 1 0 1 0 0 0 1 0 0 0 0 0 1 1 0 0 1 0 0 1 0 0 1   sum to r3
```

Figure 5.1 Another example of binary addition

The result of the addition is 1 0000 0000 0100 0001 0000 0110 0100 1001 which cannot be stored in a register as the value is over 2^{32}-1, the largest unsigned integer using 32-bits. There is a **carry out** of 1 in the position to the left of the most significant bit. It is called a carry, it is **not** called an overflow as by convention the term overflow is used for a different quantity in computer arithmetic. The value of the result bit one place to the left of the most significant bit of the result is the **carry**. The CPU always produces a value into the carry position after every addition, hence the value of the carry out is 0 if the result is less than 2^{32} and is 1 if it greater than or equal to 2^{32}. The instruction ADD does not move the carry produced into the C bit in the CPSR whereas ADDS does move the new value of the carry into bit C in the CPSR. The actions of *'set flags'* for several instructions are examined later.

When execution of an instruction causes a flag to have the value 1 the instruction **sets** the flag. The value 1 represents **set** and is also used to represent the Boolean condition **true**, a bit with the value 1 is set or true. When execution causes a flag to take the value 0 the instruction **clears** the flag. The value 0 represents **clear** and also represents the Boolean condition **false**, a bit with the value 0 is clear or false.

If the branch instruction is examined in detail there are sixteen variants, a few are

B	unconditional, branch always (BAL may be used instead of B for clarity)
BCC	branch if the carry is clear, C = 0, usually called branch on carry clear
BCS	branch if the carry is set, C = 1, usually called branch on carry set

The unconditional branch, B or BAL, has already been examined and used to illustrate the specification of branch destinations. BCC and BCS are two examples of conditional branches which are used to implement conditional and loop structures.

5.3 Using conditional branches

BCC   <label>, branch on carry clear, is such that when a program runs and the CPU executes this instruction it examines the C bit in the CPSR. If the bit is clear, 0, then the instruction behaves in exactly the same way as branch, B <label>, and the program counter is set to the new position defined by the label. If the C bit is set, 1, then the branch is not performed and the program moves on to the instruction that immediately follows the BCC instruction.

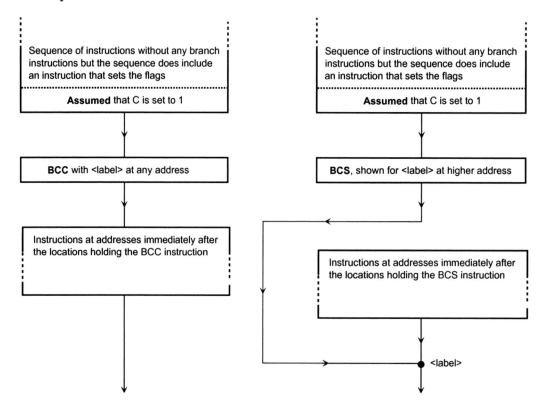

Figure 5.2 Example of program flow paths using BCC and BCS when C is set, C = 1

BCS *<label>*, branch on carry set, makes the decision to branch in the opposite manner to that used by BCC; it performs the branch to the label if C is set, 1, and does not branch if C is clear, 0. Figure 5.2 illustrates the program flow for BCC and BCS instructions assuming that previous actions have set C to 1 and the label is at a higher address than the branch instruction. Obviously if the label is at a lower address than the conditional instruction the program flow will branch backwards to a lower address when the condition is met.

Return to Program 5.1 and replace B *loop* by BCC *loop* and ADD by ADDS to produce Program 5.2. This revised program sets the contents of r3 to zero then repeatedly adds one to the value in r3 until the total in r3 exceeds the value with all bits 1. Each time ADDS is executed the flag bits in CPSR are loaded with new values that indicate features of the result. As r3 is initially loaded with zero and r7 always holds one then the first time, and on many subsequent occasions, when ADDS is executed the result of the addition is put back into r3 and a carry value of 0 is put into C. When the BCC instruction is executed C is clear and the instruction performs the branch action, the program counter is changed to the address of the instruction immediately after the label *loop*. After executing BCC the program performs the ADDS instruction again. Only when the program has executed the loop many times will r3 hold the value with all bits 1. The next execution of the ADDS instruction sets C to 1 and when the BCC instruction is executed as C is set the instruction does not perform the branch. The program counter is only changed by the automatic addition of four immediately after the instruction fetch and the program executes the instruction located immediately after BCC. That is the program performs the ADDS instruction 2^{32} times then leaves the loop; even on a fast ARM system this takes a very long time.

```
; Simple loop with exit in file Prog5_2.s
; Date:-      4th July 2007
; Revisions:- 5th July 2007, Prog5_1.s modified to exit loop
; Author:-    J.R. Gibson
; Performs a simple repeated addition loop with an exit mechanism

            AREA    Add_loop, CODE, READONLY
            ENTRY
;           WARNING - insert lines with Reset_Handler for Keil systems
mystart     MOV     r3, #0          ; load initial value
            MOV     r7, #1          ; load value added each loop
loop                        ; ** loop entry point
            ADDS    r3, r3, r7      ; repeatedly add value (set as 1)
            BCC     loop            ; loop for a long time
; For ARM systems the next 3 lines return control to the IDE, replace with
; the line    stop    BAL   stop    for other systems
stop        MOV     r0, #0x18
            LDR     r1, =0x20026
            SWI     0x123456
            END
```

Program 5.2 A simple program with a loop exit mechanism

When one is repeatedly added to the contents of a register so that it reaches the value with all the bits of the register 1 a further addition of one causes all the register bits to become all 0. Similarly if one is repeatedly subtracted from the contents of a register it eventually reaches the value with all bits 0. A further subtraction of one results in all the register bits becoming 1.

The action of adding one to some value **increments** the value; subtracting one from some value **decrements** the value. The terms increment and decrement are used to describe program actions of increasing or decreasing by one. In some cases the addition or subtraction may be by a fixed value other than one. For example ARM uses values at four successive addresses to hold a 32-bit value, increasing the address by four moves from the address of the start of one 32-bit value to the address of the start of the next. This addition of four is sometimes referred to as incrementing the address. That is increment or decrement usually means change the value by one but the terms are sometimes used to indicate increase or decrease by a fixed amount necessary to move by one position in a list of items.

It is important to devise testing processes that confirm conditional branch instructions behave as required because a large proportion of program faults arise from errors in conditional structures. Program behaviour at each conditional branch is determined by some Boolean value; although the branch actions depend on simple flag settings the Boolean value may be the result of evaluation of a complex logical requirement. In such cases testing must check that the flags are correctly set for a wide range of conditions; complex conditions are examined later. Once tests confirm that the flags are set as intended further tests must cause the program to follow both routes at the conditional branch; that is it is essential to test all possible execution paths. A method is required that indicates passage through each path. For small programs tests can be performed manually using debug facilities of a development system, large programs require inclusion of trace test mechanisms similar to those used by SQA tools.

5.4 Flag settings

Most decisions in computer programs are made by testing the state of one or more flags. To develop assembly language programs **a complete understanding of the way the flags are changed** is essential.

ARM is unusual because the programmer chooses if instructions change the flags or do not affect the flags. Instructions for most other CPUs are usually in two groups; those in one group always change some flags, those in the other never change any flags. For ARM a few instructions can never affect the flags; there is no optional {S} field in their specification; branch instructions have this form. Most other instructions affect some or all flags provided the {S} field is used. Those instructions that only affect some flags do so in a complicated way; MOVS is one such instruction. Finally a few instructions, not yet introduced, always affect the flags and for these the {S} field is not added to the mnemonic.

If the destination register, Rd, is r15 the behaviour of an instruction with the set flags option {S} is different. These settings are ignored at present as this special case involves several advanced features; this is another reason why r15 should not be used in the same manner as other registers.

For arithmetic operations the flags indicate features of the result. Another example of the execution of ADDS   r3, r2, r5 is illustrated by Figure 5.3.

```
0 0 0 0 0 1 1 0 1 1 0 0 0 1 1 1 0 0 1 1 0 1 0 1 1 1 0 0 1 1 1 1   addend in r2
1 1 0 0 1 1 1 1 0 0 1 0 0 1 0 1 0 0 0 0 0 0 1 1 1 1 0 0 1 0 0 1   augend in r5
0  1 1 0 1 0 1 0 1 1 1 1 0 1 1 0 0 0 0 1 1 1 0 0 1 1 0 0 1 1 0 0 0   sum to r3
 C  N
```

Figure 5.3 Example of execution of ADDS

N is the **sign flag** and is a copy of the MSB of the result in the destination register, r3. In Figure 5.3 the result is such that the N flag is set to 1.

Z is the **zero flag** and is set to 1 when all the bits in the destination register are 0; otherwise it is cleared to 0. In Figure 5.3 the result is not all zeros so the Z flag is cleared to 0; the case is *'not zero'*. The zero flag is sometimes confusing as the case when the result is zero, all register bits 0, causes the flag to be set to 1 whereas when the result is not zero Z is cleared to 0. Another feature that may appear odd is that when the result of an addition is exactly 2^{32} the Z flag is set to 1 because the 32-bits in the register are all zero; that is the total is very large but the Z flag indicates zero. The important feature of the Z flag is that it only indicates properties of the 32-bit part of the result of executing an instruction.

C is the **carry flag** and is a copy of the carry out from the MSB position. In the example illustrated in Figure 5.3 the carry, C, is cleared to 0. For some other instructions, especially subtraction, the behaviour of C is not obvious; subtraction is examined in section 5.7.

V is the **overflow flag**. The programmer decides if register contents represent signed integers, with the MSB indicating the sign, or they are unsigned positive integers using all the bits to represent the magnitude. The value of the overflow flag, V, is generated assuming that values are signed numbers in twos complement form, Appendix C. The V flag indicates signed number overflow. For ARM the V flag is set when overflow occurs into the thirty second place, the MSB position, from the thirty first. The example does not overflow so V is cleared to 0. A simple rule for determining the value of V for addition of numbers in twos complement is that if the MSBs of both numbers are different V is always 0. If the MSBs are the same then V is 0 if the result MSB is the same as the MSBs of the original numbers, V is 1 if the result MSB is not the same as that of the original numbers. For subtraction the opposite rule applies. If the MSBs of both numbers are the same V is always 0; if the MSBs are different then V is 0 if the result MSB bit is not the same as the MSB of the number which was subtracted otherwise V is 1.

Further discussion of flag settings for many situations is in section 5.7. The problems at the end of the chapter should be performed to develop an understanding of the flag behaviour.

5.5 ARM flag use

The flags can be set by any of the instructions which include the optional field {S} in their definition. Therefore to set the flags when executing ADD the form ADDS must be used. Similarly MOVS must be used to set the flags when executing the move instruction; **care must be taken with MOVS** because there are some features which are not obvious. MOVS affects the N and Z flags by the normal rules but, as no arithmetic is performed, there is no carry. The carry flag setting for MOVS is complicated and is sometimes difficult to predict. Unless the rules for setting the C flag, Chapter 9, are fully understood the programmer should regard the C flag state as unknown after MOVS; any instruction that follows MOVS should not test the C flag until a later instruction puts it into a defined state. **Note that MOVS does not change V**, after execution of MOVS the V flag has the value it had before MOVS was executed.

The manner in which the flags are set by all instructions which have the program counter, r15, as the destination register is different. These are **special cases** involving additional hardware features briefly described in Chapter 13. Simple programs do not require these special features and if good design rules are followed the program counter will only be the destination register in well defined situations that never require the use of the *'set flags'*.

IT IS VERY IMPORTANT TO REMEMBER to add the S, set flags, to the mnemonic when the programmer requires that the flags are to be set. Even experienced programmers sometimes accidentally omit to type the S in a single line of a program. Discovering that this error has been made is difficult because omission of a single letter is not easily detected and the effect on program behaviour may only appear when executing a section of program that is a long way from the error.

The flags are used to make decisions. For many types of CPU the only instructions which have conditional forms are the branch instructions but once again ARM has **an unusual feature**. All ARM instructions can be conditional; full definitions of the instructions introduced so far are:-

```
ADD{<cond>}{S}   <Rd>, <Rn>,  <shifter_operand>
SUB{<cond>}{S}   <Rd>, <Rn>,  <shifter_operand>
RSB{<cond>}{S}   <Rd>, <Rn>,  <shifter_operand>
MOV{<cond>}{S}   <Rd>, <shifter_operand>
MVN{<cond>}{S}   <Rd>, <shifter_operand>
B{<cond>}        <label>
```

Every ARM instruction has the optional field {<cond>} which may be any of sixteen different cases although only fifteen are allowed. Where ever {<cond>} appears in the instruction the programmer may add one of the conditional extensions to the mnemonic. Writing AL for always is optional; omitting the {<cond>} field completely or using AL both produce the same instruction code. Table 5.1 lists all the possible ARM conditions, note that NV or *'Never'* was implemented in early ARM versions but is not allowed for current versions. Care is necessary because some older assemblers produce an instruction code with NV but the action of the processor is unpredictable when it attempts to execute the code.

Mnemonic extension	Meaning	Flag status for condition to be met (action performed)
EQ	Equal / equals zero	Z set
NE	Not equal	Z clear
CS or HS	Carry set / unsigned higher or same	C set
CC or LO	Carry clear / unsigned lower	C clear
MI	Minus / negative	N set
PL	Plus / positive or zero	N clear
VS	Overflow	V set
VC	No overflow / in range	V clear
HI	Unsigned higher	C set and Z clear
LS	Unsigned lower or the same	C clear or Z set
GE	Signed greater than or equal	N and V the same
LT	Signed less than	N and V different
GT	Signed greater than	Z clear with N and V the same
LE	Signed less than or equal	*either* Z set *or* N and V are different
AL	Always (AL optional, usually omit)	Irrelevant, always met
NV	Never – **DO NOT USE**	None

Table 5.1 Mnemonic extensions for conditional execution

Examination of the condition codes in Table 5.1 shows that each flag can be tested individually to determine if it is clear, 0, or if it is set, 1. In addition some combinations of flags can be tested providing tests for conditions such as *'higher'*, *'less than'*, etc., after arithmetic operations with both signed and unsigned numbers. The mnemonic extensions, the two letters put in place of {<cond>}, are chosen to indicate the most common reason why a programmer uses the test. When two mnemonic extensions are shown for the same test either may be used; the assembler produces the same binary instruction code for both. There are two forms because there are two different tasks with the same flag test requirement. For clarity a programmer should use the extension that best indicates the reason the condition is being tested.

The exact meaning of extensions such as *'higher'* and *'greater than'* requires careful interpretation. These are usually used after subtraction; however after SUBS <Rd>, <Rn>, <Rm> does a test for *'greater than'* indicate that the contents or Rm are greater than those of Rn or does the test

Operation	Case (A,B)	Numbers	Result cases	N	Z	C	V	EQ	NE	CS	CC	MI	PL	VS	VC	HI	LS	GE	LT	GT	LE
ADD A+B	Not both 0	Unsigned	$0 < \text{result} < 2^{31}$	0	0	0	0	No	Yes	No	Yes	No	Yes	No	Yes	No	Yes	Yes	No	Yes	No
ADD A+B	Not both 0	Unsigned	$2^{31}-1 < \text{result} < 2^{32}$	1	0	0	X	No	Yes	No	Yes	Yes	No	X	X	No	Yes	X	X	X	X
ADD A+B	Neither 0	Unsigned	$\text{result} = 2^{32}$	0	1	1	X	Yes	No	Yes	No	No	Yes	X	X	No	Yes	X	X	No	Yes
ADD A+B	Neither 0	Unsigned	$\text{result} > 2^{32}$	X	0	1	X	No	Yes	Yes	No	X	X	X	X	Yes	No	X	X	X	X
ADD A+B	Sum > 0	Signed	$0 < \text{result} < 2^{31}$	0	0	X	0	No	Yes	X	X	No	Yes	No	Yes	X	X	Yes	No	Yes	No
ADD A+B	Sum < 0	Signed	$-2^{31} < \text{result} < 0$	1	0	X	0	No	Yes	X	X	Yes	No	No	Yes	X	X	No	Yes	No	Yes
ADD A+B	Sum > $2^{31}-1$	Signed	invalid	1	0	0	1	No	Yes	No	Yes	Yes	No	Yes	No	No	Yes	Yes	No	Yes	No
ADD A+B	Sum < $-2^{31}+1$	Signed	invalid	0	0	1	1	No	Yes	Yes	No	No	Yes	Yes	No	Yes	No	No	Yes	No	Yes
ADD A+B	A = B = 0	All	zero	0	1	0	0	Yes	No	No	Yes	No	Yes	No	Yes	No	Yes	Yes	No	No	Yes
SUB A-B	A > B	Unsigned	$0 < \text{result} < 2^{31}$	0	0	1	0	No	Yes	Yes	No	No	Yes	No	Yes	Yes	No	Yes	No	Yes	No
SUB A-B	A >> B	Unsigned	$2^{31}-1 < \text{result} < 2^{32}$	1	0	1	0	No	Yes	Yes	No	Yes	No	No	Yes	Yes	No	No	Yes	No	Yes
SUB A-B	A < B	Unsigned	invalid	X	0	0	X	No	Yes	No	Yes	X	X	X	X	No	Yes	X	X	X	X
SUB A-B	A = B	All	zero	0	1	1	0	Yes	No	Yes	No	No	Yes	No	Yes	No	Yes	Yes	No	No	Yes
SUB A-B	A > B	Signed	$0 < \text{result} < 2^{31}$	0	0	X	0	No	Yes	X	X	No	Yes	No	Yes	X	X	Yes	No	Yes	No
SUB A-B	A < B	Signed	$-2^{31} < \text{result} < 0$	1	0	X	0	No	Yes	X	X	Yes	No	No	Yes	X	X	No	Yes	No	Yes
SUB A-B	Result > $2^{31}-1$	Signed	invalid	X	X	1	1	X	X	X	X	X	X	Yes	No	X	X	X	X	X	X
SUB A-B	Result < $-2^{31}+1$	Signed	invalid	X	X	1	1	X	X	X	X	X	X	Yes	No	X	X	X	X	X	X

Table 5.2 Flag settings and conditional execution performed for flag settings after common arithmetic operations (see main text)

indicate the reverse case? Careful examination of the operations and flag values in Table 5.1 for each case shows that *'greater than'* corresponds to the contents of Rn being greater than the contents of Rm.

Condition tests are best illustrated by determining if a particular condition {<cond>} is met immediately after an arithmetic operation which sets the status bits. Table 5.2 illustrates the flag settings and shows which conditions are met using ADDS and SUBS instructions to perform $A + B$ and $A - B$ respectively with A in Rn and B in Rm. The register contents are either unsigned 32-bit integers or twos complement 32-bit integers, Chapter 10 and Appendix C. Many situations are possible so only the most common are shown; the values of A, B and the result all represent the same type of number as indicated in the column *'Numbers'*. The column *'Case'* indicates features of the values of A and B for the situation examined and *'Result'* indicates features of the result. Where the *'Result'* is *'invalid'* this means that it is not a valid number of the type in the *'Numbers'* column; however the CPU always produces a result because it always executes the instruction. When either a flag or a condition is indicated as *'X'* this is because both values of a flag are possible for the operation and that tests of the flag could yield either a true or false result. In a small number of cases where the condition is formed by a combination of several flags the condition may be determined even if one of the flags involved in the test may take either state.

The following illustrate a very small number of uses of conditional execution:-

ADDCC   r3, r4, r5   Performs the addition if C is clear and puts the result in r3; if C is set it does nothing and the contents of r3 are unchanged.

BCS   <label>   Performs the branch, jumps, if C is set otherwise it continues with the instruction immediately after the BCS instruction.

SUBEQ   r2, r9, r8   Performs the subtraction if Z is set and the result is put into r2 otherwise it does nothing and the contents of r2 are not changed.

MOVLT   r9, r2   Performs the move if N and V are different. This is used after the flags are set by an instruction performing A - B using twos complement signed numbers. The move is performed when B is less than A.

BHI   <label>   Performs the branch if C is set and Z is clear, this is used after subtraction of unsigned integers, A - B, the branch is executed if A was greater than B

Most ARM instruction definitions include {<cond>} and {S}; both fields are optional with every possible combination allowed. If both options are used simultaneously the risk of creating program faults, that is a program that does not behave as planned, is extremely high. This is because the flags are set to enable a conditional test to be made. When a program is designed it is essential to know when the flags were set so that the test is for a single purpose. If the set flags and conditional test are both performed by a single instruction it is not clear which instruction caused the flags to be in the condition detected when subsequent flag tests are made. **Do not use conditional execution and flag setting simultaneously**.

Once an instruction is executed which sets the flags they remain in the condition set until changed by execution of another instruction which changes them. Hence a sequence such as that in Program 5.3 is not clear and incorrect, not intended, behaviour is very probable. Causes of incorrect, that is unintended or unspecified, actions by such a program sequence will be very difficult to determine.

Program 5.3 contains features that make it difficult, or impossible, to predict its actions when it is part of a larger program. These are associated with the action of BCC which depends on the state of the carry flag. On quickly examining the program a reader could easily assume that the carry flag is set by the addition as a common requirement is to test the carry after addition. However there is no set flags field 'S' with ADD so this is not the case; if the program execution follows the path from the SUBS instruction to BCC then the flags are set by the SUBS instruction. There is a further major cause of uncertainty because BCC follows *label_1*. It is possible that BCC is reached by a branch to this label and the flag is set by the section of program executed just before the branch is performed. Therefore when BCC is executed it is not certain in which part of the program the carry flag was set. There are two important rules that should be followed when using conditionally executed instructions.

Rule 1 Put the instruction which sets the flags immediately before the instruction which acts conditionally on the flag state. When this is impossible put the instruction that sets the flags extremely close to the conditional instruction and include comments to indicate which instruction sets the flags.

Rule 2 Never put a label between the instruction that sets the flags and the one which tests them. If program design follows good structural methods these two rules will usually be satisfied.

```
         .   .   .   .
         SUBS    r5, r3, r7      ; find difference for some reason
         MOVEQ   r1, #22         ; if values equal set r1 to 22
         MOV     r2, r5          ; preserve duplicate copy of result
         ADD     r9, r5, r1      ; sum to meet some requirement
label_1                          ; ** a possible entry point
         BCC     label_2
         .   .   .   .
```

Program 5.3 An example of poor program construction

5.6 Does ARM have a small instruction set ?

For many instructions both {<cond>} and {S} are optional so a very large number of instructions can be created; for example the versions of the ADD instruction are listed in Figure 5.4.

```
┌─────────────────────────────────────────────────┐
│ Unconditional versions of ADD                    │
│      ADD         ADDS                             │
│ ................................................ │
│ Conditional versions of ADD                      │
│      ADDEQ       ADDEQS      ADDNE       ADDNES   │
│      ADDCS       ADDCSS      ADDCC       ADDCCS   │
│      ADDMI       ADDMIS      ADDPL       ADDPLS   │
│      ADDVS       ADDVSS      ADDVC       ADDVCS   │
│      ADDHI       ADDHIS      ADDLS       ADDLSS   │
│      ADDGE       ADDGES      ADDLT       ADDLTS   │
│      ADDGT       ADDGTS      ADDLE       ADDLES   │
└─────────────────────────────────────────────────┘
```

Figure 5.4 Forms of the ADD instruction

A total of thirty different ADD instructions exist. Six other mnemonics are allowed although they do not produce different instruction codes. The extension AL, for always, can be added to the two unconditional versions ADD and ADDS giving the ADDAL and ADDALS which assist the reader but do not produce different instruction codes. Similarly CS may be replaced by HS and CC by LO.

A possible confusion is that some conditions, such as CS, end with the letter S. However S is usually added as the last letter of a mnemonic to show that the flags are to be updated and condition cases such as CS can cause confusion. ADDCS appears as if it has S to update the flags **but it does not**, the update flags form is ADDCSS. It was stated earlier that flag setting and use for ARM is complicated; it was also indicated that combining conditional execution and flag setting in one instruction should be avoided as program behaviour may be very difficult to predict in many situations.

There are thirty variations of ADD and many forms of <shifter_operand> are still to be examined. **Is this a small instruction set?** The feature that should be apparent is that ARM can perform a small number of simple actions; however several can be performed simultaneously by one instruction. The ARM assembly language programmer constructs instructions using a small number of elementary components. Most programmers familiar with a CISC processor will not have met this concept. The mnemonics for CISC instructions tend to be names for complete instructions whereas for ARM the full mnemonic name is constructed by the programmer; further additions are possible when all the features of <shifter_operand> are examined. There are only a small number of basic mnemonics but the programmer adds additional components to them. The ARM instruction set is possibly best described as a *'build your own instruction'* system; a small number of components are combined to build a large number of instructions.

5.7 Details of flag setting and tests for common tasks

In most cases flag settings are obvious; even so the ARM Architecture Reference Manual [12] should be used to check the exact behaviour. Table 5.2 gives examples of flag settings for common arithmetic operations and consequent conditional instruction behaviour. Tables 5.3 to 5.6 list the possible results of addition and subtraction of unsigned and signed numbers and the effects on the flags. *Not relevant* is used to show that the flag does not provide useful information when the instruction is used to perform the arithmetic operation for the purpose stated although **all the flags are affected** by the normal rules.

5.7.1 Addition of two unsigned integers

	Carry, C	Overflow, V	Sign, N	Zero, Z
i) Result less than 2^{32}	0	0 or 1, not relevant	0 or 1, not relevant	1 only if both numbers are zero
ii) Result exceeds 2^{32}-1	1	0 or 1, not relevant	0 or 1, not relevant	0 or 1

Table 5.3 Unsigned number addition

For unsigned addition the only problem the programmer normally wishes to detect is that a result is too large to fit in the 32-bit register, this is indicated by the carry. In a few cases a result of zero shown by Z may be of interest. The N flag may be used to determine if the most significant bit of the result is 0 or 1 and is useful in some situations. V does not perform any useful function when adding unsigned integers.

5.7.2 Addition of two signed integers in twos complement form

	Carry, C	Overflow, V	Sign, N	Zero, Z
i) Result magnitude less than 2^{31}	0 or 1, not relevant	0	0 or 1	0 or 1
ii) Result magnitude exceeds 2^{31}-1	0 or 1, not relevant	1	0 or 1, not relevant	0 or 1

Table 5.4 Signed number addition

For signed addition problems arise when the magnitude of the result exceeds 2^{31}-1; the result is greater than or equal to $+2^{31}$ or less than or equal to -2^{31}. The addition of the magnitude parts of the signed numbers causes the most significant bit of the 32-bit result to be changed; the magnitude overflows into the sign position and the sign is wrong. Overflow can only occur if both numbers are positive or both are negative and is indicated by the overflow flag, V, which is set to 1 when overflow occurs.

The value of C has no significance for signed number calculations. N shows if the result is positive or negative which often provides useful information for signed number calculations. Z shows if the result is zero and may be used to determine if the numbers have equal magnitude but opposite sign.

5.7.3 Subtraction of two unsigned integers (A minus B)

	Carry, C	Overflow, V	Sign, N	Zero, Z
i) Result greater than or equal to 0	1	0 or 1, not relevant	0 or 1, not relevant	0 or 1
ii) Result below 0	0	0 or 1, not relevant	0 or 1, not relevant	0

Table 5.5 Unsigned number subtraction

When subtracting unsigned numbers problems occur if the number subtracted, the subtrahend, is the larger one; that is *B* is greater than *A* when performing *A* minus *B*. This is indicated by the carry which is now used as a **borrow**. The behaviour of borrow varies in different designs of CPU; the ARM designers chose a form which is not the most obvious. When *B* is greater than *A* the subtraction proceeds as if a 1 is put to the left of the MSB of number *A* (*A* then has 33-bits with the MSB set to 1); this extra bit is called a borrow. If a borrow is necessary C is cleared to 0 and if no borrow is required C is set to 1; hence C has the value that is the inverse of the borrow required, the carry indicates **'not borrow'**.

Z shows if the result is zero and is used when testing to find if two numbers are equal. N shows if the most significant result bit is 0 or 1; V does not have any use when subtracting unsigned integers.

5.7.4 Subtraction of two signed integers in twos complement form (A minus B)

	Carry, C	Overflow, V	Sign, N	Zero, Z
i) Result magnitude less than 2^{31}	0 or 1, not relevant	0	0 or 1	0 or 1
ii) Result magnitude exceeds 2^{31}-1	0 or 1, not relevant	1	0 or 1, not relevant	0 or 1

Table 5.6 Signed number subtraction

The flag rules for subtraction of signed numbers are closely related to those for addition of signed numbers as *A* - *B* is *A* + (-*B*); as the allowed values of *B* are from -2^{31}-1 through 0 to $+2^{31}$-1, all the same cases arise. The only difference is that overflow can only occur if both numbers have different signs. Again the value of C has no significance. N shows if the result is positive or negative which is useful when comparing two numbers to find the larger. Z shows if the result is zero and is useful when testing numbers for equality; that is for cases where both sign and magnitude are the same.

5.8 Summary

Status bits, flags, are changed by executing instructions which have the S suffix added to the instruction mnemonic. Some instructions do not allow the use of the S suffix and a very small number of instructions, still to be introduced, always set the flags and do not require that S is added to their mnemonics. The condition of the flags allows the programmer to conditionally change the flow of the program by addition of the appropriate conditional {<cond>} field to any instruction mnemonic.

Great care should be exercised in the use of flags and in **checking the conditions** indicated by them. The most important rules are to set the flags to the testable state just before a test is made and avoid more than one program execution route leading to a flag test instruction. Generally if program design is restricted to use only the structural forms described in Chapter 2 problems should not occur.

5.9 Problems

Solve all the following **without** writing and running programs; these are *'paper and pencil'* exercises.

5.1   If an ARM processor completes one loop of Program 5.2 every 5×10^{-8} seconds how long will the program remain in the loop?

5.2   a)   How many times does BCC branch to the label *loop* when executing Program 5.2?

   b)   If BCC is replaced by BPL how many times does BPL branch to the label *loop* when executing this revised form of Program 5.2?

   c)   Repeat again with BCC replaced by BEQ.

5.3   For each of the following pairs of values what are the flag values and contents of r4 after execution of ADDS r4, r5, r10 for the values in r5 and r10? Only attempt to determine the value of V if you understand overflow in twos complement arithmetic. Give the result in r4 in hexadecimal form.

   a)   r5 contains 0xc1567af9 and r10 contains 0x2f2b8017

   b)   r5 contains binary 0101 1100 1111 1000 0101 1110 1010 1100
         r10 contains binary 0001 0000 1111 0010 1101 0100 0010 0100

   c)   r5 contains 0xab98147e and r10 contains 0x5467eb82.

5.4   Repeat question 5.3 when the instruction executed is SUBS   r4, r5, r10; also repeat for the instruction RSBS   r4, r5, r10.

5.5   For each of the following what are the flag values and contents of r4 in hexadecimal form after execution of MOVS   r4, r7 if the value in r7 is as indicated? Ignore V and C.

   a)   r7 contains 0xc1567af9

   b)   r7 contains binary 0101 1100 1111 1000 0101 1110 1010 1100

   c)   r7 contains binary 1101 0010 1111 1010 1001 1100 0110 0110

   d)   r7 contains 0x2f2b8017

5.6   Repeat all parts of Problem 5.6 for execution of MVNS r4, r7.

6 Program Structures

Chapter 2 stated that every program may be built using only three elementary structures. Programs that only use the three elements are usually well organized, can be tested, and rarely contain obscure difficult to find faults. In many high level languages the structures are components of the language; using assembly language the programmer must create them. The three structures are:-

  o   Sequences - *one action after another in strict order.*

  o   Conditional structures - *if structures* and *case selection.*

  o   Loops - *while* and *repeat structures.*

Assembly language programs directly implement sequences of actions. For most types of CPU conditional and loop structures are created with conditional and unconditional branch instructions; those for ARM were introduced in Chapter 5. An assembly language does not restrict the use of branch instructions; the programmer must ensure that programs only contain correctly formed structures.

6.1 Sequences

Sequential operation is an inherent property of any processor that follows the von Neumann cycle. Assembly language programs are closely related to the von Neumann cycle; the order of the program statements is the order of opcodes in memory and is also the order in which most instructions are executed. All examples so far, except programs with simple loops, consist only of sequences.

The form of an assembly language program with instructions written in order of execution directly defines a sequence of actions. Almost any section of an assembly language program that does not include branch instructions is a sequential structure.

6.2 Building simple conditional structures

The most simple conditional structure is one that implements

  IF   *condition true*   EXECUTE (THEN)   *sequence of actions*

with no actions performed when the condition is not true.

Usually the condition is simple but some tasks require evaluation of complicated conditions; however, even a complicated condition can always be reduced to a single value which is either true or false. Values which can only be true or false are Boolean ones and an ARM assembly language program tests a Boolean value using one of the fourteen condition codes represented by the mnemonic extensions EQ, NE, CS, *etc.*, listed in Table 5.1. Strictly only seven conditions are necessary, the conditions are in complementary pairs with tests for both true and false values of each of the flag combinations. Provision of both conditions simplifies programming and can make the program easier to understand; the ability to create two versions producing the same result using opposite conditions is a consequence of the **dual** nature of Boolean algebra. Any reader not familiar with duality and its algebraic description by de Morgan's theorem should study an introduction in a logic circuit design textbook.

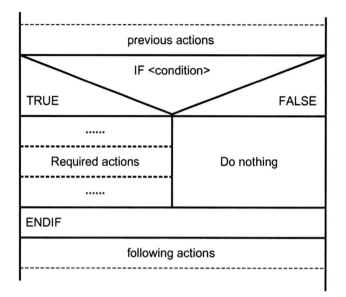

Figure 6.1 NS chart for a simple conditional structure

The most simple conditional structural form is one which tests if some condition is true and only if it is true does it perform a specified sequence of actions. If the condition is false nothing is done. This may be represented by an NS chart with the form in Figure 6.1. The structure is implemented by an assembly language program which follows the steps outlined in Figure 6.2.

```
        . . . . .
        Previous program actions
        Perform the actions to set the flags to a single testable condition
        Conditional branch - if test is false branch to label skip
            Sequence of actions performed when test is true
skip    Continue program actions
        . . . . .
```

Figure 6.2 Sequence to implement 'IF *condition true* DO *actions* (else/otherwise do nothing)'

A consequence of the dual nature of Boolean quantities is that inverse conditional tests may always be used; that is the opposite flag settings can be generated and the opposite branch test used. For every conditional branch structure in a program it is possible to create an equally valid inverse form.

The sequence in Figure 6.2 can be described using a flowchart, Figure 6.3, which implies a *'goto'* element. However the program meets the requirements that it has a good structure because the program was derived from the NS chart. It is only the reverse engineering producing a flow chart from the final program code that includes the *'goto'* generated by the branch instruction.

The next program example includes simple 'IF' structures implemented with branch instructions. Some ARM instructions introduced later would allow this task to be performed with fewer instructions but the branch form is used to illustrate the general form of the structure. The program overcomes the problem that the largest unsigned integer that can be held in an ARM register has the value $2^{32}-1$. When larger values are required two registers must be used to hold a 64-bit number with one register holding the upper 32-bits and the other the lower 32-bits. Obviously this can be extended to 96-bits, 128-bits, *etc.*

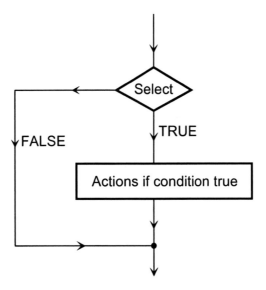

Figure 6.3 Flowchart of a simple 'IF' structure

To add two 64-bit unsigned integer values X and Y assume that X is formed using two 32-bit unsigned integers A and B such that $X = A \times 2^{32} + B$ and similarly Y is $Y = C \times 2^{32} + D$. To determine the sum $X + Y$ a program must add A to C and also add B to D. It is possible that the result of $B + D$ can exceed $2^{32}-1$ but it is impossible for it to exceed $2^{33}-1$. Whenever the result of the addition $B + D$ is over $2^{32}-1$ an additional 1 must be added to the result obtained by adding A to C. If it is necessary to detect results of 64-bit addition that exceed $2^{64}-1$ it must be noted that the excess value may occur either when A and C are added or in cases when an extra 1 is added to their sum.

Figure 6.4 is a structure chart for a section of program that forms a 64-bit sum. It uses two extra quantities, *increment* to indicate a carry from the low 32-bit addition to the high part and *carry2* to indicate when the final result exceeds $2^{64}-1$; *low* and *high* hold the two 32-bit parts of the 64-bit result. Quantities such as *increment*, *carry2*, *low* and *high* that change during program execution are known as the program **variables**. In addition to being a plan to meet the program requirements Figure 6.4 illustrates the practice of **using names for each variable**. Identifying all variable quantities with short but meaningful names is an essential feature of well documented software. The plan also sets some important variable values such as *increment* and *carry2* to default, initial, values at the start of the section involving their use so that there is no risk of using them before they have a value. It is obvious that this program will always set *high* and *low* to defined values so they are not initialised.

In complicated programs it is usually, but not always, good practice to **set all variables to known initial values**. This reduces the risk of using values which have not been set; using unset values usually causes a program to behave unpredictably. Faults arising when a variable is used before it has a defined value have been the cause of several serious software problems; such faults are often difficult to find and in some cases the program may behave differently each time it is run.

When setting variables to initial values some can be set to expected default results. Variables which do not have well defined default values are often set to zero although there are situations where this may cause problems. A good test of any program is to include a temporary initialisation section as the first instructions of the program; this section may be removed after testing is complete. The initialisation sets all variables, including those with known default values, to the same value. The results of all program tests are noted then the tests are repeated with a different initial value; if the results of the two sets of tests differ it is probable that the program is using a variable before it has a defined value.

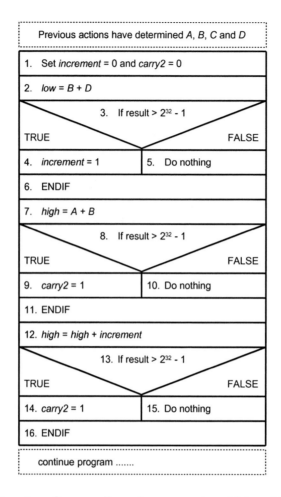

Figure 6.4 Structure for a section of program to add two 64-bit numbers

A few decisions are necessary to convert Figure 6.4 into a well structured program. At this point in studying program preparation the only places introduced that can be used to hold variable quantities are the registers. To develop the 64-bit addition program it is necessary to decide which registers will hold the initial variable values *A*, *B*, *C* and *D* and which will hold the other variables. Generally register selection is not important although ARM programmers tend to use registers in their numeric order. Later it is suggested that for larger tasks there should be some differences in the choice of variables held in registers r0 to r3 and those in r4 to r11. A section of comments at the head of the program section indicates the choices made by the programmer, for example

```
; initially A is in r0, B is in r1, C is in r2, D is in r3
; increment is put into r4, carry2 into r5, low into r6 and high into r7
```

The program is created by preparing code corresponding to each action in the NS chart working methodically downwards; the form of Figure 6.2 is used to implement the 'IF' structures. The first chart action requires that *increment* and *carry2* are set to initial values of zero, this directly translates into

```
MOV     r4, #0          ; initialise increment = 0
MOV     r5, #0          ; initialise carry2 = 0
```

Note that experienced programmers who have used other CPUs might perform this initialisation by

```
MOV     r4, #0          ; initialise increment = 0
MOV     r5, r4          ; initialise carry2 = 0
```

or they may use SUB   r4, r4, r4 to set the contents of r4 to zero and follow this by copying the result to r5. Methods of setting register contents to initial values are discussed in Chapter 12. For ARM processors setting small values using multiple MOV instructions with immediate operands is clear and efficient so it is recommended; for many other processors the equivalent form is often inefficient and should be avoided.

The second action shown in Figure 6.4 is the addition of the two low 32-bit parts of the 64-bit numbers. As the action after this is to test if the result is greater than 2^{32}-1 it is essential to remember to use the *'set flags'* feature when performing addition so that an indicator is created to show if the result exceeds 2^{32}-1. For many other types of CPU the flags are always set by addition instructions and such forward planning is not necessary. This second action in the NS chart is performed with a single ADDS instruction.

The conditional structure described by statements 3 to 6 in the NS chart is constructed by following the form in Figure 6.2 producing

```
          BCC    no_incr        ; skip if not over 32-bits
          MOV    r4, #1         ; set increment = 1
no_incr
```

This process of creating program code that follows the chart is continued and Program 6.1 is the section of program for 64-bit addition. Although preparation of a structure chart takes time the restrictions it imposes are such that the program is quickly prepared from the chart and even the first version is unlikely to have major errors. Any errors will probably be small typing mistakes or arise because some requirements were not obvious and were omitted from the plans. Overall producing a detailed plan before creating a program is quicker than attempting to write a program without plans because far fewer program faults occur. Although the time from starting the design to writing the first version is increased the time required to find and correct faults is reduced to such an extent that the total development time is much less.

```
     ; assumed A is in r0, B is in r1, C is in r2, D is in r3
     ; increment is put into r4, carry2 into r5, low into r6 and high into r7
             MOV    r4, #0         ; initialise increment = 0
             MOV    r5, r4         ; initialise carry2 = 0
             ADDS   r6, r1, r3     ; low = B + D
             BCC    no_incr        ; skip if not over 32-bits
             MOV    r4, #1         ; set increment = 1
no_incr      ADDS   r7, r0, r2     ; high = A + B
             BCC    no_Cy2         ; skip if not over 32-bits
             MOV    r5, #1         ; set carry2 = 1
no_Cy2       ADDS   r7, r7, r4     ; high = high + increment
             BCC    alt_nCy2       ; skip if this part not over 32-bits
             MOV    r5, #1         ; set carry2 = 1
alt_nCy2                           ; continue
```

Program 6.1 A partial program performing 64-bit addition

6.3 More complex conditional structures

An alternative conditional structure that considers the selection of either of two sets of actions is one which implements

IF   *condition true*   EXECUTE (THEN)   *action sequence 1*   ELSE   *action sequence 2*

This more general *'if-else'* structure, also called *'if-otherwise'*, has the NS chart form of Figure 6.5.

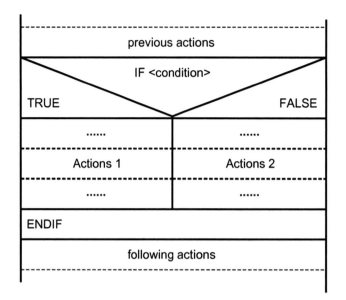

Figure 6.5 Structure chart for an *'if-else'* structure

Figure 6.5 has parallel sections for the true and false cases. However any CPU following the von Neumann sequence can only perform one action at a time; to implement the structure of Figure 6.5 the program must perform the sequence of steps in Figure 6.6. Obviously the dual nature of Boolean algebra allows the opposite conditional test to be used with the order in which the two alternative actions appear in the program reversed; either form of program produces identical results.

```
          . . . . .
          Previous program actions
          Perform the actions to set the flags to a single testable condition
          Conditional branch - if test is false branch to label do_two
              Sequence of actions performed when test is true
          Unconditional branch, always go to label done
do_two        Sequence of actions performed when test is false
done      Continue program actions
          . . . . .
```

Figure 6.6 Implementation of 'IF *condition* EXECUTE *actions* 1 ELSE *actions 2'*

As for the simple conditional statement the behaviour can be described by a flow chart; Figure 6.7 corresponds to this structure. Again it is essential to understand that the flow chart is a description of the program behaviour; **it is not a plan from which a program should be developed**.

To illustrate the construction of an *'if-else'* structure in assembly language assume that a program has reached a point where two 32-bit unsigned integer variables X and Y have been computed. At this point the specification requires that the larger number is output to a display without changing either variable; if they are equal either is output. As methods of output have not been examined assume the output is by a sequence of instructions which implements the action *'output the contents of r0 to the display'*. At present ignore how the output system functions and the reason why register r0 was specified.

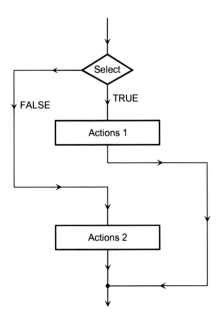

Figure 6.7 Flow sequence for execution of an '*if-else*' structure

The partial program must implement the conditional requirement

IF *X >= Y output X* ELSE *output Y*

with either > or >= acceptable. It is probable that the output will require several instructions. As both branches end with output of a value the same result is obtained by changing to

IF *X >= Y* copy *X* to *temp* ELSE copy *Y* to *temp*
Always output the value *temp*

temp is a program variable which only has a purpose within a short section of program; it is a **local variable**. The modified form may not run faster than the original but will not be slower and will probably use less memory to hold the program codes. This second version also more clearly shows that the program always performs an output operation. Figure 6.8 is the structure of this partial program. The modification to reduce the number of instructions is an example of optimisation, this is examined later.

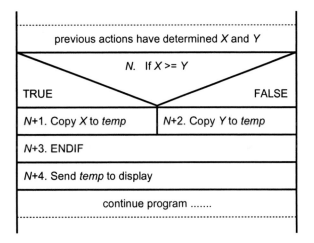

Figure 6.8 Structure for 'IF *X >= Y output X* ELSE *output Y*'

The partial program to implement this can be constructed following the structure chart as for the previous program to perform 64-bit addition except that the '*if-else*' structure must be created to follow the sequence of actions in Figure 6.6. After selecting which registers to use to hold variables Figure 6.8 is easily converted to ARM assembly language; one possible version is Program 6.2.

```
            ; Y is in r5 and X is in r2, temp is held in r0 for output
            SUBS   r3, r2, r5   ; compute X - Y so carry is clear¹ if Y > X
            BCC    Y_larger     ; skip setting temp = X if Y larger (or =)
            MOV    r0, r2       ; set temp = X as X is larger
            B      loaded       ; branch to the output point
Y_larger    MOV    r0, r5       ; set temp = Y
loaded                 ; here put the instruction(s) to send temp to the display
```

Program 6.2 A partial program to implement 'IF *X* >= *Y* output *X* ELSE *output Y*'

General methods that can be applied to most processors have been used in the example. It is possible to *'improve'* the program using techniques specific to ARM. A minor variation is that a test such as *'Is A greater than B?'* requires a subtraction. Using the subtract instruction the result must be placed in a register; if the only reason for subtraction is to test if an inequality is true the result is not required. To save using a register for the result ARM has an instruction that performs the subtraction, sets the flags according to the result then discards the result. The instruction is compare, CMP; the full definition is

```
            CMP{<cond>}   <Rn>, <shifter_operand>
```

There is no optional {S} field for the compare instruction as the flags are **always updated** and there is no destination register, Rd, because there is no result to store. CMP behaves exactly as SUBS except that the numeric result is discarded.

The powerful multiple choice conditional form known as a **case structure** or **switch** is not examined at this time. It is introduced later as it requires knowledge of several topics still to be introduced.

6.4 Simple loops with an exit condition

The only program structures, other than conditional ones, that break sequential execution of instructions are loops. Well designed programs contain only the two loop forms described in Chapter 2 with the structure charts in Figure 6.9. Some strict adherents of good programming practice do not allow the repeat form as it is difficult to guarantee correct program operation in every possible case. However the repeat version is often easier to implement and both loop forms are usually used in program design.

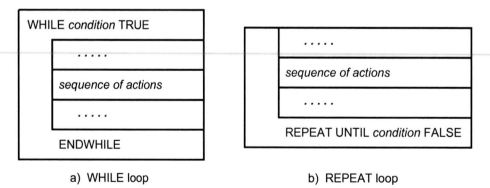

a) WHILE loop   b) REPEAT loop

Figure 6.9 Possible loop structures

---

[1] Reminder: ARM subtraction instructions put an inverse of the borrow into the carry flag.

The sequences of program actions to implement the while loop are shown in Figure 6.10 and that for the repeat loop in Figure 6.11.

> ⋯⋯
> *while_start* Evaluate Boolean condition for loop to single testable quantity
> Branch if test condition false to *while_exit*
> ***Sequence of actions performed inside loop***
> Unconditional branch, always go to label *while_start*
> *while_exit* Continue program actions
> ⋯⋯

Figure 6.10 Program sequences to implement a while loop structure

> ⋯⋯
> *rep_start* ***Sequence of actions performed inside loop***
> Branch if test condition true to *rep_start*
> Continue program actions
> ⋯⋯

Figure 6.11 Program sequences to implement a while loop structure

Implementation of the two loop structures using the action sequences in Figures 6.10 and 6.11 leads to programs that follow the flow chart sequences shown in Figure 6.12. Again these are produced as a result of creating the structures, they are not the basis of the loop designs.

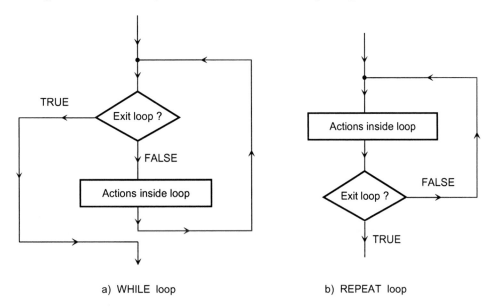

a) WHILE loop   b) REPEAT loop

Figure 6.12 Flow sequences of loop structures

The most simple loops are those to perform a set of actions a fixed number of times, X, set when the program is written; these are **count loops**. Programs where the count, X, is not fixed but is determined by the program when it runs are similar but require greater care in preparation. They also require extra testing as the programmer must test that the calculation of X never produces results with values outside the expected range. If the only action inside the loop is one that changes the count value then the only function of the loop is to create a simple delay. Electronic systems operate at high speed and delays have many uses when the processor interacts with humans or mechanical systems. Figure 6.13 outlines the NS charts for simple delay counter loops using both loop forms.

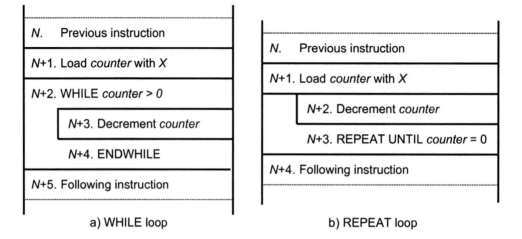

a) WHILE loop   b) REPEAT loop

Figure 6.13 Structures of simple counter loops to execute loop *X* times

Notes on designing loops.

- Counting down is often simpler than counting up because conditional tests include a test for zero; that is the Z flag indicates zero.

- When the initial value of X is less than 2^{31} the N flag may be used for a test for minus 1 because the subtraction of 1 from a value with all bits 0 produces a result with all bits 1.

- The use of *'equals'*, *'not equals'*, *'greater than'*, *'greater than or equal'*, *'less than'*, *'less than or equal'* in the loop exit test will depend on the exact specification.

- Programmers using any language must always be careful when writing loops and must perform tests to ensure that execution is for the required number of times. A common fault is the creation of loops which execute either one too many or one too few times.

The first aim of the programmer should be clarity. To show clearly what is being implemented it is often advisable to test for equality using the Z flag with the ARM condition EQ. In cases when it is possible to make the reason for exit obvious using alternative test conditions do so. If there are program faults there are more situations in which the loop will exit if the test is for inequality; consequently there is a lower chance of a fault causing the program to stick in a loop; this fault is sometimes difficult to find.

```
          . . . .
          LDR    r4, =<value X>    ; load X into counter
while_st  MOVS   r4, r4            ; set flags for check of count
          BEQ    while_nd          ; exit loop when done X times
          ;** any other actions in the loop are included here
          SUB    r4, r4, #1        ; decrement counter
          B      while_st          ; back to the start of the WHILE structure
while_nd  ; following instructions
```

Program 6.3 WHILE loop to execute *X* times

The most simple program loop is one that only produces a delay; either to wait for some external system to complete an operation or to slow a program during testing to make it easier to examine behaviour. After deciding where to hold the variable *counter* the structures in Figure 6.12 can be converted into the sequence forms of Figure 6.10 to create delay loops. Partial programs 6.3 and 6.4 show typical ARM code for the two forms of delay loop; the programmer decided to use register r4 to hold the loop counter. For the repeat version the initial value of the variable *counter* must not be zero unless an actual count value of 2^{32} is required; the while form will correctly perform the loop zero times.

```
          . . . .
          LDR    r4, =<value X>    ; load X into counter
loop_st

          ;** any other actions in the loop are included here
          SUBS   r4, r4, #1        ; decrement counter
          BNE    loop_st           ; continue looping if not done X loops
          ; following instructions
```

Program 6.4 REPEAT loop to execute *X* times

It is apparent from these examples that the instruction sequence using REPEAT is simpler than that using WHILE. The REPEAT loop executes fewer instructions and therefore executes more quickly; this is an advantage for some applications and a disadvantage in others. However, because it is safer, programmers should use the WHILE form when it is reasonable to do so.

The examples have shown loop structures where the loop is executed a fixed number times, the number of times is determined when the program is written. Alternative programs may be devised with the number of times the loop is executed determined by the program during execution.

Loop exit decisions are made using logical true or false conditions so programs may be constructed with exit conditions that are more complex than the completion of simple count loops. However, if programs are well designed, loop exit conditions are rarely extremely complex.

6.5 An example using all three structure elements

Although ARM has a multiply instruction it has not been introduced. Ignoring that this instruction is available this example multiplies two unsigned integers by repeated addition; *A* multiplied by *B* is addition of *A* to itself *B* times. A difficulty of multiplication is that results may be a large; in general if two *N*-bit numbers are multiplied the result has 2*N*-bits. A structure for multiplying two 32-bit unsigned integers producing a 64-bit result is Figure 6.13. The numbers multiplied are variables *A* and *B* and the 64-bit result has two 32-bit parts *high* and *low*; the value *B* is destroyed by the multiplication process. The while structure ensures a correct result if *B* is zero; this is an example where a repeat structure causes problems.

Creation of a program described by Figure 6.14 follows the straightforward processes already illustrated for conditional statements and loops. The program code lines closely match the chart lines and with care a program is quickly produced which is unlikely to contain obscure errors. Partial program 6.5 illustrates one implementation of this multiplication structure.

There are alternative methods of implementing the conditional 'IF' structure when using ARM processors that may be used when there are only a few actions inside the alternative paths. These must be used with care; the methods and possible problems that arise are examined in Chapter 12. Such special techniques should be ignored until general methods of creating the structural forms are well understood.

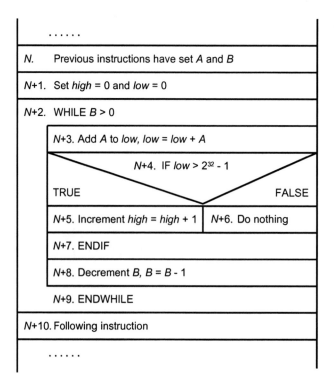

Figure 6.14 Structure of a program to perform multiplication by repeated addition

```
; assumed A is in r0, B is in r1
; the result low will be in r2 and high in r3
        MOV   r2, #0        ; initialise low = 0
        MOV   r3, #0        ; initialise high = 0
check_B     ; while loop entry point to check if B has reached 0
        MOVS  r1, r1        ; set to test for B equals zero
        BEQ   all_done      ; exit loop if completed
        ADDS  r2, r2, r0    ; add A to low
        BCC   high_OK       ; skip if not over 32-bits (don't change high)
        ADD   r3, r3, #1    ; increment high
high_OK SUB   r1, r1, #1    ; B = B -1, count down times added A to itself
        BAL   check_B       ; go to start of while loop
        ; ENDWHILE - loop is complete
all_done    ; ****  continue after loop
```

Program 6.5 A partial program performing multiplication by repeated addition

6.6 Summary

When preparing assembly language programs it is the responsibility of the programmer to create good structural forms. The fundamental structures requiring decisions are readily created in most assembly languages with branch instructions as in Figures 6.2, 6.6 and 6.10. Their implementation in ARM assembly language is straightforward. Although minor improvements may be made to programs utilising particular features of an individual type of CPU most programs should be restricted to the general structural forms to create reliable and easily maintained software.

6.7 Problems

6.1 Partial program 6.1 outlined the addition of two 64-bit numbers. Design, create and test a program that performs the subtraction of two 64-bit numbers.

6.2 Partial program 6.2 selected the larger of two numbers and copied it to a variable *temp* ready for output. Develop a structure chart then use it to create and test a partial program to find the smallest of three numbers and load this into a variable *temp*.

6.3 Program 6.6 is a section of program that implements a simple loop.

```
        MOV    r4, #8        ; load counter
loop           ; Actions in loop which do not change contents of r4
        SUBS   r4, #1        ; decrement counter
        BNE    loop          ; exit loop when done ? times
```

Program 6.6 A partial program creating a simple loop

a) How many times are the actions inside the loop performed?

b) If BNE is replaced by BCC how many times are the actions inside the loop performed?

c) If BNE is replaced by BCS how many times are the actions inside the loop performed?

d) If BNE is replaced by BPL how many times are the actions inside the loop performed?

6.4 Programs may contain loops within loops, nested loops. A simple form is one loop inside another to produce a very long delay. Create a program with an inner loop that is executed X times and an outer loop that is executed Y times. Test that it operates correctly and that the execution times are the same for the following two cases

a) $X =$ one hundred and $Y =$ fifty thousand

b) $X =$ one thousand and $Y =$ five thousand

Provided the hardware test system or simulator is not a high performance one the execution time will exceed 20 seconds and a wrist watch is adequate for checking times. If the time is less than 20 seconds double both values of X; if the time is still less than 20 seconds double both values of X again and continue doubling both values of X until the time exceeds 20 seconds.

6.5 Many CPUs, including ARM, do not have divide instructions. A simple slow method of division is to repeatedly subtract a positive divisor from a positive dividend counting the number of times this is possible before the result is negative. The count is the quotient and the value left in place of the dividend is the remainder. Often the subtraction is repeated until the dividend is negative, the divisor is added back to give the correct remainder and the count value is corrected by subtracting one.

This method takes a long time if a large number is divided by a small one but it is easy to produce a program. Develop and test a program to perform division that produces a quotient and a remainder. Test your program, in particular test it for the following cases.

0x00001000 divided by 0x00000008
0x0f0f0f0f divided by 0x00000000
0x0f0f0f0f divided by 0x0000000e

7 Simple Data

The elements of ARM assembly language required to build most structures that control the flow of program execution have been introduced. An essential feature of all programs is manipulation of existing data values to produce new data values, results. Programs obtain input data values from some source and send the results to some destination. The purpose of every possible computer program may be defined as

- o   Obtain the data.
- o   Perform operations on the data.
- o   Send the resulting data to the destination.

Only simple methods of obtaining input data have been introduced; they only apply to programs that require a few values known when a program is written. No techniques have been introduced to input values that are unknown when a program is written or to send results to destinations other than registers.

The instruction already introduced to copy values is MOV with the extended forms MOVS, MOVCC, etc.; it has the full definition

```
MOV{<cond>}{S}  <Rd>, <shifter_operand>
```

MOV is used to copy values from one register to another and to load fixed values in the range 0 to 255 into registers. Execution of the sequence

```
MOV         r2, #1
MOV         r3, r2
MOV         r4, r2
```

loads the binary value 0000 0000 0000 0000 0000 0000 0000 0001 into registers r2, r3 and r4. This sequence uses immediate data to register and register to register data transfers. The pseudo instruction LDR is provided for loading registers with known values that are not in the restricted range.

Registers can only hold a few values whereas most programs manipulate many data items. For a RISC processor, such as ARM, all the input values used for calculations and all the results produced must be in registers. As there are only a small number of registers they are used to hold values which are currently required; **registers are not used for long term storage**. When a program has many variables they are held in read and write memory, RAM; values are moved into registers when they are required.

In addition to manipulating data values in memory programs must obtain input data from external sources and send results to output devices. Input and output devices are connected to ARM systems in the same manner as memory devices; ARM has memory mapped IO. Therefore the methods for input and output are similar to those for transfer of values between the CPU and memory.

7.1 Instructions to transfer data to and from memory

CPU designers can devise many forms of instruction to transfer data between registers and memory. ARM simultaneously executes one instruction, decodes the next one and fetches the following one, Figure 3.5. The fetch is a memory read operation from the address equal to the contents of the program counter. As the processor is always fetching instructions the bus system is always in use. Any execution action to transfer data to or from memory must use the same bus system as the instruction fetch. The need to access memory simultaneously by the fetch and execute steps creates problems for the CPU designer. To reduce the problems RISC processors usually have a **load-store** form; this does not remove the problem but reduces effects on the CPU performance. Load-store means that the only memory transfer instructions in the instruction set are to load registers with copies of the contents of memory locations and to store copies of register contents in memory locations. Unlike many CISC processors there are no instructions that use memory contents as operands in arithmetic instructions.

There are very few ARM instructions that transfer data to and from memory. The primary memory transfer instructions are LDR and STR with the general definitions

```
LDR{<cond>}  <Rd>, <addressing mode>
STR{<cond>}  <Rd>, <addressing mode>
```

LDR loads register Rd with a 32-bit value from memory while STR stores the 32-bit contents of register Rd in memory. Both LDR and STR can be conditionally executed but **neither has the set flags {S} field**.

There is a risk of error because the pseudo instruction LDR has the same mnemonic as the actual instruction. Generally the two forms of LDR are easily distinguished because the pseudo instruction operand is preceded by an equals sign and a memory transfer instruction operand usually has square brackets to indicate addressing mode. However there is a version of the LDR instruction which does not use square brackets; accidentally omitting the equals sign when typing the pseudo instruction does not always cause the assembler to indicate an error. This is one of many cases where the programmer must check the source program very carefully after it is typed.

An unusual assembly language feature of STR is that the **order of operands** for the instruction is not directly related to the **direction** in which the **data moves**. In **almost all cases** the direction of data movement indicted by an ARM assembly language instruction is from right hand operand to left hand operand; for example for MOV <Rd>, <Rn> and ADD <Rd>, <Rn>, <Rm>. However for STR, and also for RSB introduced in Section 4.10, the transfer is in the opposite direction; the instruction STR{<cond>} <Rd>, <addressing mode> copies the contents of register Rd to some location in memory; in this case the transfer direction is left hand operand to right hand operand.

ARM is a 32-bit processor therefore most instructions operate using full 32-bit values, words, as data values. However there are memory transfer instructions to transfer 8-bit values, bytes, and 16-bit values, half-words, as well as full 32-bit words.

7.2 Data transfer between registers and memory

The operand of LDR and STR instructions indicated by <addressing mode> defines the method of determining the memory address to be used when the memory transfer is performed. The concept of **addressing mode** is common to all processor systems; addressing mode describes how an operand is obtained or stored. The forms of ADD and MOV instructions already introduced have two addressing modes. Both ADD r2, r3, r4 and MOV r5, r6 use **register addressing** as the mode for all their operands, values are obtained from registers and are put into registers. MOV r7, #123 uses **register addressing** for the destination operand and **immediate addressing** for the source operand. Further addressing modes are used to transfer data to and from memory; these are **memory addressing modes** and are only available with the small number of instructions that perform load and store operations.

ARM has a reasonable number of memory addressing modes for a RISC processor but fewer than many CISC designs. **Only some memory addressing modes are examined** at this point; brief details of all modes are in Appendix D and full specifications are in the ARM Architecture Reference Manual [12].

Note that the syntax, the form of text, only differs slightly for several modes. Care must be taken to use the correct syntax for the mode required. Errors created by minor typing mistakes can produce a valid addressing mode which is not that intended; such errors are difficult to detect.

All ARM addresses are 32-bit values and the simple way to manipulate 32-bit values is to hold them in registers. Using register contents as addresses for memory transfers are addressing modes that are called **indirect addressing**. Alternative names are register indirect addressing or indexed addressing. The ARM assembly language uses square brackets to indicate *'use the contents of the item inside the square brackets as an address'*. The square brackets, [and], must be typed when writing a program.

The instruction LDR   r5, [r11] loads r5 with the contents of the memory location whose address is the 32-bit value in r11 when the LDR instruction is executed. As registers hold 32-bits and each byte has a different address the CPU processor automatically obtains values from four memory locations. It uses the four addresses starting with the value in r11 provided that the contents of r11 are divisible by four; that is the two least significant bits of the address are zero. If the address does not have the lowest two bits zero it is **not aligned** and the behaviour is complicated; see Appendix D for details. For most tasks only aligned data structures should be used and most data addresses used will be those of data structures set up by the programmer. The directive ALIGN, Section 7.5.1, assists in ensuring that starting addresses of data structures are aligned when complex data structures are created.

Program 7.1 is a section of a program similar to Program 4.1 whose function is to add together two numbers. This revised program differs as requires that the numbers to be added are held in memory; it is assumed that the previous section of program has put the address of one number into r10, the address of the second into r7, and the result will be placed in memory at the address held in r3.

```
. . . .
LDR    r0, [r10]      ; load first input number
LDR    r1, [r7]       ; load second input number
ADD    r0, r0, r1     ; form the sum of the two numbers
STR    r0, [r3]       ; store the result in assigned location
. . . .
```

Program 7.1 A simple partial program using values held in memory

Program 7.1 illustrates that using an ARM system to perform an arithmetic operation with operands held in memory *'spare'* registers must be allocated as temporary stores to hold such operands. As usual there are restrictions when r15 is used as an operand with the LDR or STR instructions and there are situations where the behaviour is unpredictable. However there are cases where the programmer uses r15 to define the operand address in a memory transfer operation or as the source or destination register; such actions involve using ARM features still to be introduced.

7.3 More complex addressing modes

The instructions LDR{<cond>}   <Rd>, [<Rn>] and STR{<cond>}   <Rd>, [<Rn>] are shortened versions of general versions of the addressing mode with the form

$$LDR\{<cond>\}   <Rd>, [<Rn>, \#\pm offset]$$
$$STR\{<cond>\}   <Rd>, [<Rn>, \#\pm offset]$$

where ±offset is a 12-bit magnitude signed integer which allows specification of any value in the range from -4095 through 0 to 4095. When the offset is zero it is not necessary to indicate this when writing the assembly language instruction; the versions of LDR and STR used in Program 7.1 are this mode with a zero offset value. As for branch instructions, Chapter 5, the term **offset** is used to indicate that a specified amount must be added to some address, a **base address**, to produce a new address. Often the base address is determined by the program when it runs. In the form of addressing `[<Rn>, #±offset]` Rn is the **base register** and the offset is a fixed amount determined when the program is written; some alternative addressing modes allow the offset to be computed by the running program.

Offset addressing provides additional methods of forming the address used when transferring data to and from memory; an example of this form of addressing is described when an example requires it. Although this mode is sometimes used in assembly language programs it is more often found in the code produced by high level language compilers for programs that manipulate complex data structures.

Program 7.1 illustrates simple access to data in memory but is restricted because it requires the individual addresses of every data item. Many programs process large amounts of data by systematically working through lists of data. The most simple form of data list is an **array**; a set of data items of the same type held in successive memory locations. Usually the number of items, **elements**, in the array is fixed. To use array elements in order with the addressing mode of Program 7.1 an extra instruction to change the contents of Rn is required after each memory access. An addressing mode that removes this requirement is one with a **post-indexed** or **post-increment** operation. If a third operand of a signed immediate value of 12-bits plus sign is placed after the operand in square brackets the contents of the register inside the brackets are changed by adding the signed value **after** the memory transfer has been performed. The general forms of load and store using post-indexed addressing are:

```
LDR{<cond>}   <Rd>, [<Rn>], #±offset
STR{<cond>}   <Rd>, [<Rn>], #±offset
```

The only text difference between this mode and the previous one is the position of the closing square bracket. However, the two modes `[<Rn>, #±offset]` and `[<Rn>], #±offset` perform different operations. The first computes an address using the contents of Rn plus the signed offset and uses this as the load or store address; the contents of Rn are not changed. The second form uses the original contents of Rn as the load or store address and afterwards changes the contents of Rn by adding the signed offset. The form `[<Rn>], #±offset` is called post-indexed addressing or more fully register indirect addressing with post-increment; if the offset value is negative it is register indirect addressing with **post-decrement**. In all ARM addressing modes Rd and Rn may be the same register; however if they are the same and a post-indexed, or other, addressing mode alters the base register contents the result is unpredictable.

Program data often includes lists of values and some program actions systematically process the lists using a **pointer** or an **index** to indicate the member of the list being used. The terms pointer and index are sometimes confused; usually the value of a pointer is the memory address of the item in a list whereas an index is an element's numeric position in the list. That is a pointer is related to the true or absolute address of a list item whereas an index is a position relative the start position of a list. Usually the index value for the first element of a list is zero rather than one. Also an index is increased by one for each list item regardless of how many memory locations are required to hold items whereas a pointer is increased by the number of memory locations required to store an individual list item.

A common method of manipulating lists of data is to hold a pointer in a register; often it is changed to point to the next list item after each data transfer. Using ARM simple 32-bit value transfers require that the pointer is increased by four because ARM uses byte addressing. Provided that the value in r3 is divisible by four, that is the two least significant bits are both zero, the instruction

```
STR   r9, [r3], #4
```

stores the contents of register r9 in the four bytes of memory starting at the address which is held in r3 then adds 4 to the contents of r3 so that it points to the next 32-bit quantity. The use of indirect addressing with post-increment or post-decrement assists in creation of programs that process lists of values. The ability to use a range of post-increment values means that list elements are not restricted to 4-bytes and the offset sign allows lists to be processed upward, increasing addresses, or downward, decreasing addresses.

An example of a list processing task is finding the maximum value in a list of 32-bit unsigned integers; that is find the largest value in an array of 32-bit unsigned integers. Searching tasks are frequently required; one sequence of actions to find the maximum value in a list is outlined in Figure 7.1.

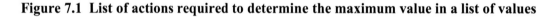

> . . . . .
> Values are already placed in memory by previous program actions.
> The following actions find the maximum.
> - Set *ptr* as a pointer to the address of the first list value
> - Set *count* to the number of items in the list
> - Set *result* to zero (the smallest possible unsigned integer)
> - Create a loop which performs the next four steps *count* times
>   1. Set *value* = contents of memory at address *ptr*
>   2. If *value* > *result* set *result* = *value*
>   3. Advance *ptr*
>   4. Decrement *count*
> Continue program, variable *result* is the largest value in the list
>
> . . . . .

Figure 7.1 List of actions required to determine the maximum value in a list of values

In Figure 7.1, as in Chapter 6, quantities which change, variables, have been given names; clear identification of variables is an essential feature of good documentation. The list is easily converted into an NS structure, Figure 7.2. A repeat loop was chosen as it is assumed that the program will never be used to find the largest member of a list with fewer than two items; for critical applications the program should include a check to ensure this. Problem 7.1 is an exercise to perform the same task using a while loop.

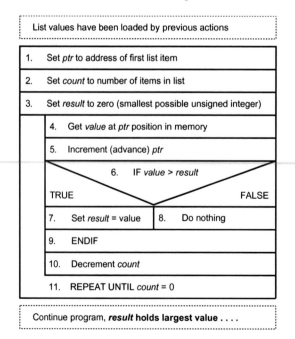

Figure 7.2 Structure to find the maximum value in a list of values

Because the post-increment addressing mode was known to exist when designing the program Figures 7.1 and 7.2 show *index* incremented immediately after the data read. Experienced programmers usually increment an index at this point. One reason is that many CPUs, and some high level languages, have a post increment feature similar to that of ARM. Another important reason is that program clarity is improved and the risk of programmer's mistakes is reduced if **all actions involving a variable quantity are performed close together** in the program whenever possible.

An assembly language program, Program 7.2, is easily developed from the NS chart. The condition branch if carry set, BCS, is used because CMP   r0, r7 sets the flags to the condition obtained by subtracting the contents of r7 from those in r0. If a borrow is required C is cleared to 0, otherwise it is set to 1; the ARM carry is the inverse of the borrow. When *value* in r7 is greater than the largest value found so far, that is *result* in r0, a borrow is required and the carry is cleared. The loop exit is also performed with BCS; extensive testing is necessary to ensure that the loop exits correctly.

```
            .  .  .  .
        LDR     r4, =list_start   ; list_start is the address of the first
                                  ; list element (often defined by a label)
        LDR     r5, =list_len     ; list_len is the number of items in the
                                  ; list (defined elsewhere)
        ; r4 is used as ptr and r5 as count
        MOV     r0, #0            ; r0 holds result, initial value zero is
                                  ; the smallest possible unsigned integer
loop_st
        LDR     r7, [r4], #4      ; load memory value at ptr, advance ptr
        CMP     r0, r7            ; test for value > than largest so far
        BCS     small            ; if value was smaller then skip load
          ; reminder SUB and CMP set carry = inverted borrow
        MOV     r0, r7            ; make value new largest result
small
        SUBS    r5, r5, #1        ; count down number to do
        BCS     loop_st          ; continue looping if more to do
            .  .  .  .
```

Program 7.2 A simple partial program to find the maximum value in a list of numbers

When the address of both the start and end of a list are known an alternative design without a counter may be preferable. Instead of counting down a register is loaded with the address of the last item in the list before the entry to the loop and the loop exit is changed to *'REPEAT UNTIL ptr > address of last list item'*.

So far only a small number of memory addressing modes have been described. These are adequate for the simple data handling used in most examples. Another mode is introduced in Section 7.7 and all ARM addressing modes are described in Appendix D. Again the experienced programmer of CISC processors will find a feature of ARM that differs from most CISC processors; ARM does not support **direct addressing**[1] of memory operands. The reason is the same as that restricting the range of immediate data values; the RISC structure does not allow the 32-bit value which is necessary to provide a complete address to be incorporated in the instruction code.

---

[1]   A direct addressing mode includes the full address of the memory location used as part of the instruction code. Because both addresses and instruction words are fixed size 32-bit values this is impossible for an ARM processor.

7.4 Using byte size values

It has been assumed that all values transferred to and from memory are 32-bit ones. ARM is capable of transferring 8-bit (byte) and 16-bit (half-word) values. Transfer of byte values is a frequent requirement because it is common practice to represent the individual characters in a section of text by 8-bit code numbers. Many programs manipulate large amounts of text and if a full 32-bit word was used to hold each character code a large amount of memory would be wasted. There are versions of LDR and STR for manipulating bytes, these have the modified mnemonics LDRB and STRB. They have the same operands and behave in exactly the same way as the 32-bit versions **except** that

- only the eight least significant bits in the register are stored by STRB regardless of the values in the other bits.

- as every address is used the address value does not have to be divisible by four.

- using LDRB the value obtained from memory is put in the eight least significant bits and the **other bits are cleared to zero**. Readers familiar with some other types of CPU should note this forcing of other bits to zero when loading a register with a byte value; many other types of CPU do not behave in this manner.

Using the forms

```
LDR{<cond>}B   <Rd>, [Rn], #±offset
STR{<cond>}B   <Rd>, [Rn], #±offset
```

with an offset of ±1 allows lists of characters, strings, to be manipulated. Note that the mnemonic for the conditional forms of LDRB and STRB has the two letter condition code between the LDR or STR part and the letter B, not after B. The letter B is regarded as indicating part of an addressing mode of the general mnemonics LDR{<cond>} or STR{<cond>} so appears at the end. However the newer RealView assembler allows both LDR{<cond>}B and LDRB{<cond>} to be used with similar forms for STR; ARM state that the second is now the preferred form. However most assemblers, including the ADS and GNU ones, do not accept the second form so the older version will be used in all examples.

Using byte data with items in successive locations has the effect that the data items will not always be at addresses with the two least significant bits both zero. If data structures store a mixture of byte and 32-bit data values it is possible for 32-bit items to start at addresses with the low two bits not both zero; the programmer must be aware of this and arrange that it does not happen.

There are also versions of LDR and STR to transfer 16-bit values. LDR{<cond>}H transfers the 16-bit memory contents to the low sixteen bits of the destination register and forces the remaining bits to zero while STR{<cond>}H stores the low 16-bits of the source register in memory regardless of the contents of the high 16-bits. There are more restrictions for 16-bit transfers than for byte and 32-bit ones; some addressing modes are modified and some are not allowed. Instructions LDRH and STRH require that addresses used are half word aligned, that is they must have the LSB zero; brief details of these modes are in Appendix D.

7.5 Assembly language data

The data on which programs operate may be either constant data or as variable data. Constant data items are values that never change and are known when the program is written; they are built into the program. One typical example of a constant data item is text that gives information to the user. For example a message with the form *'Please enter your PIN'* that is displayed when a user puts a card into the automatic machines used by banks and credit card companies is a constant, fixed, string built into the program controlling the machine. Variable data items, **variables**, are changed by the program as it runs; for example the amount of cash requested by a customer using a cash issuing machine is a variable quantity, as is the customer's balance.

Assembly languages provide mechanisms to support both constant and variable data items. Usually when planning a program the programmer, or in some cases the development system operating automatically, will allocate different regions of memory to different functions such as program code, constant data, variable data, and other purposes not yet described. Most ARM development systems force variable data and the program code to be in separate memory regions; the programmer may select that constant data is either part of the code memory region or it is in an extra, separate, region. At present it is assumed that constant data is in the code section of memory.

7.5.1 Constant data

There are many reasons for requiring constant data in a program. A common one is a system that includes an output device that can display text to give information to the user. Most systems use 8-bit codes for each character that can be displayed, frequently these are ASCII codes, Appendix B. Usually one character code is stored in every memory byte, a list of characters is a string and the assembly language includes methods of easily including strings and other constant values in the program.

Strings are one particular type of array; usually all the strings in a program have different numbers of characters, different **lengths**, whereas most numeric data arrays can be organised to have a fixed number of items. Variable size arrays, such as strings, cause several programming difficulties. One of these is that some method is required by which the size, string length, can be determined when a program manipulates the array. For strings the most simple method is to reserve one character, a terminator, to mark the end of the string; a common choice is to use the value zero as the terminator giving a **null terminated string**. Other methods are possible; they have advantages in many applications but they are usually more complicated and therefore are more difficult to implement.

Constant data is included in a program by use of some additional directives. These are **DCB**, **DCW** and **DCD** which are define constant byte, define constant half word and define constant data word respectively. In their most simple form these can be used as

```
xyz      DCB      34
abc      DCW      1234
pqr      DCD      0x3f123abc
```

Here *xyz, abc* and *pqr* are labels that allow the address of the constant value in memory to be identified. 34, 1234 and 0x3f123abc are the values which, as usual for numeric quantities, are decimal values unless the printed form indicates otherwise. A list of several values can be created by separating the values by commas as in

```
xyz      DCB      34, 0xc7, 99
```

To use the code for a text character as a constant data value the required character is enclosed in single quotation marks, for example

```
xyz      DCB      34, 'A', 99
```

If a sequence of characters, a string, is required this is written using double quotation marks as

```
xyz      DCB      "Hello world", 0
```

The addition of a comma and the value zero adds a null terminator at the string end. For most ARM assemblers the form with double quotes is only allowed with the directive DCB whereas a single character with single quotes is allowed wherever a numeric value may be used, it may be an immediate operand when one is required. There are very large variations in the manner used to indicate individual characters and strings in assemblers from different suppliers. It is essential to read the documentation that defines the rules for the assembler used; here the forms for the ADS and RealView assemblers are used.

If byte and 32-bit values are mixed in a list of constant values the position of a 32-bit value in memory might not start at an address with the last two bits both zero. For the DCD and DCW directives ARM assemblers correctly position the data in memory. However there is an additional directive ALIGN; using ALIGN after defining data using DCB or DCW will indicate that there is a risk of unaligned data and will ensure that the next data item is correctly positioned in memory. ALIGN only solves problems if they exist and is ignored if there are no problems, an example of its use is shown later in Program 7.6. As ALIGN is ignored if it is not necessary excessive use of the ALIGN directive does not lead to extra use of memory. Therefore ALIGN should always be used after data that is defined by DCB or DCW, it improves documentation even if it is not essential.

7.5.2 Variable data

In most cases the values of variable data items will be held in memory; registers are only used for variables while they are being manipulated. Variables must be stored in RAM whereas the program code and constant data are fixed and may be placed in ROM. A simple method of implementing the variable data is to set up a separate section of memory using a second AREA directive.

An example illustrating the creation and use of variable data is a program to add together five variables ignoring the possibility that the result may exceed 32-bits. At this time it is assumed that some process, for example a tool in the development system, has put the five numbers in successive memory locations using four bytes for each number. The program must perform the actions illustrated by the NS chart of Figure 7.3. As *'count'* is set to five just before the loop it is safe to create a repeat loop in this case; creation of the same action using a while loop with additional testing is an exercise, Problem 7.3.

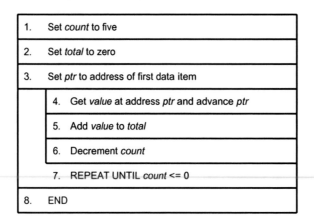

Figure 7.3 NS chart add five values from a list in memory

Some important decisions are required when preparing a program that matches the structure chart. For example this is a small program so the variables *count* and *total* may be held in registers rather than in memory. The address held as *ptr* may also be in kept a register and is initially loaded with the start address of the region of memory used to hold the data.

The use of registers to hold some variables is possible for small programs but is not possible, nor is it good practice, for large programs as the number of CPU registers is limited. The programmer must use the relatively small number of registers efficiently. When a program has many variables most are held in memory and moved to registers when required. However access to registers is much faster than access to memory so holding frequently used variables in registers results in faster execution. Further for ARM all operands for arithmetic operations must be in registers; therefore variables in memory are transferred to registers before they are used and results are transferred from registers to memory.

Repeatedly moving values to and from memory significantly slows program execution; the effect is particularly pronounced for a pipelined RISC processor as the bus system required to transfer values is always in use fetching instructions. Memory transfer speed and the interference of data memory transfer with instruction fetch are additional reasons why the programmer should attempt to keep multiple uses of a variable close together and reduce the number of memory transfers performed.

7.6 More assembler directives

Inclusion of constant and variable data in an assembly language program requires additional directives. Directives DCB, DCW and DCD were introduced as methods of defining constant data items. Program 7.3 is defined by Figure 7.3; it allocates an area of memory to store the variables using a second AREA directive and uses further directives to arrange variables in memory.

This use of AREA has several additional parameters; DATA indicates that the section of memory holds variable data values, not instruction codes; READWRITE shows that the running program, or something else, may alter the values. Finally NOINIT indicates that the initial values are unknown and must be treated as such by the programmer. It must never be assumed that any location in RAM will have known contents at the start of a program; when power is connected to a processor system the contents of all RAM locations and most registers will settle to random values.

Another directive used is SPACE which reserves a number of bytes for a data item. SPACE allows the programmer to choose the required number of bytes for each variable such as an integer, array or string. The optional label before the SPACE directive sets the username value to the address of the variable item. The name of a variable and its address are often used interchangeably in documentation of assembly language programs. **Strictly** the value of a named variable and its address are two different quantities and different names should be used. In a high level language the distinction is clear; the name of a variable is used to imply its value and the address of a variable is the value of a pointer to it. The lack of precision in assembly language arises because an assembly language only uses names for the addresses of variables; the language does not have a use for names indicating the values stored in memory locations. In most cases the same name is used here for the value and its address; the context indicates which quantity is being referenced. For those who wish to be more precise one convention is to use the name to indicate the address and add a prefix, the symbol @ is commonly adopted, to the name to indicate the value.

A further directive; the **equate directive, EQU**; defines the number of values to be added together. The equate directive must have a label as the purpose of the directive is to set the user name defined by the label to a quantity set by the programmer. By giving the number of values a name and using this name at all parts of the program it is easy to change this number reliably if the program is modified. Without the EQU directive when a minor change is made the programmer has to search for every use of the value; when revising a large program a single use is easily missed and creates a fault in the program. Extensive use of well commented equate directives is usually good programming practice.

Labels have already been introduced as one method of defining user names. The equate directive provides a method of creating user names with fixed values which can be used anywhere a user name is required. Although the EQU directive can be positioned anywhere in a program well documented programs usually put the equate directives that define simple known numeric constant values immediately after the program's comment heading; related items are grouped together. A user name defined by EQU or its use as a label may be used anywhere an immediate value is required; for example as in MOV <Rn>,#immed or LDR <Rn>,=immed.

```
; Compute the sum of five numbers held in successive memory locations
; Program in file Prog7_3.s
; Date:-      6th July 2006
; Revisions:- none
; Author:- J.R. Gibson
Numvals    EQU       5                 ; number of items in list
           AREA      Summation,   CODE,    READONLY

           ENTRY
;          WARNING - insert lines with Reset_Handler for Keil systems

; r3 holds count and r4 holds total, r5 is the pointer to the data, ptr
           MOV       r3, #Numvals    ; initialise count
           MOV       r4, #0          ; initialise total
           LDR       r5, =datstart   ; set ptr to the start of the data
        ; start of addition loop
cloop      LDR       r6, [r5], #4    ; get value at ptr, advance ptr
           ADD       r4, r4, r6      ; add value to total
           SUBS      r3, r3, #1      ; decrement count (remember the S)
           BNE       cloop           ; loop if not done required times
           NOP                       ; NOP to help testing

; For ARM systems the next 3 lines return control to the IDE, replace with
; the line    stop   BAL   stop   for other systems
           MOV       r0, #0x18
           LDR       r1, =0x20026
           SWI       0x123456

; IMPORTANT. Before running determine where the data is located and use the
;            development system to load test values into memory
           AREA   Thedata, DATA, NOINIT, READWRITE ; define a read/write region
datstart   SPACE     20              ; reserve 20 bytes of memory for data
           END
```

Program 7.3 Computation of the sum of five numbers held in successive memory locations

Program 7.3 illustrates the creation of a simple data storage area with the name set by the label before the SPACE directive. For this program an array of five 32-bit unsigned integers is required; each byte has its own address so twenty locations are required. The LDR pseudo instruction uses the label name to load the start address of the array into register r5. The use of a label avoids the programmer having to determine the location used for the data. The memory addresses are set by the linker when it combines the output modules produced by the assembler into a single entity for loading into the target system. The linker always positions blocks, AREA sections, so they start at addresses divisible by four.

The label *datstart* may be used to identify the variable; as indicated previously *datstart* is strictly the name of a pointer to the memory location holding the variable, in this case the array of five items. In a DATA section defined by an AREA directive each program variable may be allocated a position in memory using a label to define the variable's address. Multiple SPACE directives are used to allocate memory to each variable held in memory using separate labels to create pointers to each variable.

In Program 7.3 there are some extra comments in brackets. These sections of the comments are to emphasise decisions that were made when designing the program; in most cases they are more detailed than necessary but provide extra tutorial information.

7.7 A data structure example

When using high level languages elaborate data structures are often created that link together related data items; most of the tasks of determining how to construct the structures and how to access elements of them are performed by the compiler with little programmer effort. In assembly language the programmer must create any data structures required and must determine how to access their elements. Although the tasks of constructing and maintaining data structures are best implemented in high level languages there are situations when data structures have to be created using assembly language.

A simple example is a control system using an ARM processor to perform the control task. The system has sensors to measure features of the process with the sensor output signals input to analog to digital converters, ADCs, whose 16-bit digital outputs are inputs to the processor system. The 16-bit value represents the measurement such that zero corresponds to zero and the maximum sensor output, the full scale deflection (FSD), is exactly 0xffff. The sensors are automatically read as rapidly as possible and the readings are stored in the system memory by extra hardware that implements direct memory access, DMA. The DMA hardware puts the values read into the correct memory locations without involving the CPU. A structure of several constant data items is built for each ADC so that the program can easily determine any information concerning a particular analog input whenever necessary. This structure consists of

- the 32-bit address of the ADC; required to control the behaviour of the ADC.
- the 32-bit address of the memory location where the DMA system stores the most recent 16-bit ADC reading value.
- a 16-bit unsigned number such that multiplying the ADC reading value by this converts the value to a 32-bit unsigned integer number that, when multiplied by a specified power of ten, is the true sensor reading in some standard units.
- a 16-bit signed integer value that indicates the power of ten by which the 32-bit unsigned integer must be multiplied to obtain the true reading.
- A string of exactly ten 8-bit character codes that is text showing the measurement units.

The program must contain details describing the construction of the data structure; one form for the example is Program 7.4. Any description of data structures of this form are usually placed at the head of the program data section; that is immediately after the AREA directive that defines the variable data.

In Program 7.4 a number of items could have been defined directly; for example each offset could have been calculated by the programmer. The more elaborate use of the EQU directive shown causes the computer running the assembler to evaluate these quantities; such computer calculation is much more likely to be error free than calculations performed by the programmer. Whenever possible programmers should use assembler features to make the computer running the assembler calculate values. In addition to obtaining correct results there is the advantage that if program alterations are made a single amendment will automatically make the required alterations at all points in the program; consequently the risk of introducing errors when modifying a program is reduced.

```
; Definition of the structure holding ADC channel data
; All offsets are number of bytes from start of the structure
Add_Offs   EQU    0                  ; offset of address of channel
Rdg_Offs   EQU    Add_Offs + 4       ; offset of latest reading address
Scl_Offs   EQU    Rdg_Offs + 4       ; offset of scale factor
Pwr_Offs   EQU    Scl_Offs + 2       ; offset of power of ten value
Stg_Offs   EQU    Pwr_Offs + 2       ; offset of units string start
End_Offs   EQU    Stg_Offs + 10      ; end of structure allowing ten
                                     ; bytes for the units text
```

Program 7.4 Header defining the data structure for the ADC example

Performing calculations as part of the assembly process is a very important task of the assembler. It removes the need for programmers to make calculations with the consequent chance of accidental errors. In well constructed programs it also reduces the risk of mistakes if the program is modified. For example Program 7.4 can be improved by defining sizes for each item in the structure as in Program 7.5. If the hardware is later changed and the sizes of some elements change an alteration of this revised definition automatically updates the whole program. A brief examination of the ability of an assembler to perform calculations is provided in Chapter 14; at this point it is sufficient to know that the assembler can combine any numeric quantities, that is actual numbers and values defined by user names, using simple arithmetic operations. The assembler performs calculations using values that it must be possible to determine at assembly time, it cannot use the values of quantities such as variables that only exist when the program runs.

```
; Definition of the structure to hold ADC channel data
; All offsets are number of bytes from start of the structure
Siz_Adr   EQU    4              ; number of bytes for channel address
Siz_Rdg   EQU    4              ; number of bytes for reading address
Siz_Sca   EQU    2              ; number of bytes for scale factor
Siz_Pwr   EQU    2              ; number of bytes for power of ten
Siz_Str   EQU    10             ; number of bytes for string

                  ; the total structure size is
Siz_ADC   EQU    Siz_Adr+Siz_Rdg+Siz_Sca+Siz_Pwr+Siz_Str

Add_Offs  EQU    0                     ; offset of address of channel
Rdg_Offs  EQU    Add_Offs + Siz_Adr    ; offset of latest reading value
Scl_Offs  EQU    Rdg_Offs + Siz_Rdg    ; offset of scale factor
Pwr_Offs  EQU    Scl_Offs + Siz_Sca    ; offset of power of ten value
Stg_Offs  EQU    Pwr_Offs + Siz_Pwr    ; offset of units string start
End_Offs  EQU    Stg_Offs + Siz_Str    ; total size of structure allowing ten
                                       ; bytes for the string
```

Program 7.5 Revised data structure for the ADC example

An alternative, equally valid, statement for the total structure size is

```
Siz_ADC    EQU    End_Offs
```

Assuming there are two temperature sensors, a pressure sensor and a flow meter then storage space is reserved in the DATA segment for the data structure corresponding to each sensor by statements such as those in Program 7.6. The ALIGN directive, not strictly necessary using ADS, is used after allocating space for each structure to ensure that structures always start at addresses divisible by four.

```
Tempr1    SPACE   Siz_ADC       ; data structure for temperature sensor 1
          ALIGN
Tempr2    SPACE   Siz_ADC       ; data structure for temperature sensor 2
          ALIGN
Press     SPACE   Siz_ADC       ; data structure for pressure sensor
          ALIGN
Flow      SPACE   Siz_ADC       ; data structure for flow meter
          ALIGN
```

Program 7.6 Reservation of data space for data structures

Using these structures development of general purpose modules that perform commonly required tasks for any ADC channel is straightforward; additions of more ADC channels are simple and involve little programmer effort. If extra items are added to the data structure all features are adjusted correctly without the programmer having to determine all the consequential changes and ensuring that they are implemented. Although a reasonable data structure has been created the example is very simple; even so the programmer performs a number of tasks that a high level language performs automatically.

The controller data structure allows the use of the addressing mode `[<Rn>, #±offset]` to be illustrated. A common task is converting an ADC reading, raw value, into a scaled value for display. Using the data structures a module can be devised to perform this task for any of the ADC channels. Program 7.7 performs this task and uses the addressing mode to obtain the values of elements of the structure.

```
; the program heading must include Programs 7.5 and 7.6. xxxx indicates use
; any structure label, that is any one of Tempr1, Tempr2, Press or Flow
       LDR    r0, =xxxx            ; set a pointer to this ADC's structure
       LDR    r1, [r0, #Rdg_Offs]  ; get address of latest ADC reading
                                   ; (32-bits)
       LDRH   r1, [r1]             ; get latest ADC reading (16-bits)
       LDRH   r2, [r0, #Scl_Offs]  ; get 16-bit scale value
; MUL (described in Chapter 10) multiplies contents of r1 by contents of r2.
; As LDRH sets high 16-bits all zero the result cannot exceed 32-bits
       MUL    r2, r1, r2           ; product to r2
       . . . .
```

Program 7.7 A partial program illustrating the use of indexed offset addressing

7.8 Another addressing mode

An important requirement of many programs is the use of an address with an offset that is computed as the program runs and depends on two program variables. It is possible to perform such an operation using a sequence of instructions with the addressing modes already introduced but it can be performed more efficiently using one of the other addressing modes available. One mode has the instruction forms

```
LDR{<cond>}   <Rd>,  [<Rn>,±<Rm>]
STR{<cond>}   <Rd>,  [<Rn>,±<Rm>]
```

This addressing mode is similar to the mode that uses `[<Rn>, #±offset]` except that the contents of register Rm are added to or subtracted from the contents of Rn and the result used as the memory address. The contents of Rn and Rm are not changed when this addressing mode is used.

Situations that require the more complicated addressing modes for efficient programming tend to arise when complex data structures are used; as a result simple examples to illustrate their use tend to be artificial. A situation where this mode is useful can be illustrated by modification to Program 7.2. In this program the address of the first number in a list is copied to a register and the address held in the register, the pointer, is changed as each list item is obtained from memory. In many programs which perform more complicated tasks the programmer wishes to examine items in a list several times; using the addressing mode adopted in Program 7.2 the list start address must be repeatedly reloaded into the register holding the pointer. One method of avoiding repeatedly reloading the list start address is to use the addressing mode `<Rd>, [<Rn>,±<Rm>]`; using this mode Program 7.8 performs the same task as Program 7.2 but leaves the *'base address'* in register Rn unchanged. In Program 7.2 the register whose contents are being changed is a pointer because it holds the full address to be used, in Program 7.8 the register being changed is related to an index as it identifies the element in the list by an offset from the list start. It is not exactly an index because it is increased by four each time, rather than by one. This addressing mode is even more effective when a program uses elements from the same index position in two or more lists.

```
        . . . .
        LDR    r4, =list_start    ; list_start is a label giving the
                                   ; address of the first list element
        MOV    r5, #0             ; this is the offset from
        LDR    r6, =(4*list_len)  ; keep a copy of the list length
                                   ; (length defined elsewhere)
        ; r4 is used as ptr and r5 as index
        MOV    r0, #0             ; r0 holds result, initial value zero is
                                   ; the smallest possible unsigned integer
loop_st
        LDR    r7, [r4,r5]        ; load value from address list_start + index
        CMP    r0, r7            ; test for value > than largest so far
        BCS    small             ; if value was greater then skip load
        MOV    r0, r7            ; make value the new largest result
small
        ADD    r5, r5, #4        ; move index to next position in list
        CMP    r5, r6            ; all done ????
        BLS    loop_st           ; continue looping if more to do
        . . . .
```

Program 7.8 A partial program illustrating the use of a register to provide indexed offset

The two different addressing modes of Program 7.2 and Program 7.8 illustrate the difference between a pointer and an index. This difference is subtle and the use of the two terms causes many inexperienced programmers difficulty. Selecting when to use a pointer and when to use an index is also often difficult and requires practise in the use of both. The ARM memory addressing modes are such that in many situations the selection does not affect program size or speed. When this is the case use of an index often produces a program that is more easily understood.

7.9 Summary

Some methods of using memory to hold data values using the ARM instructions to store and retrieve data have been described and illustrated with simple examples. The most noticeable feature when manipulating memory contents using an ARM processor is the absence of a direct addressing mode; because of this it is always necessary to hold addresses, or parts of addresses, in registers. The full ARM instruction set provides several additional addressing modes; brief details are provided in Appendix D and full specifications are in the ARM Architecture Reference Manual [12].

The data handling techniques that have been described are adequate for most assembly language programs. A program that requires large amounts of data or complex data structures should be prepared in a high level language, the compiler will use all the addressing modes available efficiently.

A feature of ARM assembly language is that LDR and STR are two frequently used instructions but are also the two instructions which can most easily lead to program faults when small typing errors are made. The syntax of some addressing modes differ only slightly in the order of brackets and other punctuation marks; a typing error can easily change one valid mode into another and the assembler will not report an error. Additionally the use of LDR as the mnemonic for the pseudo instructions and the availability of another form of LDR with very similar syntax can also mask small typing mistakes. Finally there are restrictions on the use of some modes, restrictions of the use of certain registers or combinations of registers, and complicated effects occur if addresses which are not aligned are used. The restrictions and effects of using non-aligned addresses are described in Appendix D.

7.10 Problems

7.1 Design an alternative version of Program 7.2 to determine the maximum value of a set of unsigned integer numbers which uses a count up from zero method instead of a count down method. Prepare and test such a program. Comment on the differences between your program and Program 7.2.

Also develop versions of Program 7.2 with both count up and count down forms that are constructed using a while loop instead of a repeat loop.

7.2 Develop, prepare and test a program that finds both the largest and smallest 32-bit unsigned integer numbers in a list of numbers.

7.3 Program 7.3 computes the sum of five numbers held in successive memory locations and is constructed using a repeat loop. Design, prepare and test a program that performs the same function using a while loop.

7.4 Develop a program that sorts a list of 32-bit unsigned numbers into ascending order. Start by developing an NS chart for a bubble sort; this method is simple to program and is reasonably fast provided the lists are not large. The following sequence is not the most efficient but is clear and easily understood.

i)   Set a pointer to the first position of the list (two pointers might be found to be useful).

ii)   Set an indicator variable to a value you define as *'complete'*.

iii)   Compare the value at the pointer with the value at the next position in the list. If the second is less than the first exchange the positions of the two values in memory and set the indicator to show *'not complete'*.

iv)   Repeatedly advance the pointer then perform step (iii) until the end of the list is reached, that is until the loop is executed with the second value as the last list value.

v)   If the indicator value is *'not complete'* repeat from step (i)

Perform the complete (i) to (v) loop as many times as necessary.

7.5   Develop a program that copies a null terminated string that is a constant data item into a another position in memory so that the copy is a variable data version of the string.

7.6   Program 7.9 illustrates a method of creating a string that does not use a terminator. Instead the number of characters in the string is stored as a full 32-bit word at the address defined by the label at the head of the string. Repeat Problem 7.5 using this method to create the string.

```
;           note that the -4 removes the number of memory locations used to
;           hold the string length
string      DCD   str_end - string - 4   ; number of string characters
            DCB   "This is the string"
str_end                                  ; mark string end
```

Program 7.9 Definition of a string with the length at its start

8 Program Modules

A program that only uses the techniques already described is a single list of instructions; even for a simple task the list is long. Chapter 2 stated that well designed programs should be built of small modules. As the amount of text readily viewed is about one page of normal typescript a guideline is that the program text of a module should not exceed this. This suggests that modules, including comments and headings, should have no more than forty to fifty lines. This is a guideline, not a rigid rule, but modules significantly larger than this are probably too complicated; complexity leads to a high risk of faults [9].

To illustrate division into modules consider a program for a simple system with a keyboard for input and an output device to display text. The specification is that messages are displayed requesting users to input two unsigned decimal integer numbers, after both are input the program computes and displays their sum. The NS chart, Figure 8.1, is a top level structure that meets the specification.

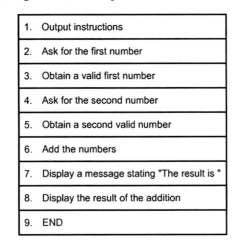

| 1. Output instructions |
| 2. Ask for the first number |
| 3. Obtain a valid first number |
| 4. Ask for the second number |
| 5. Obtain a second valid number |
| 6. Add the numbers |
| 7. Display a message stating "The result is " |
| 8. Display the result of the addition |
| 9. END |

Figure 8.1 Top level actions of the decimal addition example

Each task in Figure 8.1 is moderately large; if the whole program is written *'in line'* as a list of assembly language statements the list is very long. It would be too large to be clear to readers and would be difficult to prepare, test and modify. Another feature is that the same task is performed at several points using different data. For example text is displayed in at least four places; if possible a single program section should perform all text outputs. Similarly each number should be obtained using the same module. Multiple use of modules is an important feature of good program design. It reduces development effort, costs are lower, and the number of undetected errors is lower because use of a module many times leads to frequent execution during testing increasing the probability of error detection. Finally libraries of modules can be developed for common tasks; this further reduces development costs and the occurrence of errors.

8.1 Subroutines

The most common, but not the only, module form in an assembly language program is a **subroutine**. A subroutine is a section of code to perform a specific task that is reached by a special branch instruction, a **call**. A call differs from a normal branch because after executing the program at the call destination address the program **returns** to the **calling point**; it continues by executing the instruction immediately after the call instruction. Therefore a call to a subroutine must be by a branch instruction that remembers where it came from; the flow of a simple program calling a subroutine twice is illustrated by Figure 8.2.

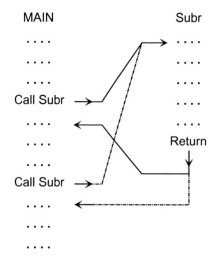

Figure 8.2 Program flow sequence using a subroutine

Because of its RISC structure the ARM instructions for subroutine call and return perform fewer actions than similar instructions of CISC type CPUs. Consequently the ARM programmer has to perform more tasks than a CISC programmer to create a subroutine. The ARM subroutine call instruction is **branch with link,** mnemonic **BL**; as usual all the conditional forms are allowed.

Branch with link performs all the actions of a normal branch; it also puts the address of the instruction that immediately follows the branch with link instruction into register r14. This is the special use of r14, it is the **link register;** the assembler accepts the names lr, LR, r14 and R14. At the end of the execution of all the subroutine instructions the return is performed by copying the contents of r14 into the program counter, pc; one method is by using the instruction MOV pc, lr.

This return from a subroutine is one of the very few special cases where the programmer changes the contents of the program counter by moving a new value directly into it instead of using a branch instruction. Such explicit loading of the program counter is not necessary for most CISC processors because they have a return instruction that performs this automatically. Moving the return address into the program counter is required for ARM because the programmer must create part of the mechanism for saving return addresses and restoring return addresses at the end of subroutine execution.

Constructing subroutines using branch with link is straight forward but a problem arises if the code of one subroutine includes a call to another subroutine, a process called **nesting** of subroutines. Figure 8.3 illustrates a main program calling two subroutines with the first subroutine also calling the second; this has only two levels of nesting whereas many more levels of nesting are common.

In Figure 8.3 the second subroutine is called by the first. If the first subroutine return address is in r14 when the second subroutine is called the return address for the first is lost, it is replaced by the return address for the second. Most CISC type CPUs automatically save return addresses in memory instead of registers. The area of memory used for return addresses is operated as a **last in first out, LIFO**, store; when it holds return addresses and related items it is the program **stack**. Another description of this store is that it is a push in or push down and pop out or pop up memory; each item added pushes previous ones more deeply into the memory and each retrieval causes remaining items to rise upwards.

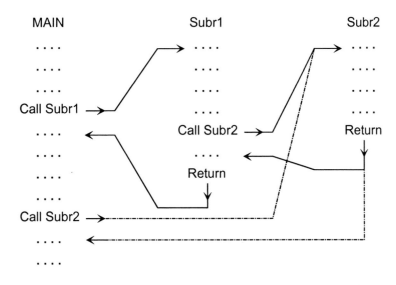

Figure 8.3 Program flow sequence with nested subroutines

Large programs contain many subroutines with many levels of nesting; a stack is essential for storing return addresses and other items. A RISC processor cannot perform several memory accesses when executing one instruction so BL cannot store the return address in memory at the same time as it performs a memory read to fetch the code of the first instruction of the subroutine. The link register is a temporary store for the return address. It is the programmer's responsibility to copy the return address from its temporary position in the link register into the stack memory. Therefore when using ARM assembly language the programmer must set up and manage storage and retrieval of return addresses using the stack; however:

i)   ARM define a standard method to be used. **Always** use this standard so that other features operate correctly.

ii)   The ARM instruction set includes features which help in stack use provided that the standard method of creating and using subroutines is followed.

8.2 Stacks

A stack must be created as a LIFO memory within the normal processor system memory address space. The standard method for an ARM system is to use r13 as the **stack pointer;** the assembler allows sp or SP to be used instead of r13 or R13. One of the first instructions of any program is to load the stack pointer. For early exercises using ARM development tools such as the ARMulator or Evaluator-7T set the initial stack address to 0x010000. This address places the stack at much higher RAM addresses than those usually used for code and data by small programs. For other development systems an alternative setting may be required; for example if the Keil tools are set as suggested in Appendix E the stack should be set to 0x40001000. To set the stack to 0x010000 the following line should be included as soon after the ENTRY directive as possible.

```
        LDR     sp, =0x10000        ; set up the stack
```

Usually this is the first instruction after ENTRY although it is sometimes necessary to put a small number of instructions to configure the system hardware before setting the stack. Once set at the start of the program never use instructions to change the contents of the stack pointer directly; use only the automatic LIFO memory manipulations to be described.

Storage of subroutine return addresses is an important function of the stack; another is storage of copies of register contents when they are changed by the subroutine. In most subroutines the programmer uses registers to hold temporary values, **local variables**, which are only required within the subroutine and are discarded on return. The program that calls the routine may be using many registers for its own local variables which should not be changed. For large programs with many levels of subroutine nesting it is difficult to determine which registers must not be changed. A simple method to avoid problems is to save all registers used by a subroutine on the stack. ARM suggest a better, slightly more complicated, method which requires that certain registers never contain values that must be saved; values in other registers must always be preserved if the registers are used by the subroutine. These rules are outlined in Section 8.7; they are adopted by compilers for high level languages so must be used in mixed language programming.

Except for very simple subroutines that do not call other subroutines the contents of the link register must be stored on the stack near the start of a subroutine and must be restored to the program counter by the return process. It may also be necessary to save the contents of other registers to prevent their loss. The values could be saved using multiple STR and LDR instructions; this is cumbersome and requires that the programmer correctly changes the stack pointer. Two ARM instructions perform stack operations efficiently. **Store multiple, STM,** copies the contents of multiple registers to the stack and **load multiple, LDM**, performs the reverse process; both instructions correctly adjust the stack pointer. There are many forms of STM and LDM; a description of all forms and their use is beyond the level of this book. Only the form that is most frequently used to create and manipulate the program stack is described.

The STM and LDM instructions do not satisfy the specification of RISC processor instructions. This is an ARM feature where the designers followed a pragmatic approach; the instructions provide an efficient method of performing an essential task so have been included in the instruction set. Because the number of values transferred to or from memory by STM and LDM is chosen by the programmer their execution time is not fixed. Programs should transfer the minimum number of registers necessary to the stack as each memory transfer significantly slows program execution.

Stacks are operated so the stack pointer automatically moves in the correct manner as items are stored and retrieved; usually the action to store something on the stack is called **push** and retrieval is **pop**. The stack could operate so that as items are added the next address to be used is higher, **ascending stack**, or alternatively it could be lower, **descending stack**. Many CPUs restrict operation to one form whereas ARM allows the programmer to choose the form. In most cases a descending stack is used because the start of the stack is placed at the highest possible address in the available memory. The descending version is regarded as the standard form and is used here; in all cases the full 32-bit contents of a register are stored and retrieved. The versions of STM and LDM to store 32-bit values in a descending order have the mnemonic names STMFD and LDMFD (with alternative names STMDB and LDMIA). The letter **F** indicates **full** meaning that the memory at the current address indicated by the stack pointer contains a value that has been placed on the stack; the stack pointer must be changed **before** anything is added to the stack and changed **after** anything is retrieved from the stack. An alternative **empty** method of operating the stack exists, do not mix the two methods. The letter **D** indicates **descending**, as items are placed on the stack the stack pointer is decreased, the stack grows towards lower value addresses.

The instruction to store register contents of on the stack, push, using the full descending form is:

```
STM{<cond>}FD  sp!, {register list}
```

The corresponding instruction to retrieve values from the stack, pop, is:

```
LDM{<cond>}FD  sp!, {register list}
```

where {*register list*} is a list of all registers to be pushed or popped. There is possible **confusion** because this is the one case when the curly brackets { and } are typed as part of the instruction. The register list is the names of the registers to be transferred with the individual register names separated by commas. If a group of registers is to be transferred the first and last separated by a hyphen may be used instead of typing the full list. For example STMFD sp!, {r3, r4, r6-r9, r12} means that the contents of registers r3, r4, r6, r7, r8, r9 and r12 are copied to the stack; writing r6-r9 is exactly the same as writing r6, r7, r8, r9. The **exclamation mark** means correctly adjust the value in the register to the left of the mark, in this case r13 also called sp, each time the contents of one register are transferred to or from memory.

As for LDRB and STRB, the use of {<cond>} with LDM and STM requires that the two letter conditional code, {<cond>}, is placed between the basic instruction and its mode of use, such as FD. For the limited uses introduced here the conditional forms are never required. Stack manipulations **should not be conditional** as this would cause major structural problems in a program.

Because the full versions of the ARM instructions used to create and manipulate the stack are general in form it is possible to create multiple stacks using registers other than r13 as the pointers to these additional stacks. Multiple stacks provide very powerful programming techniques but these are advanced methods and should be avoided until operation and use of stacks is fully understood.

8.3 Subroutine construction

To avoid problems subroutines should be constructed in a standard manner. The subroutine entry point should always be the first instruction of the subroutine and, although not essential for very simple cases, the first instruction should always be

```
STMFD    sp!, {list of registers which must include lr}
```

Although it might appear that the safe method would be to push all registers using {r0-r15} this must be avoided; it would cause sixteen 32-bit values to be written to memory and the corresponding LDMFD instruction required would read sixteen 32-bit values from memory. Read and write operations are slow therefore a program should only put onto the stack those registers which will be changed inside the subroutine and whose change will affect other sections of the program. Section 8.8 examines which registers to store and retrieve in more detail. Further storage of r15, the program counter, would cause problems if it were restored at the end of the subroutine so it should not be included in the register list of the STMFD instruction. The subroutine exit should have as final instructions:

```
LDMFD    sp!, {list of registers pushed, must include lr}
MOV      pc, lr
```

In general the push and pop register lists of a subroutine **must always be identical**. However after the return is completed the value in the link register is of no interest; therefore most ARM programmers, and the code produced by high level language compilers, use the single instruction form

```
LDMFD    sp!, {list of registers including pc instead of lr}
```

In this version pc is used **instead of** lr but all other registers in the list are the same. This storage of lr and retrieval of pc is the only case where the rule of the push and pop lists being identical may be broken; even in this case the push and pop lists are identical except that lr in the push list is replaced by pc in the pop list. As well as not being a safe programming technique the trick of pushing one register onto the stack and popping the value into another will not work in general; detailed knowledge of the operation of STM and LDM is essential to determine which cases will behave correctly.

To minimize the risk of creating complex errors the only instruction to push values onto the stack should be the first instruction of a subroutine and the only instruction that pops values off the stack should be the subroutine's last. The push and pop should always be performed even in trivial cases for which it is not essential to put the link register onto the stack; developing the habit of always following standard techniques greatly reduces the risk of errors when preparing programs. More complex use is made of push and pop instructions by high level languages.

```
; Compute the sum of five numbers held in successive locations in memory with
; addition of a simple counter type delay subroutine to slow program
; Program in file Prog8_1.s
; Date:-      7th July 2007
; Revisions:- addition of delay routine to Prog7_3.s
; Author:-    J.R. Gibson
Numvals    EQU       5                  ; number of items in list
           AREA      Summation,  CODE,  READONLY
           ENTRY
;  WARNING add lines with Reset_Handler and use different sp value for Keil

; r3 holds count and r4 holds total, r5 is the pointer to the data, point
           LDR       sp, =0x10000       ; initialise stack pointer
           MOV       r3, #Numvals       ; initialise count
           MOV       r4, #0             ; initialise total
           LDR       r5, =datstart      ; set point to the start of the data
        ; start of addition loop
cloop      LDR       r6, [r5], #4       ; get value at pointer, advance point
           ADD       r4, r4, r6         ; add value just obtained to total
           BL        delay              ; wait to slow program
           SUBS      r3, r3, #1         ; decrement count and set the flags)
           BNE       cloop              ; loop if not done required times
           NOP                          ; NOP to help testing

; For ARM systems the next 3 lines return control to the IDE, replace with
; the line  stop    BAL stop  for other systems
           MOV       r0, #0x18
           LDR       r1, =0x20026
           SWI       0x123456
; Software counter delay routine (can be placed at any reasonable point)
; This does not corrupt any registers (used registers are saved on the stack)
; Inputs:-   None
; Outputs:-  None
delay      STMFD     sp!, {r5, lr}      ; save used registers and return address
           LDR       r5,=0x234567       ; use r5 as the delay counter
Wait       SUBS      r5, r5, #1         ; decrement delay count (S to set flags)
           BNE       wait               ; if not zero (done required times) loop
           LDMFD     sp!, {r5,pc}       ; pop and return
           ; Note - pop list should be identical to push list BUT push lr and
           ; pop pc is a standard ARM technique (see main text)

           AREA      Thedata, DATA, NOINIT, READWRITE ; define a read/write region
Datstart   SPACE     20                 ; reserve 20 bytes of memory for data
           END
```

Program 8.1 Example of a simple subroutine

Program 7.3 computes the total of five integer numbers. Program 8.1 is a modified version of Program 7.3; it includes a subroutine that causes it to run much more slowly because the subroutine contains a loop which is executed a large number of times. As the register used as the loop counter is already used by the main program the contents of the register must be saved on the stack.

8.3.1 Some notes concerning features of Program 8.1

The **subroutine has a comment heading** that defines its function. The heading describes values required from the program that calls it and values it sends back to the calling program; no values are transferred in this example. A clear heading stating what a subroutine does, how it obtains values used and where it returns results is an essential part of program documentation.

Because the delay subroutine does not call any other subroutines the LDMFD and STMFD instructions are not strictly necessary. However always following the standard method to construct subroutines reduces the risk of errors.

Software delay loops are a convenient method of slowing program execution. However they should not be used when accurate timing of actions is essential; accurate timing must be implemented using hardware timer circuits. Microcontrollers, for example in development boards such as the Unique ML67Q4000 and Evaluator-7T, usually include several hardware timers because microcontrollers are frequently used for control tasks requiring accurately timed actions.

The order in memory of the main program, subroutines and items such as constant data is usually unimportant. For small assembly language programs the main program is often first; with the subroutines or constant data second. Those familiar with the C language may prefer to put the subroutines before the main program. In larger programs the constant data may be separated into data belonging to each routine with the data belonging to a routine stored immediately after the routine.

The problems of starting up any processor system have been ignored; it is assumed that it is handled by a development system. For an independent system that runs a single fixed program as soon as power is supplied there must be start up code to initialise features of the system hardware. The start up code ends with a branch to the ENTRY point in the main program; when using a development system it performs all the start up tasks then branches to the entry point. Therefore the order of items in memory is not important at this time. It is only when a complete program, including start up code, is developed that the programmer must consider where components are placed in memory.

8.4 Passing information to and from subroutines

Some subroutines, such as the delay in Program 8.1, do not require the calling program to provide any values and do not return values to the calling program. This is unusual; most subroutines require that values are transferred, **passed**, to them and most pass values back to the calling point. The values passed to a subroutine are the **subroutine inputs**, often just called inputs, and the values returned are **subroutine outputs** or outputs. The terms input and output must not be confused with real electrical inputs and outputs such as signals from keyboards or signals to displays. The values passed as inputs to a subroutine or returned as outputs from it are **parameters** and may be explicitly referred to as input parameters and output parameters. The process of transferring values is **parameter passing**. Here only subroutines with a small number of parameters are examined; a full discussion of the possible nature of parameters, methods of passing large numbers of parameters and related tasks are advanced topics.

In simple cases only a few values are passed to a subroutine and only a few are returned. For example program 8.1 may be modified so different delays are created by different count values with the value chosen by the calling program instead of being fixed. A simple way is to pass the count value to the subroutine in a register as in program 8.2. Conventional ARM practice is to pass a single parameter in r0; usually values passed are not preserved so r0 is not pushed onto the stack at the start of the subroutine.

```
; Compute the sum of five numbers held in successive locations in memory with
; a simple counter type delay subroutine to slow program
; Program in file Prog8_2.s
; Date:-  8th July 2007
; Revisions:- modified Prog8_1.s to allow variable delay
; Author:- J.R. Gibson

numvals     EQU       5                   ; number of items in list
            AREA      Summation,  CODE,  READONLY
            ENTRY
;  WARNING add lines with Reset_Handler and use different sp value for Keil

; r3 holds count and r4 holds total, r5 is the pointer to the data, point
            LDR       sp, =0x10000        ; initialise stack pointer
            MOV       r3, #numvals        ; initialise count
            MOV       r4, #0              ; initialise total
            LDR       r5, =datstart       ; set point to the start of the data
      ; start of addition loop
cloop       LDR       r6, [r5], #4        ; get value at pointer, advance point
            ADD       r4, r4, r6          ; add value just obtained to total
            LDR       r0, =23456          ; select delay count
            BL        delay               ; wait to slow program
            SUBS      r3, r3, #1          ; decrement count and set the flags
            BNE       cloop               ; loop if not done required times
            NOP                           ; NOP to help testing
; For ARM systems the next 3 lines return control to the IDE, replace with
; the line stop   BAL  stop for other systems
            MOV       r0, #0x18
            LDR       r1, =0x20026
            SWI       0x123456
; Counter delay routine which corrupts r0 (passed parameter)
; Inputs:-   Delay count passed in r0
; Outputs:-  None
delay       STMFD     sp!, {lr}           ; save return address
wait        SUBS      r0, r0, #1          ; decrement delay count (S to set flags)
            BNE       wait                ; if not zero (done required times) loop
            LDMFD     sp!, {pc}           ; return
            ; Reminder - push lr and pop pc is a common ARM technique

            AREA      Thedata, DATA, NOINIT, READWRITE ; define a read/write region
datstart    SPACE     20                  ; reserve 20 bytes of memory for data
            END
```

Program 8.2 Modified example of delay subroutine using a single parameter

Program 8.2 illustrates passing one parameter to a subroutine; the parameter is passed in a register. Similarly a register can be used to return values to the calling point. Passing parameters in registers may be used when only a small number of parameters are involved. When a subroutine has a large number of parameters passed in either direction a more complex method of passing parameters by putting them into a well defined position in memory is required; often, but not always, the stack is used. Most programs that pass a large number of parameters to and from subroutines are those that manipulate large amounts of data; programs of this nature should normally be prepared using a high level language.

8.5 An example of a subroutine with several parameters

ARM does not have a division instruction. For all CPU types division is avoided whenever possible as even CPUs with division instructions perform it very slowly. However sometimes division is essential and for a limited range of situations a simple subroutine may be developed with the following specification.

- Both values (dividend and divisor) are 32-bit unsigned integers.
- Unsigned integer division is performed; that is both an unsigned integer result, quotient, and an unsigned integer remainder are returned.
- Any attempt to divide by zero is detected, an indicator is returned to show it occurred.
- The suggested ARM rules described later for passing parameters are adopted.

The method of division selected is repeated subtraction of the divisor from the dividend counting the number of times this is possible before a negative result is produced. This is simplified by performing the subtraction once too often producing an easily detected negative result. The divisor is added back, restored, to provide a correct remainder and the count value is reduced by one to give the quotient. To avoid looping for ever a test for division by zero is performed before the first subtraction and an error indicator is returned, 0 for no division by zero and 1 for attempted division by zero. The subroutine has two input parameters, *dividend* and *divisor*, and three outputs. The outputs are the quotient, *quot*; the remainder, *remain*; and *error* used to indicate an attempt to divide by zero. Obviously *quot* and *remain* do not have meaningful values if *error* = 1. Figure 8.4 is a subroutine structure that meets this specification.

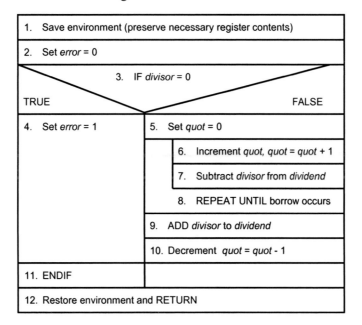

Figure 8.4 Structure of a simple division subroutine

An ARM assembly language subroutine that matches the structure of Figure 8.4 is Program 8.3; the comments contain additional details added for tutorial purposes. For example a typical comment with STMFD is 'save environment' while that with LDMFD is 'restore environment and return'.

This division routine is extremely slow; any reader with a requirement for an efficient division routine for ARM should study the sections of the book by Shloss *et.al.* [13] that examine division using both high level language and assembly language for several forms of number representation.

```
; Software division routine for division of unsigned 32-bit integers
; This does not corrupt any registers except those used for parameter return
; Inputs:-   dividend in r0, divisor in r1
; Outputs:-  remainder remain in r0, integer result, quotient quot in r1,
;            error code in r2 (0 for no error, 1 for division by zero)

divi        STMFD   sp!, {r4, lr}   ; save used registers (except those for
                                    ; parameters) and the return address
            MOV     r2, #0          ; set default error code (no error)
            MOVS    r1, r1          ; test for divisor zero
            BNE     not_div0        ; skip to divide if not divide by zero
            MOV     r2, #1          ; set error code for divide by zero
            B       endif           ; skip division actions

not_div0    MOV     r4, #0          ; working value of quot result

rep_Lp      ADD     r4, r4, #1      ; increment quot (count times subtracted)
            SUBS    r0, r0, r1      ; subtract divisor from dividend
            BCS     rep_Lp          ; loop if no borrow, dividend still > 0
            ADD     r0, r0, r1      ; restore excess subtraction
            SUB     r4, r4, #1      ; correct count quot
            MOV     r1, r4          ; put quotient quot into return register

endif       LDMFD   sp!, {r4,pc}    ; restore used registers (except those
                                    ; to return parameters) and perform return
```

Program 8.3 Simple division subroutine

8.6 Safe use of the stack

If errors are made in manipulating the stack the effects are catastrophic. An error causing stack faults may be very difficult to find as the point at which effects of the mistake are observed may be many instructions after execution of the incorrect instructions. Additionally some stack faults cause different effects each time the program is run while other faults may destroy some of the program code or data if these are held in RAM. The following rules should be followed at all times.

- Always put the instruction that defines the position of the stack in the memory near the start of the program. Usually the first program instruction after essential initialisation tasks should set the stack pointer to the top of the memory area chosen for the stack.
- Only change the value of the stack pointer using the sp! form of addressing to adjust it automatically. Once the stack pointer is set at the start of the program never write new values directly to the stack pointer.

- A subroutine should only have a single entry point which should be at the first instruction of a subroutine.
- The push instruction, STMFD, should be a subroutine's first instruction.
- Enter subroutines by a branch with link to the first instruction of the subroutine; **never** enter by branch without link or any other instruction that changes the program counter.
- Never enter at any point other than the entry point.
- Only have one return in a subroutine which must be the subroutine's last instruction.
- Leave subroutines by the standard return method; never leave by a branch instruction.
- The pop instruction, LDMFD, to restore registers and load the program counter with the return address should be the last instruction.
- Do not use operations that push and pop values on and off the stack anywhere other than at the start and end of a subroutine; make another stack if such operations are essential.
- Develop a fixed set of rules for passing values to and from subroutines; for ARM systems the recommendations in Section 8.8 should be adopted.
- Have fixed rules that define which registers must have their contents preserved and which will not have their contents preserved.
- Fully test the subroutine by itself and also when it is incorporated into a program.
- In extreme cases define a maximum amount of memory to be used for the stack and include instructions to check that the stack pointer indicates an address in the allowed memory after each STMFD instruction.

It is difficult to break most of these rules if good design methods are adopted leading to well structured programs that are fully designed before any attempt is made to prepare the code.

It is possible to determine the address of each item placed on the stack; this should be avoided if possible as there is a high probability of errors. Advanced techniques using the stack for purposes other than those that have been described are adopted by high level languages; these techniques should be copied if assembly language is used for more advanced tasks than those that have been described.

8.7 Subroutine testing

Subroutines should be tested as fully as all other software. Because they perform well defined functions they can often be tested independently; such tests should ensure that they produce correct results for a wide range of input values. Choice of values that are used as inputs to the subroutine will depend upon its function; for simple numerical functions selections should be similar to those suggested in Table 2.5.

Tests must also ensure that the correct addresses are used on call and return and that the stack operates correctly. The following tests should be sufficient to check these features.

- Set a breakpoint at the address of the BL instruction. At the break note the values of the program counter, stack pointer and all registers except those specified as corrupted.
- Single step from the breakpoint checking that the next instruction to be executed is the STMFD instruction at the start of the subroutine; that is test that the branch and link instruction is executed and reaches the correct destination.
- Step past the STMFD instruction checking that the value of the stack pointer has decreased by four times the number of registers pushed onto the stack.
- Set a second breakpoint at the address of the LDMFD instruction and when it is reached check and note the values of the program counter and stack pointer.

- Single step through LDMFD and check that the instruction to be executed after LDMFD is the one immediately after the branch with link that called the subroutine. Check that the stack pointer has returned to the value noted and that all registers that should be unchanged contain the expected original values.
- Check that the returned values are correct and are in the specified registers.

Some development systems provide trace facilities which allow register values at specified points in a program under test to be recorded in a text file without stopping the program. These facilities reduce the need for manually setting breakpoints and noting register contents at each point.

8.8 ARM conventions for subroutine operation

ARM define the ARM Architecture Procedure Call Standard [14], AAPCS; this is a complex document covering all possibilities for the most complex parameter passing methods that are ever required. Within the AAPCS the Base Procedure Call Standard, BPCS, defines the use of registers by subroutines in simple situations. In all cases r13, r14 and r15 must be used as stack pointer, link register and program counter respectively. In large programs r12 should be reserved for a purpose not examined here; also r9 has a special function in some advanced systems but this use may be ignored by simple programs.

These restrictions leave registers r0 to r11 available for use inside subroutines; in some cases r12 is also available. Following the BPCS rules the registers r4 to r11 (and r12 if available) are used to hold the local variables of the subroutine. Always assume that the subroutine may be called by another subroutine as it is difficult to check large programs if it is assumed that this never happens; this also ensures that future program modifications will not cause problems. If a subroutine is called from another the registers r4 to r12 may be holding local variables of the calling routine, a higher level routine, or main program. Therefore if any of the registers r4 to r12 are used within the subroutine their previous values should be saved on entry to the subroutine and restored at exit.

The BPCS requires that when parameters are passed to a subroutine the first is passed in r0, if there is a second it is passed in r1, a third is in r2 and a fourth in r3. Any further parameters are passed on the stack; passing parameters on the stack is complicated and should only be attempted by experienced programmers. The BPCS indicates that subroutines do not have to preserve the values of parameters passed to them and the registers must not be assumed to hold the original input parameter values after the return. In general the BPCS requires that values in r0 to r3 are not preserved even if not used for parameter passing. Programs should be written assuming that the values of r0 to r3 may be changed by any subroutine call; this avoids having to check if this is true at each subroutine call and also reduces the risk of program errors being created when programs are modified.

When a subroutine returns values to a calling program the first value is in r0, the second in r1, the third in r2 and the fourth in r3. Implementation of this strict form may require inclusion of extra MOV instructions in a subroutine. For example one extra MOV instruction was needed in Program 8.3 to put the return quotient value in the correct register. However it is worthwhile adhering to standard rules as this significantly reduces the risk of program errors. When more than four values are returned the additional values are returned on the stack; again this is an advanced technique that is not examined here.

The description given for passing parameters assumes that they are 32-bit values, for larger data structures two or more registers must be used to hold the value. If several values each less than 32-bits are packed into a 32-bit value it is the programmer's responsibility to arrange this and to ensure that packing and unpacking is performed correctly.

8.9 Example of stack behaviour

Some readers will find it helpful to understand the detailed stack operation while others find the behaviour confusing and should ignore this example. Program 8.4 is an outline, a **framework**[1], of a program that includes two subroutines where the second is called by the first; the functions performed by the program and subroutines are not important for this examination.

```
; Framework of a program that calls two subroutines in file Prog8_4.s
; Date:-   9th July 2007
; Author:- J.R. Gibson
            AREA     Sub_frame,  CODE,  READONLY
; Insert lines that inform the IDE of the start position
            LDR      sp, =XXXX       ; initialise stack pointer as required
            ; some program actions which don't use the stack
test_pt1    BL       sub1            ; call first subroutine
test_pt2
            ; further program actions up to end of main program

; Insert exit lines required for the IDE bring used

; First subroutine
; Assumed it corrupts r0 (passed and returned parameters) and uses r4
; Inputs:-   single parameter passed in r0
; Outputs:-  single parameter returned in r0
sub1        STMFD    sp!, {r4, lr}   ; save return address and used register
s1_pt1
            ; initial subroutine actions (no further stack use)
            BL       sub2
            ; further subroutine actions (no further stack use)
s1_pt2
            LDMFD    sp!, {r4, pc}    ; return and restore environment
; Second subroutine
; Assumed it corrupts r0 (passed and returned parameters) and uses r4 and r7
; Inputs:-   single parameter passed in r0
; Outputs:-  single parameter returned in r0
sub2        STMFD    sp!, {r4,r7,lr}  ; save return address and used registers
s2_pt1
            ; subroutine actions
s2_pt2
            LDMFD    sp!, {r4,r7,pc}  ; return and restore environment
            END
```

Program 8.4 Framework of a program using two subroutines

---

[1] The term framework describes an incomplete program, or program definition, that indicates how the whole is to be constructed. Here it shows where to insert the main program and subroutine actions.

Figure 8.5 shows how the value of the stack pointer and memory contents change as the program is executed. Note that, as always when a value is read from memory, the memory contents are unchanged by the read action. This is emphasised by use of bold print to indicate a value that is held in the stack memory and will be read, that is popped off the stack. Italic print indicates a value that has been read, popped, but the memory still holds the value although it will not be read. *'undef'* is used to indicate memory contents that have not been written at all by the program so are an unknown, undefined, value.

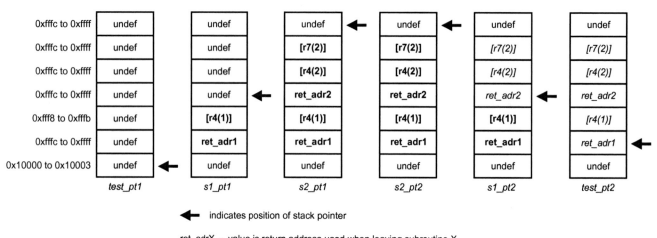

Figure 8.5 Stack contents as Program 8.3 executes (sequence order left to right)

8.10 More advanced topics

It is advised that readers should ignore these topics until they have experience in preparing assembly language programs. The topics are included here as they are associated with creation or use of subroutines.

When the stack pointer is initialised, for example by LDR sp, =0x10000, there is often no memory fitted at the address set. This is because the stack is usually positioned at the highest addresses in the RAM fitted to the system. Because the stack pointer is always decremented first before STMFD pushes items onto the stack it may be set to the address just above that of the last address at which memory is present. Available RAM using ARMulator or Evaluator-7T extends from 0x8000 to 0xffff while that using the LPC2102 with the Keil tools is from 0x40000000 to 0x40000fff.

An important feature of subroutines is the manner in which the programmer passes information to and from them. When converting from the program plan to the code there are two significantly different methods although some readers may find the difference subtle and difficult to understand. Consider a main program which has labels *varA*, *varB* and *varC* to define the memory locations to hold items with values *@varA*, *@varB* and *@varC* respectively. A subroutine is created to perform some arithmetic process which combines two values and returns the result of this action. The programmer can design the subroutine in two different ways, both require the use of three parameters.

Method 1. The program is designed so that the current values of *@varA* and *@varB* are loaded into r0 and r1 as input parameters then the subroutine is called. The subroutine combines these values according to the rules for the process it performs then puts the result into r0; after the return the main program must transfer the value from r0 into the location with address *varC* so that the value of *@varC* becomes the value of the result.

Method 2. The program is designed so that the values of addresses *varA*, *varB* and *varC* are loaded into r0, r1 and r2 as input parameters then the subroutine is called. The subroutine obtains the values of @*varA* and @*varB* from the addresses passed as parameters then combines the values according to the rules for the process it performs putting the result into the location with address *varC*. On return the main program need take no action as the result is already the value in the location *varC*.

Method 1 is referred to passing parameters **by value** while method 2 is called passing parameters **by name**. Obviously the methods can be mixed with some parameters passed by name and some by value. Each method has advantages and disadvantages. Passing by name often requires less code although with careful program design the difference may be very small. However some programmers consider passing by name dangerous as it causes the subroutine to change contents of memory locations that hold data items belonging to the calling module; this makes it difficult to determine points in a program where variables change value. However passing by name is very useful when a subroutine requires the values of a large data structure; transferring every item by value would be very slow. For example strings are almost always passed to and from subroutines by name.

8.11 Summary

Subroutines are the primary method used to create program modules in assembly language. To minimise the risk of errors the programmer must follow a well defined set of rules to create the stack and construct subroutines. Complex faults often arise if such discipline is ignored.

The CPU designer usually incorporates features to assist in subroutine use; full benefit of these is only obtained if the related standard method defined for construction and use of subroutines for the particular CPU are followed. For ARM processors the methods of the Base Procedure Call Standard should be used. ARM encourage this so strongly that the RealView version of their assembler introduces the mnemonics PUSH and POP as alternatives for STMFD and LDMFD respectively and ARM state that these new versions are the preferred forms. The PUSH and POP instructions are

```
PUSH{cond}    {register list}
POP{cond}     {register list}
```

Note that these forms do not require the register used as the stack pointer to be specified, they always use r13 whereas the general forms allow any register to be the stack pointer. The mnemonics PUSH and POP are not accepted by the ADS and GNU assemblers.

8.12 Problems

These problems all require the development of subroutines. The Base Procedure Call Standard should be used and the routines should be tested by creating test programs for a wide range of test cases. When performing the tests using a development system adopt the methods suggested in Section 8.7

8.1 For the test system you use develop a subroutine to create a delay of approximately one second; use trial and error to determine the count value. Develop a second subroutine that calls the one second delay subroutine. The second produces a delay of *N* seconds where *N* is the single parameter passed to this subroutine. *N* may take any value within some range of values that you clearly state.

8.2   One method of performing 64-bit arithmetic was described in Chapter 6. Develop and fully test a subroutine that has as input two 64-bit unsigned integer values and returns their 64-bit sum. It should also return a value to indicate the carry output from the 64-bit addition.

8.3   Develop a subroutine that examines a list of N values; all are 32-bit unsigned integers held in successive memory locations. The subroutine returns the value of the largest number in the list. The parameters passed to the subroutine should be the address of the first list member and the value of N.

Revise your design of the solution of problem 8.3 so that the subroutine returns both the largest and smallest values in the list.

8.4   ARM development systems that support semihosting, Chapter 11, can display the character corresponding to a single ASCII code in a window on the development system screen. Register r1 must hold the address of the byte holding the ASCII code; note that r1 holds the address, it does not hold the ASCII code. To output the character to the display the sequence of instructions

```
MOV    r0, #3     ; semihosting function 3 (display character)
LDR    r1, =xxx   ; pass address where ASCII code is stored
SWI    0x123456   ; perform semihosting function
```

is executed; SWI to be introduced in Chapter 13 implements a form of subroutine call.
Develop and test a subroutine to output a null terminated character string. To test your subroutine create a program that uses the directive DCB to include a constant data string in your program. (The Keil tools allow a similar output and display mechanism to be created by simulating hardware).

8.5   Develop a subroutine to compare two null terminated strings of characters held in memory. It should return a value that indicates if the strings are identical or not. The parameters passed to the subroutine should be the start addresses of the two strings.

9 Manipulating Bits and Bit Patterns

A few instructions and several types of operand have not yet been introduced. Some of these allow more efficient methods of implementing some tasks; others provide methods of performing tasks still to be examined. In particular methods of manipulating single bits or groups of bits within 32-bit words have not been considered; these are tasks that require experience to implement in the most efficient ways.

9.1 Logical instructions

The instruction sets of almost all types of CPU include several instructions that perform **logical** operations, also called **bitwise** operations. The exact set of logical instructions provided varies slightly from one CPU type to another. The ARM processor supports four logical operations; these are

```
AND{<cond>}{S}  <Rd>, <Rn>, <shifter_operand>
BIC{<cond>}{S}  <Rd>, <Rn>, <shifter_operand>
EOR{<cond>}{S}  <Rd>, <Rn>, <shifter_operand>
ORR{<cond>}{S}  <Rd>, <Rn>, <shifter_operand>
```

The four logic instructions have the same format as the addition and subtraction instructions already met. The conditional execution and flag setting fields are optional and there are two source operands and one destination operand. The operands allowed are the same as those for add and subtract instructions. As indicated assembly language programmers should be familiar with Boolean algebra; these instructions perform Boolean operations.

The laws of Boolean algebra define the three operations NOT, AND and OR. These are performed on quantities, variables, which can only have two different values; therefore Boolean variables can be represented by single bits. NOT or **inversion** is performed on a single bit producing a single bit result while the operations AND and OR combine two or more single bits to produce a one bit result. The Boolean operations are defined for single bit values; they do not involve groups of bits whereas an arithmetic and logic unit, ALU, operates on many bits simultaneously; 32-bits in the case of ARM.

The ARM logical instructions for AND and OR operations simultaneously perform Boolean logical operations between corresponding bits, bits in the same position, of the operands. The result is put into the same position as the original bits; hence the alternative name for these operations is bitwise ones.

The definition of the Boolean AND operation between two single bits A and B is that A **and** B equals 0 unless both A and B are 1; in this case only the result is 1. The AND operation is often written symbolically as $A.B$ or as $A \wedge B$. When two 32-bit patterns are combined in an AND operation the corresponding bits in each pattern are simultaneously combined by thirty two separate AND operations as in Figure 9.1.

```
1 1 0 0 1 1 1 1 0 0 0 0 1 1 1 0 1 1 0 0 0 1 0 1 0 0 1 1 0 1 0 1    A
0 0 1 1 0 1 1 1 0 1 0 0 0 0 1 0 0 1 0 0 0 0 0 1 0 0 0 1 0 1 0 0    B
0 0 0 0 0 1 1 1 0 0 0 0 0 0 1 0 0 1 0 0 0 0 0 1 0 0 0 1 0 1 0 0    A.B
```

Figure 9.1 Logical AND of register contents

When the AND instruction is executed and both input operand bits in a column, in the same bit position, are 1 then the result in that column is 1; in all other cases the result in the column is 0. Unlike add and subtract operations there is no propagation of values from one column to the next; that is there is no carry from one bit position to the immediately adjacent bit position. Therefore the result bit in any column is completely determined by the values of the bits of the source operands in the same column.

The other ARM logical instructions are logical OR with mnemonic ORR; Exclusive-OR with mnemonic EOR; and bit clear with mnemonic BIC. The ORR instruction implements the Boolean OR operation. The OR operation combining two single bits is such that the result is 1 if either bit is 1 or if both are 1; only if both bits are 0 is the result 0. That is A **or** B equals 1 unless both A and B are 0 in which case the result is 0; the common algebraic representations of OR are $A + B$ and $A \vee B$. Figure 9.2 illustrates the action of the ORR instruction for the same values that were used to illustrate AND.

$$1\,1\,0\,0\,1\,1\,1\,1\,0\,0\,0\,0\,1\,1\,1\,0\,1\,1\,0\,0\,0\,1\,0\,1\,0\,0\,1\,1\,0\,1\,0\,1 \quad A$$
$$0\,0\,1\,1\,0\,1\,1\,1\,0\,1\,0\,0\,0\,0\,1\,0\,0\,1\,0\,0\,0\,0\,0\,1\,0\,0\,0\,1\,0\,1\,0\,0 \quad B$$
$$1\,1\,1\,1\,1\,1\,1\,1\,0\,1\,0\,0\,1\,1\,1\,0\,1\,1\,0\,0\,0\,1\,0\,1\,0\,0\,1\,1\,0\,1\,0\,1 \quad A+B$$

Figure 9.2 Logical OR of register contents

Bit clear, BIC, is slightly more complicated than the AND and OR instructions as it combines two Boolean operations. BIC performs the AND of a bit in Rn with the inverse of the corresponding bit of the value given by <shifter_operand>. The bit clear operation of bits with values of A and B produces the result of A **and not** B; that is if bit A is 1 and bit B is 0 then the result is 1, in all other cases the result is 0. In Boolean Algebra NOT, inversion, is often indicated by an overline so the bit clear operation is written as $A.\overline{B}$. Because not all word processing systems can overline symbols inversion is sometimes indicated on other ways, foe example by an exclamation mark ! or the symbol ¬ immediately before the quantity to be inverted. An example of the action of BIC is illustrated in Figure 9.3. For this logic operation **the order of operands** is important and B is the lower initial operand in the figure.

$$1\,1\,0\,0\,1\,1\,1\,1\,0\,0\,0\,0\,1\,1\,1\,0\,1\,1\,0\,0\,0\,1\,0\,1\,0\,0\,1\,1\,0\,1\,0\,1 \quad A$$
$$0\,0\,1\,1\,0\,1\,1\,1\,0\,1\,0\,0\,0\,0\,1\,0\,0\,1\,0\,0\,0\,0\,0\,1\,0\,0\,0\,1\,0\,1\,0\,0 \quad B$$
$$1\,1\,0\,0\,1\,0\,0\,0\,0\,0\,0\,0\,1\,1\,0\,0\,1\,0\,0\,0\,0\,1\,0\,0\,0\,0\,1\,0\,0\,0\,0\,1 \quad A.\overline{B}$$

Figure 9.3 Example of the bit clear instruction

The exclusive-OR action is closely related to the OR action but differs because the result is 0 when both bits are 1. The result of the exclusive-OR operation between two single bits is such that the result is 1 if either of the bits is 1 but is 0 if both bits are 0 or if both are 1; the operation is OR **excluding** the case of both bits 1. Exclusive-OR performs a test of *'are the bits the same?'* An important use is to test if two patterns are identical because a result with all bits 0 indicates that the patterns are the same. A common algebraic representation of the exclusive-OR is $A \oplus B$; it may be performed by a combination of the fundamental Boolean operations as $A \oplus B = A.\overline{B} + \overline{A}.B$. An example showing the behaviour of the exclusive-OR instruction is shown as Figure 9.4; again the same input patterns are used as previously.

For all logical instructions the flags N and Z are set according to the usual rules for these flags provided that the programmer adds the {S} field to the mnemonic; that is the instruction mnemonics used are ANDS, BICS, EORS and ORRS. The carry flag, C, behaves in the same complicated way as it does for MOVS and usually it should be assumed to have an unknown value. As overflow cannot occur when logic instructions are executed the overflow flag, V, is not changed by logic instructions.

$$1\ 1\ 0\ 0\ 1\ 1\ 1\ 1\ 0\ 0\ 0\ 0\ 1\ 1\ 1\ 0\ 1\ 1\ 0\ 0\ 0\ 1\ 0\ 1\ 0\ 0\ 1\ 1\ 0\ 1\ 0\ 1 \qquad A$$
$$0\ 0\ 1\ 1\ 0\ 1\ 1\ 1\ 0\ 1\ 0\ 0\ 0\ 0\ 1\ 0\ 0\ 1\ 0\ 0\ 0\ 0\ 0\ 1\ 0\ 0\ 0\ 1\ 0\ 1\ 0\ 0 \qquad B$$
$$1\ 1\ 1\ 1\ 1\ 0\ 0\ 0\ 0\ 1\ 0\ 0\ 1\ 1\ 0\ 0\ 1\ 0\ 0\ 0\ 0\ 1\ 0\ 0\ 0\ 0\ 1\ 0\ 0\ 0\ 0\ 1 \quad A \oplus B$$

Figure 9.4 Exclusive-OR of register contents

The rules of Boolean algebra are defined in terms of three fundamental operations AND, OR and inversion. The instructions implementing the AND and OR operations and those for the compound operations bit clear, BIC, and exclusive-OR, EOR, have been described. No description has been given in this chapter of an instruction to perform inversion; that is an instruction to implement the Boolean NOT function which changes the value of a bit to the other, opposite, value. In many CPUs inversion of all bits in a register is provided by an inversion instruction, often with the mnemonic NOT. There is an inversion instruction in the ARM instruction set but it **does not** have the mnemonic NOT; it is the instruction MVN introduced in Chapter 4. This instruction could be classed as a logical one but it can be used for more tasks than simply inverting the contents of a single register and ARM documentation describes it as a data transfer instruction. Hence when Boolean inversion, the NOT function, is required the instruction move-negate, MVN, described in Chapter 4 is used.

9.2 Masking and bit forcing

Logical operations provide efficient methods of performing frequently required tasks. Two important tasks are masking to extract and test several bits at a time, and bit forcing to set or to clear selected bits. If, following a calculation, only the result in some bit positions of a 32-bit word is of interest then the result should be logically ANDed with a value with 1 in those bits of interest and 0 in other bits; the required bits are extracted because all bits not required are forced to 0. Suppose only the least significant 16-bits of a value in a register are required. Put the binary value 0000 0000 0000 0000 1111 1111 1111 1111 into another register; the pseudo instruction LDR <Rd>,=0x0000ffff will achieve this; then perform an AND operation using this pattern as one operand and the value being examined as the other. The unwanted most significant sixteen bits will be cleared to zero as illustrated by Figure 9.5.

b_{31}	b_{30}	b_{29}	b_{28}	b_{27}	b_{26}	b_{25}	b_{24}	b_{23}	b_{22}	b_{21}	b_{20}	b_{19}	b_{18}	b_{17}	b_{16}	b_{15}	b_{14}	b_{13}	b_{12}	b_{11}	b_{10}	b_9	b_8	b_7	b_6	b_5	b_4	b_3	b_2	b_1	b_0
0	0	0	0	0	0	0	0	0	0	0	0	0	0	0	0	1	1	1	1	1	1	1	1	1	1	1	1	1	1	1	1
0	0	0	0	0	0	0	0	0	0	0	0	0	0	0	0	b_{15}	b_{14}	b_{13}	b_{12}	b_{11}	b_{10}	b_9	b_8	b_7	b_6	b_5	b_4	b_3	b_2	b_1	b_0

Figure 9.5 Masking to extract selected bits using logical AND

AND must have both bits 1 to produce a result of 1, if the mask bit is 0 the result is always 0 because b_n **and** 0 is 0. If the mask bit is 1 then the result is 1 if $b_n = 1$ but is 0 if $b_n = 0$; that is the result is the same as b_n because b_n **and** $1 = b_n$. The pattern used to extract selected bits is a **mask** and the process of extracting certain bits is **masking**.

The masking process forces selected bits to a required value and is useful in many other situations. For example the 8-bit codes often used to represent letters of the alphabet, ASCII codes, are the same for upper and lower case letters except that bit 5 is 1 for lower case letters and is 0 for upper case letters. Letters can be forced to have a required case by masking without determining which case they are in; to ensure a letter is in lower case combine the letter code with 00100000 using an OR operation. If the code was for a lower case letter it is not changed, if it was for an upper case letter it is changed to the code for the corresponding lower case letter. Problem 9.2 is to perform lower case to upper case conversion.

Another function assisted by logical operations is multiple bit testing. If a program is examining the results that are in a register in groups of 4-bits and it is necessary to determine if a particular group of 4-bits are all zero a masking operation enables this to be performed by a single test. In Figure 9.6 it is assumed that the 4-bits of interest are the most significant ones then masking by an AND operation with the pattern illustrated produces a result containing zeros in all bits other than those being examined.

b_{31}	b_{30}	b_{29}	b_{28}	b_{27}	b_{26}	b_{25}	b_{24}	b_{23}	b_{22}	b_{21}	b_{20}	b_{19}	b_{18}	b_{17}	b_{16}	b_{15}	b_{14}	b_{13}	b_{12}	b_{11}	b_{10}	b_9	b_8	b_7	b_6	b_5	b_4	b_3	b_2	b_1	b_0
1	1	1	1	0	0	0	0	0	0	0	0	0	0	0	0	0	0	0	0	0	0	0	0	0	0	0	0	0	0	0	0
b_{31}	b_{30}	b_{29}	b_{28}	0	0	0	0	0	0	0	0	0	0	0	0	0	0	0	0	0	0	0	0	0	0	0	0	0	0	0	0

Figure 9.6 Masking to test bit values

Provided that the *'set flags'* form of the AND instruction, ANDS, is used then checking the Z flag enables several bits to be tested simultaneously to determine if all are 0. In the example if Z = 1 then the four most significant bits were all zero otherwise Z = 0 and at least one of the bits was a 1. Other tests, or combinations of tests using logic instructions to set the flags, allow any bit pattern to be detected.

The AND operation allows selected bits to be forced to 0 leaving other bits unchanged. The OR operation allows selected bits to be forced to 1 leaving other bits unchanged. It is left as an exercise, Problem 9.1, for the reader to determine the very useful effects of using EOR and BIC with masks.

9.3 Further forms of <shifter_operand>

Assembly language programming has been introduced by describing how to perform single tasks using ARM instructions. This is similar to introductions to assembly language for any type of CPU. Some features introduced are not present in CISC type CPUs; in particular the features that all instructions may be executed conditionally and that most have the optional *'set flags'* field. These enable the ARM programmer to modify an instruction so that it performs several actions simultaneously with the combination of actions selected by the programmer. Most CISC processors only perform a single well defined set of actions; an instruction may perform a complicated combination of actions but it is always the same combination and cannot be modified by the programmer.

ARM has other features that differ from those of many general purpose CPUs. All move, arithmetic and logic instructions include *<shifter_operand>* as one of the source operands. Only cases with this quantity as the contents of a register, or a simple fixed value in the range 0 to 255, have been introduced. Other forms are possible and when these are combined with optional conditional execution and flag setting programmers they allow the programmer to produce a large range of different actions.

Readers who have programmed CISC systems will have noticed that one common group of instructions is missing; the list of ARM instructions does not include shift or rotate instructions. Inspection of the ARM structure, Figure 3.1, shows that all binary values being sent to a general purpose register come from the ALU output. Even an instruction such as MOV <Rd>, <Rn> passes the value from Rn through the ALU to copy it to Rd; for this simple form no change is made to the value as it passes through the ALU. One input path to the ALU includes a unit labelled shifter, Figure 3.1; any value that passes through the shifter may have a shift operation performed on it before it is processed by, or just passed through, the ALU. This is another action that ARM can perform in combination with others in a single instruction.

When using a register or an immediate value as <shifter_operand> with the forms described previously the instruction code generated by the assembler sets the shifter unit so that it makes no changes to the values passing through it. However the shifter can be used to perform several different actions; some are complicated and there are some peculiar restrictions.

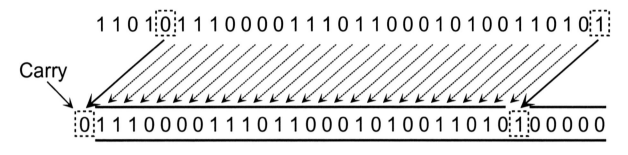

Figure 9.7 Logic shift left by five places

A simple left shift operation moves a binary pattern left a specified number of places, this is logical shift left denoted by LSL. The bits of the pattern are moved left; the bits moved out are lost and 0 values are put in the low bits. Any instruction with <shifter_operand> as part of its specification may use <Rm> by itself as <shifter_operand> or It may also use the form <Rm>, LSL #<immediate>. The field <immediate> is replaced by any value from 0 to 31 and there must be at least one space between LSL and the # character. This form is more completely called logical shift left immediate. For example if register r4 contains 0xd70ec535 and the instruction MOV r7, r4, LSL #5 is executed then after execution the value 0xe1d8a6a0 will be in r7 as shown by Figure 9.7.

Obviously a shift amount to zero has no effect and the assembler does not require LSL #0 to be included if no shift is required. All the instructions introduced with <Rm> as <shifter_operand> are regarded as having the operand <Rm>, LSL #0 but the comma and LSL #0 are not typed.

Flag settings have been described for each instruction as it was introduced but some complicated settings were ignored. For **logic and move instructions, but NOT for arithmetic instructions,** when S for *'set flags'* is appended to the mnemonic the value of the C flag is the carry from the shifter unless the destination register is r15. Chapter 13 and reference manuals describe the actions for the **special case of r15 as the destination register**. The carry from the shifter is the discarded bit that was the last one output by the shifter; that is if a multiple place shift is considered as a sequence of one place shifts the carry is the last bit shifted out. For a shift of zero places the carry is the value of the C flag that existed before execution of the instruction. This behaviour is complex and is why the carry flag was previously regarded as unknown after logic and move instructions. There are situations where the value of C set by these instructions is useful but these are in advanced programming situations; the experienced programmer should refer to the ARM Architecture Reference Manual [12] for full details of carry setting by logic and move instructions.

There is a second form of logical shift left which uses the contents of a register at execution time to provide the number of places shifted, this is **logical shift left by register**. The printed form of this form of <shifter_operand> is <Rm>, LSL <Rs> with <Rs> indicating any register r0 to r15. The number of bits shifted is given by the lowest eight bits of the contents of register Rs; it is important to **note** that if the value of these eight bits equals or exceeds 32 decimal the shift amount is always zero. Using r15 for Rs has unpredictable effects and must be avoided.

A left shift by *n* places corresponds to multiplication by 2^n and, although ARM does have a multiply instruction, a left shift operation is the faster method of multiplying an unsigned integer by a power of two.

Both   LSL #<immediate> and LSL <Rs> have corresponding **logical right shift** operations, LSR #<immediate> and LSR <Rs>. Logical shift right discards bits moved out to the right and moves zeros into the empty bits at the MSB end. A right shift of *n* places has the same effect as division by 2^n. The shifter carry again is the last bit shifted out, that is it is the bit that was originally just to the right of the LSB of the result. When the shift amount is zero the carry is not changed.

There is an additional right shift operation **arithmetic shift right, ASR,** with both **immediate** and **register** versions. This is used for signed arithmetic and behaves as logical shift right **except** that the bits moved in are the same as the MSB of the register contents before shifting. This is an essential requirement when right shift operations are performed on signed integer numbers in twos complement.

The final shifter operations are two rotate right ones; the most important is **rotate right** with the mnemonic **ROR**. It has the same **immediate** and **register** forms as shift operations. For rotate operations bits moved out at the LSB end are moved in at the MSB end as illustrated in Figure 9.8. Rotate left is not required as rotate right thirty one places is the same as left rotate one place, rotate right thirty places equals left rotate two places, *etc.* To rotate left *X* places use right rotate *Y* places where $Y = 32 - X$. The carry behaviour for rotate is the same as for logical shift right.

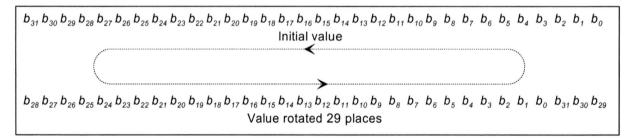

Figure 9.8 Illustration of right rotate 29 places (equals left rotate 3 places)

In most cases when <shifter_operand> performs a shift or rotate action using r15, the program counter, as any one of the operands the results are unpredictable. Once again note that r15 should not be used as a general purpose register. r15 should only be used as an operand in special cases, for example in the register list of the LDMFD instruction when it is used to perform the return from a subroutine.

The other rotate operation is rotate right with extend, **RRX**. This differs from all other shift and rotate operations as the number of places rotated is not selected; the rotate is always by a single place. All the bits in the register are moved one place right; the bit moved out to the left, from the LSB, is put into the carry flag, C, and the original carry flag becomes the MSB of the 32-bit result. That is RRX rotates a 33-bit value by one place with the carry flag added to the register contents to provide 33-bits. Many programmers will never use this operation; its most frequent use is for implementing arithmetic processes involving values with more than thirty two bits.

9.4 Immediate operands combined with <shifter_operand>

The use of an immediate value operand, restricted to 0 to 255, was introduced as a <shifter_operand>. When such operands are used the value passes through the shifter unit so the value can be changed. However left and right **shift operations are not allowed** with immediate operands, only **rotate right operations are allowed** and even these are restricted. An immediate value, as usual limited to the range 0 to 255, can be rotated right **but only by an even number of places**. Further the assembler syntax differs in an unexpected way, the name ROR and the # before the number of places shifted are not typed.

For example MOV   <Rd>, #255, 30 puts 1020 in Rd because a thirty place right rotate of a 32-bit value with at least two leading zeros is the same as left rotating two places; multiplication by four.

Summarising, shifts and rotates can be by any number 0 to 31 places when the source of the quantity shifted is a register. However when the pattern shifted is an immediate operand only rotate right by an immediate quantity is allowed; the number of places rotated must be even and the syntax form is different. Table 9.1 shows examples of shift and rotate operands, two unallowed cases are illustrated.

MOV r4, r5, LSL #13	is legal; source of value shifted is register r5
ADDS r3, r4, #182, 13	is not legal; cannot rotate immediate operands an odd numbers of places
MOV r4, #182, 12	is legal (rotate an even number of places)
MOV r4, #91, 12	is legal and is the same as #182 rotated 13 places
SUBS r6, r9, r3, ASR r7	is legal; the amount shifted is given by the 8 LSBs of r7 BUT the action is different if the value is 32 or larger (see [12])
MOV r8, #43, ROR #4	is not legal; the syntax to rotate immediate values does not use ROR

Table 9.1 Examples of legal and illegal shift and rotate operands

The complex restrictions for rotation of an immediate value are why the LDR pseudo instruction should be used instead of MOV immediate; the assembler generates a valid instruction using rotate immediate when possible. For arithmetic and logic operations there are no pseudo instructions; the programmer must create rotate operations of immediate operands if required. However the ADS and RealView assemblers produce code with a shifted immediate operand, if possible, for values over 255. For example ADD r4, r5, #4080 causes the assembler to produce the code for ADD r4, r5, #255, 28; assemblers from other suppliers may report an error. Programmers should not rely on such unusual behave of an assembler; always use instructions that most clearly indicates the actions the processor will perform.

9.5 <shifter_operand> summary

The many <shifter_operand> forms are complex but provide many useful features, Table 9.2 summarises all the forms. There are special cases for the immediate value shown as <num5> in Table 9.2 and where a value of 32 is used to produce a value of zero. In general there is no need to use these cases; they should not arise in well designed programs. The value of the carry flag for move and logic instructions is the shifter carry output, the last bit shifted out, except for shifts of zero and thirty two or larger. For shifts of zero the carry flag is unchanged; in general values above thirty one should be avoided.

<shifter_operand>	Syntax*
Immediate 8-bit value	`#<num8>`
Immediate 8-bit value rotated right by immediate	`#<num8>, <even5>`
Register	`<Rm>`
Register, logical shift left by immediate	`<Rm>, LSL #<num5>`
Register, logical shift left by register	`<Rm>, LSL <Rs>`
Register, logical shift right by immediate	`<Rm>, LSR #<num5>`
Register, logical shift right by register	`<Rm>, LSR <Rs>`
Register, arithmetic shift right by immediate	`<Rm>, ASR #<num5>`
Register, arithmetic shift right by register	`<Rm>, ASR <Rs>`
Register, rotate right by immediate	`<Rm>,ROR #<num5>`
Register, rotate right by register	`<Rm>, ROR <Rs>`
Register, rotate right with extend	`<Rm>, RRX`

*Key   `<num8>` is any 8-bit numeric value

`<num5>` is any 5-bit numeric value

`<even5>` is a 5-bit numeric value, even only

Table 9.2 ARM shift and rotate operations

9.6 Using <shifter_operand> features

To obtain the shift and rotate instructions found in many other CPUs the MOV instruction is used to copy a value from a register, shift or rotate it with <shifter_operand> set as required, then return the result to the source register. However the MOV instruction with shift and rotate allows the changed value to be put into a different register providing the useful feature that both the original and shifted values can be available if required. A further advantage is that shift and rotate may be performed in combination with all the move, arithmetic and logic instructions allowing some multiple tasks to be performed by a single instruction; a few are described in Chapter 10.

Because programmers frequently use the instruction MOV to shift or rotate a value and put the result back into the source register the RealView version of the ARM assembler allows shift and rotate operations, LSL, LSR, etc., to be used for this purpose as if they are mnemonics; that is without the need for the MOV mnemonic. However this feature is not supported by the ADS or GNU assemblers.

To determine individual bits in a pattern in a register beginners often use a sequence of many shift or rotate operations to move each bit in turn into the carry or sign flag and follow this with a flag test. Except to examine the MSB, which can be determined by using the N flag, it is better to use logical masking operations; however, as with all rules, there are situations where this not true.

Shift operations have many uses; one of the most simple is in packing and unpacking. Frequently a program requires the use of quantities with fewer than 32-bits and several such quantities are put into one 32-bit word. For example instead of simple binary number form some programs use binary coded decimal, BCD. In BCD each group of four bits represents 0 to 9 with patterns 1010 to 1111 unused. This system is often found where a large amount of numeric information is printed or displayed; it is used by many pocket calculators because every input value and result is displayed. Converting a pattern representing a pure binary number to a series of the individual digits of the equivalent decimal number for display requires execution of a large number of instructions whereas BCD values can be converted very easily. Using BCD to represent a decimal number such as 95276 requires the 32-bit BCD form

0000 0000 0000 1001 0101 0010 0111 0110

with the hexadecimal equivalent 0x00095276 rather than the pure binary value which would have the hexadecimal equivalent value 0x0001742c. Shift operations combined with masking may be used to extract the groups of four bits corresponding to the individual digits.

The use of shift and masking operations for handling packed numbers can be illustrated by examining the addition of two numbers in 32-bit BCD representation The normal ADD instruction does not correctly add such values so programs that manipulate BCD numbers usually include a subroutine to perform BCD addition.

A simple method of performing BCD addition is to take groups of four bits at a time, starting with the least significant group, and adding the groups from each number. When the result of any addition exceeds nine it is corrected by subtracting ten from the result and a BCD carry is generated and added to the next group. Figure 9.9 outlines a structure for a program that follows this method. The initial BCD values are the variables *numA* and *numB* which are the input parameters of the subroutine and the BCD sum is returned as *result* with *BCD_cy* indicating the final carry.

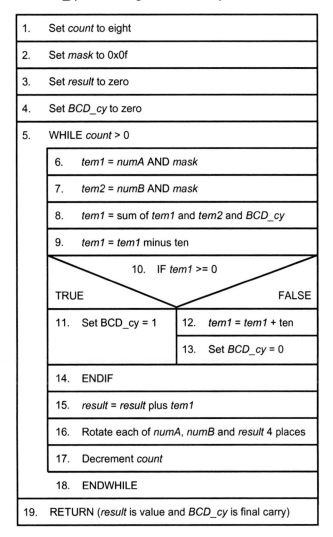

Figure 9.9 Structure of a subroutine to perform BCD addition

It is possible to use the ARM ability to shift an operand before using it and the feature that all instructions may be conditional to reduce the number of instructions required to perform BCD arithmetic. The code becomes difficult to understand so a direct approach following Figure 9.9 is used by Program 9.1 which is a BCD addition subroutine without any complex coding. Generally complicated coding should be avoided as it is a common source of errors. However if maximum speed or minimum number of instructions is essential small complex routines may be devised; thorough testing of these is essential.

Program 9.1 could be *'improved'* in several ways, some involve features of ARM not examined yet, others require care. For example instead of storing *mask* in a register and performing the AND operation using the register as one input operand the AND operation could use the immediate value 0x0f as <shifter_operand> because this is less than 255. This would reduce slightly the number of instructions required but would have a very small effect on speed.

```
; Performs BCD addition, follows the BPCS, registers r0 to r3 may be changed,
; other registers are not changed.
; Local use is r4 for count, r5 for mask, r6 for working BCD_cy, r7 for
; working result, r8 for tem1, r9 for tem2
; Inputs:-   One number, numA in r0, other number numB in r1
; Outputs:-  The sum result in r0 and carry BCD_cy in r1

BCD_add    STMFD    sp!, {r4-r9, lr}  ; save used registers BPCS requires
           MOV      r4, #8            ; initial count
           MOV      r5, #0x0f         ; set mask
           MOV      r6, #0            ; initial BCD_cy
           MOV      r7, #0            ; initial result

while      MOVS     r4, r4            ; test value of count
           BEQ      end_while         ; exit loop if all done
           AND      r8, r0, r5        ; tem1 = numA AND mask
           AND      r9, r1, r5        ; tem2 = numB AND mask
           ADD      r8, r8, r9        ; tem1 = tem1 + tem2
           ADD      r8, r8, r6        ; tem1 = tem1 + BCD_cy
           SUBS     r8, r8, #10       ; tem1 = tem1 - ten and set flags
           BMI      less              ; branch is result was less than ten
           MOV      r6, #1            ; set BCD_cy
           BAL      end_if            ; IF branch complete
less       ADD      r8, r8, #10       ; tem1 = tem1 + ten, restore value
           MOV      r6, #0            ; clear BCD_cy
end_if     ADD      r7, r7, r8        ; result = result + tem1
           MOV      r7, r7, ROR #4    ; shift result right 4 places
           MOV      r0, r0, ROR #4    ; shift numA right 4 places
           MOV      r1, r1, ROR #4    ; shift numB right 4 places
           SUB      r4, r4, #1        ; decrement count
           BAL      while             ; complete loop
end_while
           MOV      r0, r7            ; result to return register
           MOV      r1, r6            ; BCD_cy to return register
           LDMFD    sp!, {r4-r9,pc}   ; pop and return
```

Program 9.1 A BCD addition subroutine

Another possible change is that the loop test could be modified to *'While count is decremented and the result is **greater than or equal to zero**'*. Using this form and the fact that *'greater than or equal to'* is also the same as *'not negative'* the lines

```
        MOVS    r4, r4              ; test value of count
        BEQ     end_while           ; exit loop if all done
```

would be changed to

```
        SUBS    r4, r4, #1          ; decrement and test value of count
        BMI     end_while           ; exit loop if all done
```

The subtract instruction at the loop end is removed reducing the number of instructions inside the loop.

Many other modifications can be made to reduce the number of instructions but the primary objective should always be to produce a clear easily understood program. Any *'optimisation'* should be performed only if small code or high speed execution is essential. It should be done after a correctly functioning program has been produced and the resulting optimised program must be fully tested.

Another use of shifts is to obtain a byte from one position in a register and put it into another position. For example `AND r7, r2, #255, 16` followed by `MOV r7, r7, LSL #16` will put the second byte in r2, bits 23 down to 16, into the least significant byte position of r7 with all other bits of r7 zero. Packing and unpacking, especially of bytes, is needed when as little memory as possible is used to hold small data items. For ARM systems it is often faster to transfer 32-bits of data to or from memory using STR and LDR rather than use four separate byte transfer instructions.

9.7 Summary

Manipulation of binary patterns is an essential feature of most assembly language programs and the assembly language programmer must become skilled in the use of the available methods to select the most efficient one. Logical operations provide an efficient method of testing multiple bits, for forcing some bits in a pattern to a required value, and for extracting groups of bits from a larger word.

In general repeated shifts should not be used to extract several bits from a pattern if a logic operation will produce the same result; the logic operation is usually more efficient. However shifts are required when several small data items are packed and unpacked using a single 32-bit word to hold them.

9.8 Problems

9.1   It was shown in section 9.2 that AND and OR may be used to modify selected bits in a register. If the value 0xc209af16 is in one register and the mask 0x0f0f0f0f is in another determine the result (without writing a program) of performing

a) the logic AND instruction using these two values.

b) the logic ORR instruction using these two values.

c) the logic EOR instruction using these two values.

d) the logic BIC instruction using these two values with the mask as the second operand.

e) the logic BIC instruction using these two values with the mask as the first operand.

As indicated an AND of register contents with a mask pattern forces bits of a register to be 0 at all the positions where there are 0 bits in the mask pattern; an OR operation forces bits to 1 wherever the mask includes a 1. Examine your results and state the effects of masking using EOR and BIC.

9.2   Develop and fully test a subroutine which makes all the text characters in a string uppercase regardless of their present case, assume ASCII 8-bit codes are being used. A single parameter which points to the start of the string is passed to the subroutine; the end of the string is indicated by the pattern with all 8-bits zero, it is a null terminated string.

9.3   Develop and test a subroutine which makes all the text characters in a string match normal sentence case regardless of their present case, assume the text is only one sentence and is a null terminated string. The sentence may contain punctuation marks such as commas, quotation marks, *etc.* The result must ensure that the first letter of the resulting sentence is uppercase and all others are lower case. A single parameter which points to the start of the string is passed to the subroutine and the string is null terminated.

9.4   Develop and test a subroutine which changes a block of text containing several sentences to sentence case; that is ensure that each sentence has an initial capital letter. The complete block of text forms a single string and, as for problems 9.2 and 9.3, the end of the whole string is a null terminator. Individual sentences end with the ASCII code for a full stop, question mark or exclamation mark.

9.5   Text is stored in memory with one ASCII code in each byte location. Devise a subroutine which has a pointer to the start of a block of text as an input parameter and is required to determine the address of the first block of 4 ASCII codes corresponding to the word 'help'; allow for the situation in which the block is not present. The end of the block of text is indicated by the null value; 8-bit all zero code.

9.6   Figure 9.9 outlines a structure for a BCD addition subroutine. Produce a design for a BCD subtraction routine. Develop and test a subroutine that implements the design.

9.7   A 32-bit number is to be displayed in hexadecimal as 0x*hhhhhhhh* where each '*h*' is the character representing a hexadecimal digit. Design, develop and test a subroutine that converts any 32-bit value into a null terminated ASCII code string representing the number in the form 0x*hhhhhhhh*.

9.8   Using a combination of logical masking and rotate operations design, develop and test a subroutine that determines if the 6-bit pattern 011001 occurs anywhere within a 32-bit pattern. The output of the routine should only indicate yes or no, the number of times the pattern occurs is not of interest.
Your routine should be tested using many different patterns; the minimum set of tests should include the patterns

0x00000000, 0xffffffff, 0x12345678, 0x9abcdef0, 0x55555555, 0xaa998877, 0xaaaaaaaa and 0xaaaa5555.

10 Arithmetic Operations

Programs to perform complex calculations are usually developed using a high level language. However, most assembly language programs include some arithmetic even if it is only to perform a simple counting task or to rank items in order. An arithmetic operation produces a new numeric value by combining existing, known, numeric values according to a precise rule. The most elementary arithmetic operation is the combination of two numbers to produce a new number that is their sum. The other common arithmetic operations are subtraction, multiplication and division; these are completely defined for any pair of initial numbers selected from the infinite set of all real numbers.

The set of real numbers extends from an infinitely large magnitude negative value through zero to an infinitely large positive value. The interval between any two numbers, no matter how close together they are, can be divided into an infinite number of sub-divisions with each sub-division a valid number. Even restricting the set of numbers in some way, for example to unsigned integers, frequently produces a sub-set of infinite size. Any manufactured system, such as a CPU, that manipulates numeric values has a finite number of components. Numbers are manipulated using CPU components; as there are only a finite number of components a CPU can only manipulate a restricted, finite, set of numerical values.

A consequence of performing arithmetic with a restricted set of numeric values is that an operation to combine two numbers, each a member of the restricted set, may produce a result that is not in the restricted set. Therefore machines that perform arithmetic only approximately follow the rules that define arithmetic operations. When the result of a machine calculation is not a member of the allowed set the output value produced will be incorrect. Often, but not always, there are indicators to show this; the programmer must check the indicators and act appropriately when a result is not allowed. If there is no indicator the programmer must devise tests to detect incorrect cases.

Some errors caused by the limitations of a finite set of values are very large; others are minor with approximately correct results produced. However, even small errors may produce large effects if the results are used in further computations. Anyone developing programs for critical engineering, financial and similar systems should study the literature concerning the consequences of performing calculations with restricted sets of values. It is essential to understand the problems that occur and the techniques that must be used to avoid them.

For most programs prepared in assembly language numbers can be restricted to be only signed and unsigned integers within the limited ranges of values possible using a fixed number of bits. Only operations involving unsigned integers and one form of signed integer are considered here.

10.1 Number representation

Most CPUs have instructions to perform simple arithmetic operations with unsigned integer operands that have the same number of bits as the CPU registers. There is usually an instruction that assumes that values are unsigned integers and adds two values to produce the unsigned integer sum with the same number of bits. Except for very small microcontrollers instruction sets also include an instruction to subtract one unsigned integer from another producing an unsigned integer result. CPU flags are provided to indicate when the result is not an unsigned integer in the same range of values as the source operands.

In assembly language the programmer must include instructions to check for cases when the result of an arithmetic operation is not in the set of numbers being used. When invalid results are detected programs must act to overcome the error situation, this is sometimes difficult. If the program is running on a desk top computer it can display an error message and wait for actions by the user. However if the program controls an automatic system, for example an automobile engine controller, it must continue to perform the control function. Either the program must be designed so that invalid results cannot occur, or the specification must require that they are detected and define the behaviour required if they are found.

Checking results after unsigned integer arithmetic operations is straightforward. Results can only be too large, greater than the largest value a register can hold, or too small, less than zero. Usually the CPU status bits, flags, can be tested to identify the out of range cases. It is the programmer's responsibility to include flag checks and interpret them correctly; flag behaviour differs from one CPU type to another. Using ARM there is a further **essential program requirement**; the flags are only affected by arithmetic operations if the *'set flags'* extension, S, is appended to the mnemonic. When addition is performed with the *'set flags'* extension the carry, C, is set to 1 if the result of unsigned integer addition is too large, over 2^{32}-1; otherwise the carry is cleared so that C is 0. For subtraction ARM clears the carry if the result of is less than zero otherwise it sets it to 1; carry is the inverse of borrow, Chapter 5. Table 5.2 lists examples of the flag settings for common addition and subtraction operations using unsigned and signed integers.

In multiple calculations the result **must be checked after each step**. To perform a calculation such as $S = A + B + C$ two of the values must be added to obtain a partial sum, for example $PS = A + B$, then the third value is added to obtain the final result, $S = PS + C$. It is essential to check for out of range results after each addition; the addition 0xe1234567 + 0x1fedcba9 + 0x24680123 produces a carry when the first two numbers are added but not when the partial sum is added to the third number. The feature that all ARM instructions may be conditional is useful in multiple step calculations as illustrated in Program 10.1. Section 10.3 introduces another instruction that allows further improvement.

```
; Assumed that three numbers to be added are in registers r0, r1, and r2.
; Register r4 will hold a value of 0 if the result is in range, otherwise it
; will hold the number of times it has exceed 32-bits
; Register r3 will hold the 32-bit partial sum and final result

        MOV     r4, #0          ; initial excess value, 0 = none
        ADDS    r3, r0, r1      ; partial sum of first two values
        ADDCS   r4, r4, #1      ; increase excess if necessary
        ADDS    r3, r3, r2      ; add third value to partial sum
        ADDCS   r4, r4, #1      ; increase excess if necessary
```

Program 10.1 Partial program to illustrate out of range indication in multiple step arithmetic

There are many methods of representing signed integer numbers. If twos complement form, Appendix C, is used add and subtract operations for unsigned integers will correctly add and subtract signed numbers. However if the results are not in the allowed range for twos complement values the error indications are not the same as for unsigned integers. Addition or subtraction of unsigned integers produce a carry or a borrow when the results are out of range; that is when an addition result exceeds 2^N-1 and when a subtraction result is below zero for N-bit numbers. In twos complement addition or subtraction out of range results cause **overflow** or **underflow**. The magnitude of an N-bit twos complement number is held in N-1 bits; results with magnitude larger than 2^{N-1}-1 cause overflow and underflow. A negative result no longer causes a problem unless it is below $-(2^{N-1}$-1). The out of range cases are not indicated by the carry flag and are not easily detected unless the CPU has extra features. ARM has the **overflow, V,** status bit to detect overflow and underflow when twos complement numbers are added or subtracted. Hence, although any form of signed number may be used, the ARM designers included features that encourage programmers to select twos complement. **The CPU designer has provided features that influence the programmer's decisions**. Additional reasons for using twos complement are that most development tools behave as if signed numbers are in twos complement form provided their magnitudes are below 2^{31}. For example the assembly language programmer may use

```
LDR   r5, = -12345
LDR   r7, = (label - 64)    ; label is defined elsewhere
```

The value –12345 decimal is converted to the 32-bit twos complement value 0xFFFFCFC7 and if *label* is less than 64 the value loaded into r7 is the twos complement value equivalent to (*label* – 64).

10.2 Arithmetic operations with numbers in two representations

In assembly language the programmer defines what the patterns in each register and memory location represent. The type of quantity each pattern represents should be clearly stated and must only be used for this purpose; good program organisation and detailed documentation with generous use of comments is essential. This problem does not arise using most high level languages as the type of each manipulated quantity is usually defined and the compiler inserts the necessary check instructions.

The assembly language programmer may use some variables to represent unsigned integers and others, usually twos complement, to represent signed integers. The sub-set of all numbers that can be represented as *N*-bit unsigned integers is not the same as the sub-set of all numbers represented by *N*-bit twos complement integers. Normally variables of one type should not be combined with those of the other using arithmetic operations. If it is essential to perform arithmetic using values of different types, **mixed arithmetic,** the program must include instructions to check that the operation is possible using the values in the registers at the time of execution. Unlike the checks when both operands represent the same types of number there are cases where some tests are best performed before the operation in addition to further tests after the operation. All possible mixed arithmetic situations are shown in Table 10.1 for any operation that combines two input numbers *A* and *B* and produces one output number when each number may be a signed integer or an unsigned integer and all numbers have the same number of bits.

Number A	Number B	Required result
Unsigned integer	Unsigned integer	Unsigned integer
Unsigned integer	*Unsigned integer*	*Signed integer*
Unsigned integer	Signed integer	Unsigned integer
Unsigned integer	Signed integer	Signed integer
Signed integer	Unsigned integer	Unsigned integer
Signed integer	Unsigned integer	Signed integer
Signed integer	*Signed integer*	*Unsigned integer*
Signed integer	Signed integer	Signed integer

Table 10.1 Possible combinations of integer types, italic cases are unlikely to be required

The extra checking requirements for mixed arithmetic are illustrated by examining addition of a 32-bit unsigned integer and a twos complement 32-bit value to produce a 32-bit twos complement result. The following details must be considered:

- If the twos complement value is a positive quantity the operation can only produce a valid result if the magnitude of the unsigned integer is less than 2^{31}-1.
- Addition might produce an overflow whenever the twos complement value is positive.
- If the twos complement value is negative its magnitude is subtracted from the unsigned value. The unsigned value might be greater than 2^{31}-1 preventing the use of simple twos complement addition. Overflow occurs if the unsigned value exceeds 2^{31}-1 and the negative value is very small.
- Overflow cannot occur for negative signed values and unsigned values less than 2^{31}.

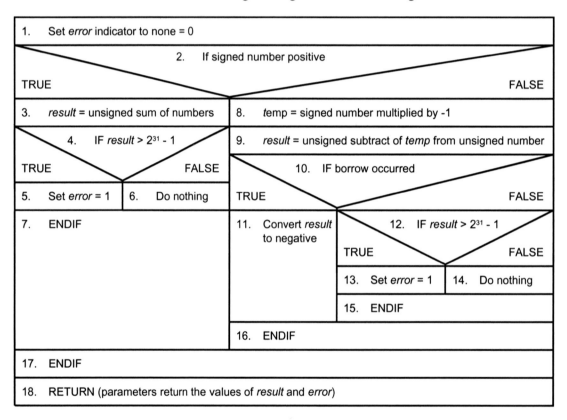

Figure 10.2 Subroutine to add an unsigned and signed number

Many situations must be considered. For simplicity a programmer may decide that if the unsigned value exceeds 2^{31}-1 the operation cannot be performed even although there are cases with valid results. If this assumption is made the binary pattern for the unsigned integer is identical to that for the equivalent twos complement value and the operation can be performed as if both numbers are in twos complement.

When the simplification is not allowed all possible error situations must be detected, instructions must be included to perform the detection, and some error indication must be produced. Figure 10.2 is one structure for a subroutine that considers all possible cases for addition of an unsigned integer and a twos complement integer to produce a twos complement result using 32-bits to hold all values. Program 10.2 is an implementation for an ARM system. After the addition when both numbers are positive a result greater than 2^{31}-1 is indicated if either the C or N flag is set to 1 but if the signed number is negative a result that is too large only sets the N flag to 1.

```
; Routine to add a 32-bit unsigned value to a 32-bit twos complement value
; producing a 32-bit signed value. Register use follows the BPCS
; Input values:-  Unsigned value in r0, twos complement value in r1
; Output values:- result signed sum in r0, error code in r1

add_mix    STMFD    sp!, {r6,lr}    ; save used register and return address
           MOVS     r6, r1          ; make copy of signed value & find sign
           MOV      r1, #0          ; initial error value, 0 = none
           BMI      add_10          ; skip if MSB=1, signed is negative
           ADDS     r0, r0, r6      ; result case signed is positive
           BCS      add_05          ; branch if much too large
           BPL      add_20          ;= exit if result correct, otherwise
                                    ;= it was slightly too large . . .
add_05     MOV      r1, #1          ; . . . indicate error in all error cases
           B        add_20          ; exit
        ; case signed is negative
add_10     MVN      r6, r6          ;= invert and add 1 to get magnitude,
           ADD      r6, r6, #1      ;= into temp
           SUBS     r0, r0, r6      ; result magnitude
           BCS      add_15          ; if no borrow* positive go to check
           MNV      r0, r0          ;= invert and add 1 to get the two's
           ADD      r0, r0, #1      ;= complement result
           B        add_20          ; exit, result must be correct
add_15     MOVS     r0, r0          ; find MSB
           BPL      add_20          ; branch if MSB zero as in range
           MOV      r1, #1          ; set error to show overflow
add_20     LDMFD    sp!, {r6,pc}    ; pop and return

; *Footnote:- reminder ARM produces an inverse borrow
```

Program 10.2 Subroutine to add an unsigned integer and a twos complement value

Program 10.2 is constructed with branches to create the 'IF' structures; a branch form is necessary when using most CISC processors. Again the ARM feature of conditional execution of all instructions allows some program reduction although this may lead to difficulty in understanding the program; in more complicated cases the program may also have a poor structural form. A simple change is to replace

```
           BCS      add_05          ; branch if much too large
           BPL      add_20          ;= exit, result correct otherwise
                                    ;= was slightly too large
add_05     MOV      r1, #1          ; indicate error
           B        add_20          ; exit
```

by the three lines without any conditional branches

```
           MOVCS    r1, #1          ; indicate error if much too large
           MOVMI    r1, #1          ; indicate error if slightly too large
           B        add_20          ; exit
```

Other more complicated changes are possible but destroy the program structure. Further description of the use of conditional execution of instructions other than branch ones are in Chapter 12.

10.3 Integer forms that do not use 32-bits

A common requirement is to manipulate numbers with more or fewer bits than the standard register size. Generally use of numbers with fewer than 32-bits is straightforward provided the programmer provides mechanisms to detect results that are too large. Unsigned integers with fewer than 32-bits are converted to 32-bit values by adding as many zeros as necessary before the MSB. Many values with fewer than 32-bits are input values from external devices; adding extra zero bits before the MSB of unsigned integers does not create any problems. For example if a system includes sensors to provide the value of a physical quantity such as temperature, pressure, speed, etc., the device which converts the measured quantity into a digital value usually produces an unsigned result with between eight and sixteen bits. If these values are converted to 32-bits by addition of leading zeros the 32-bit values formed can be manipulated using the normal methods. ARM assists in this by the behaviour of the byte and word forms of the LDR instruction

```
LDRB    <Rd>, <addressing_mode>
LDRH    <Rd>, <addressing_mode>
```

These instructions copy 8-bit or 16-bit memory or input quantities from the location, or input device, whose address is defined by <addressing_mode> into destination register Rd and also force the high, unused, bits of the register to zero. Devices providing a number of bits other than eight or sixteen are a little more complicated, additional instructions must be included to ensure that the correct input value is obtained. For example when a 10-bit value is obtained the program should ensure that all bits other than the ten input bits are zero using a sequence such as

```
LDRH    <Rd>, <addressing_mode> ; get input value
LDR     <Rx>, =0x3ff            ; mask with high bits all 0
AND     <Rd>, <Rd>, <Rx>        ; force all but the ten data bits to 0
```

Some input devices provide the measured values as signed values; usually these are in twos complement form. If the number has fewer than 32-bits the programmer must convert the input value to the correct, 32-bit, signed version. The requirement of changing the number of bits when using twos complement occurs frequently, not just in this situation. As indicated in Appendix C twos complement representation requires signed numbers having a fixed number of bits to produce correct results. However they have a property that allows their size to be increased easily; the number of bits can be increased by adding the additional bits in front of the sign bit by copying the sign bit, this is **sign extend**.

For example the values +21 and -21 decimal in 8-bit twos complement are 00010101 and 11101011 respectively. To change to 16-bit twos complement values it is necessary to extend at the MSB end by copying the sign bit to obtain 0000000000010101 and 1111111111101011. Extension to 32-bits requires a further sixteen additional leading 0 or 1 bits as appropriate. ARM provides capability for sign extend with special versions LDRSB and LDRSH of the LDR instruction to automatically sign extend the 8-bit and 16-bit values respectively to 32-bits when they are read from memory. There is also support for sign extension in some applications by use of the ASR function as part of <shifter_operand>.

If the programmer decides to use and manipulate values represented by fewer than 32-bits there are no simple methods of detecting overflow or carry using ARM instructions common to all architecture versions; the programmer must devise methods using the logical operations. Cases where manipulations with values smaller than the register size are not common, they usually have features that are unique for the application so are not considered here.

ARM provides support for operations with more than 32-bits provided that the number of bits is a multiple of thirty two. Typically larger representations will use 64-bits, in certain situations 128-bit or even 256-bit numbers may be required. If a program requires some very large integer values that can only be represented using more than 32-bits the programmer must decide how to store these in memory. A common method is to use successive memory locations; if the system is little-endian the lowest 32-bit component of the number should be first; if it is big-endian the highest 32-bit part should be first. To add two such numbers it is necessary to add the two low 32-bit parts then add the next two 32-bit parts and so on until all parts have been added. However there may be a carry out produced each time a 32-bit addition is performed; in these cases an extra one must be added to the total in the next addition stage.

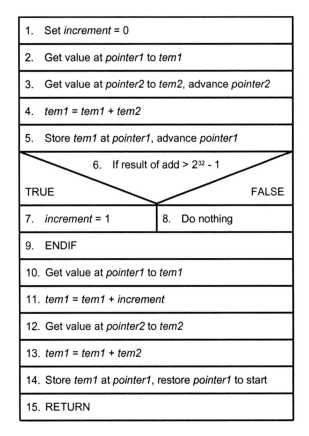

1.	Set *increment* = 0	
2.	Get value at *pointer1* to *tem1*	
3.	Get value at *pointer2* to *tem2*, advance *pointer2*	
4.	*tem1* = *tem1* + *tem2*	
5.	Store *tem1* at *pointer1*, advance *pointer1*	
6.	If result of add > 2^{32} - 1	
TRUE		FALSE
7. *increment* = 1		8. Do nothing
9.	ENDIF	
10.	Get value at *pointer1* to *tem1*	
11.	*tem1* = *tem1* + *increment*	
12.	Get value at *pointer2* to *tem2*	
13.	*tem1* = *tem1* + *tem2*	
14.	Store *tem1* at *pointer1*, restore *pointer1* to start	
15.	RETURN	

Figure 10.2 Structure of a subroutine to add two 64-bit numbers

Figure 10.2 is the structure of a subroutine to add two unsigned numbers each with 64-bits. The numbers are assumed to be stored in memory with the least significant 32-bit values first; the subroutine parameters are pointers to the numbers with the sum returned in place of the first number. This first version does not return information regarding any carry or other features of the result. One implementation is Program 10.3 which performs a similar task to Program 6.1.

Program 10.3 provides another illustration of the use of the ARM feature that all instructions, not just branches, may be executed conditionally. Even with the conditional execution of MOV the code is more complicated than necessary; further the flags do not show if a final carry is created as it could occur with either of the two ADD instructions that produce the high 32-bits. Significant improvement is possible because ARM, in common with many other CPUs, provides a mechanism to support multiple word arithmetic; for addition this is the instruction add with carry, ADC

```
ADC{<cond>}{S} <Rd>, <Rn>, <shifter_operand>
```

ADC performs exactly the same operation as ADD except that the sum produced is the value of <shifter_operand> plus the contents of Rn plus the value of the carry flag before the operation; the carry is always 0 or 1. Hence using ADC the 64-bit addition subroutine can be written as Program 10.4.

```
; Subroutine to add two 64-bit values
; Follows the BCPS, also changes the memory area of the first 64-bit number
; Input values:-    r0 and r1 hold pointers to two 64-bit numbers stored low
;                   32-bits first
; Output values:-   pointer to sum returned in r0 (by chance it is unchanged),
;                   sum is in place of the input value pointed to by r0

sum_64      STMFD   sp!, {r5-r7,lr} ; save as BPCS
            LDR     r5, [r0]        ; get low 32-bits of operand 1
            LDR     r6, [r1],#4     ; get low 32-bits operand 2, advance pointer
            ADDS    r5, r5, r6      ; add setting carry
            STR     r5, [r0],#4     ; save result low 32-bits, advance pointer
            MOVCC   r7, #0          ; do if no carry from add of low 32-bits
            MOVCS   r7, #1          ; do if carry from add of low 32-bits
            LDR     r5, [r0]        ; get high 32-bits of operand 1
            ADD     r5, r5, r7      ; add the carry from add of low 32-bits
            LDR     r6, [r1]        ; get high 32-bits of operand 2
            ADD     r5, r5, r6      ; add the two high 32-bit parts
            STR     r5, [r0],#-4    ; save result high 32-bits, restore pointer
            LDMFD   sp!, {r5-r7,pc} ; restore and return
```

Program 10.3 Subroutine to add two 64-bit values

Use of ADCS, that is ADC with *'set flags'*, sets the C and N flags in a manner such that they provide information concerning carry and sign for the complete 64-bit result. Program 10.4 behaves correctly for both unsigned and twos complement 64-bit integers. With careful design use may be made of Z and it is possible to use V to provide its usual function for signed arithmetic.

```
; Modified Program 10.3 subroutine to add two 64-bit values
; Input values:-    r0 and r1 hold pointers to the two 64-bit numbers stored
;                   low 32-bits first
; Output values:-   pointer to sum returned in r0 (by chance it is unchanged),
;                   sum is in place of the input value pointed to by r0

sum_64      STMFD   sp!, {r5,r6,lr} ; save as BPCS
            LDR     r5, [r0]        ; get low 32-bits of operand 1
            LDR     r6, [r1],#4     ; get low 32-bits operand 2, advance pointer
            ADDS    r5, r5, r6      ; add setting carry
            STR     r5, [r0],#4     ; save result low 32-bits, advance pointer
            LDR     r5, [r0]        ; get high 32-bits of operand 1 ***
            LDR     r6, [r1]        ; get high 32-bits of operand 2 ***
            ADCS    r5, r5, r6      ; add the two high 32-bit parts plus the
                                    ; carry from the low 32-bits ***
            STR     r5, [r0],#-4    ; save result high 32-bits and restore
                                    ; the pointer ***
            LDMFD   sp!, {r5,r6,pc} ; restore and return
```

Program 10.4 *'Improved'* subroutine to add two 64-bit values

A loop structure could be used to extend the subroutine to numbers with 96-bits, 128-bits, etc., but it is necessary to devise a method of storing the state of the carry, C, while performing the loop test. A direct a method is available, Chapter 12, but unless extremely large numbers of bits are used the program is shorter and execution is faster if the four lines of Program 10.4 which have their comments marked *** are changed to

```
LDR     r5, [r0]        ; get next 32-bits of first operand
LDR     r6, [r1]        ; get next 32-bits of second operand and
                        ; advance the pointer
ADCS    r5, r5, r6      ; add the two high 32-bit parts plus the
                        ; carry from the previous 32-bits
STR     r5, [r0],#4     ; save result 32-bit parts, advance pointer
```

and as many copies of these lines as necessary are included. The offset value required to restore the pointer on the last STR instruction must be amended for larger value cases. If required, the final load instruction using the pointer in r1 may use a post-decrement to restore the pointer to the entry value.

ARM also provides two subtract instructions to perform a subtract with borrow

$$SBC\{<cond>\}\{S\}\ <Rd>,\ <Rn>,\ <shifter\_operand>$$
$$RSC\{<cond>\}\{S\}\ <Rd>,\ <Rn>,\ <shifter\_operand>$$

SBC behaves as SUB except that the result is contents of Rn minus the value of <shifter_operand> minus the inverse of the carry flag. The inversion of the carry flag is necessary because ARM clears the carry flag to 0 if a subtract operation produces a borrow (i.e. if B > A for A - B) and sets the carry flag to 1 if there is no borrow (i.e. if B <= A for A - B). The instruction RSC is the subtract with borrow version of RSB, the instruction which uses the operands in the reverse order to SUB when performing subtraction. Problem 10.4 is an exercise requiring the development of a 64-bit subtraction subroutine.

Although the multiple word addition and subtraction have been described for unsigned integers they work equally well for twos complement integers provided the larger numbers are in N-bit twos complement form where N is the total number of bits of the multiple word numbers.

10.4 Multiplication

The ARM instruction set includes several multiply instructions; most are available in all current processor versions but the flag behaviour varies with architecture version. ARM documentation should be studied for full details of flag settings because the behaviour is complicated. Multiplication always introduces difficulties when performed by a CPU as, in general, the result of multiplying two numbers when each has N-bits is a number with $2N$-bits. In general program design it is usual to assume that all numbers of the same type are restricted to all having the same fixed number of bits. This doubling of the number of bits by multiplication instructions causes difficulties. In a high level language program the compiler inserts instructions to perform the tests and execute appropriate actions when problems are detected but in assembly language the programmer must ensure that the problems are identified and overcome; for most CPUs the flags only provide limited support for this process.

The first ARM multiply instruction has the general form

$$MUL\{<cond>\}\{S\}\ <Rd>,\ <Rm>,\ <Rs>$$

Note that the operand form is not as general as for addition and subtraction; the third operand may only be the contents of a register, shift operations are not allowed. There are many other restrictions on the operands for multiply instructions. The most important ones are that r15, the program counter, must not be used for any of the three registers; also Rm and Rd must not be the same register although Rs and Rd may be the same. In some cases an assembler reports an error if these rules are broken, in other cases it produces code but the program action when it executes the instruction is **unpredictable**. For unpredictable cases some, but not all, assemblers produce a warning message. The behaviour of assemblers from different suppliers, or even different versions from the same supplier, will not be identical whenever the CPU behaviour is unpredictable or not defined for certain combinations of operands.

The MUL instruction performs the multiplication of the 32-bit values in Rm and Rs and puts the lowest 32-bits of the result in Rd. The high 32-bits are discarded and there is no method of determining what they were. For the versions of multiply instructions such as MULS with the *'set flags'* field included N and Z behave normally on all ARM versions but the behaviour of C is unpredictable for ARM7TDMI whereas it is unchanged for some later architecture versions. V is not affected by multiply instructions. Because only the lower 32-bits are produced MUL behaves correctly for both twos complement and unsigned integers provided the result magnitude does not exceed 2^{32}-1 for unsigned integers or 2^{31}-1 for twos complement values.

There are several other multiply instructions, one powerful version is multiply-accumulate

$$\text{MLA\{<cond>\}\{S\} <Rd>, <Rm>, <Rs>, <Rn>}$$

Restrictions and rules are similar to those for MUL; the action is the same except that after the multiplication the contents of Rn are added to the product and the result is put into Rd. This may seem an unusual instruction but there are many situations requiring that each element of a list is multiplied by the corresponding element of a second list and the sum of all the products is formed. Rn and Rd may be the same register so a very simple loop will quickly allow corresponding elements from two lists to be multiplied and a sum formed of all the products.

The loss of the high 32-bits means that MUL and MLA instructions can only be used when the programmer is certain that the result will not exceed 32-bits, surprisingly there are many situations where this is true. For example many modern automobiles have a facility to show the outside air temperature. There is a temperature sensor that produces an electrical signal and this signal is converted to a binary value. Often this binary value will have only 8-bits and may be any value from all bits zero to all bits one. This means that the maximum value will be 255 decimal. However when the value is displayed the user will most commonly require that it is in a familiar form, for example a decimal number from zero to one hundred. A neat trick is to convert the maximum value from 255 to one thousand and permanently display a decimal point between the third and fourth digit so the display shows 100·0 as the maximum. Some simple arithmetic operations achieve this with trivial loss of accuracy. To change the input value so that one thousand is the maximum multiply the reading by 64251; the maximum that can ever be produced is $255 \times 64251 = 16384005$ which requires only 24-bits. If this result is right shifted fourteen places, that is it is divided by 16384, then the maximum is 1000·0003. As the places to the right of the point are lost in shifting the result is exactly 1000; for intermediate cases rounding up may be necessary. For example a reading value of 195 will give a result of 764·70612 so should be converted to 765; this is simple in binary as the last bit shifted out is always 1 if rounding up is required and 0 if it is not. The complicated C flag setting by ARM on a move combined with shift provides the required indication to round the result. Hence in this example the programmer can be certain that the result of multiplication will never exceed 32-bits because the largest value from the sensor is 255 and the largest result of multiplication is 255 multiplied by 16384 which only requires 24-bits.

When it is not possible to be certain that the multiplication result will fit into 32-bits multiply operations are available that produce 64-bit results. Using these instructions the 64-bit result may be accepted and further steps in the program must use the larger value; alternatively tests may be performed to confirm that the high 32-bits do not hold any significant bits (not necessarily all zero for signed multiply) and the high part of the result can be discarded. A problem now is that multiplication of signed and unsigned numbers are different; separate instructions are required for each. SMULL performs multiplication of twos complement 32-bit values producing a 64-bit twos complement result, UMULL is multiplication of 32-bit unsigned integer values producing a 64-bit unsigned integer. These have the corresponding multiply accumulate instructions SMLAL and UMLAL.

```
SMULL{<cond>}{S} <RdLo>, <RdHi>, <Rm>, <Rs>
UMULL{<cond>}{S} <RdLo>, <RdHi>, <Rm>, <Rs>
SMLAL{<cond>}{S} <RdLo>, <RdHi>, <Rm>, <Rs>
UMLAL{<cond>}{S} <RdLo>, <RdHi>, <Rm>, <Rs>
```

As for 32-bit multiply the source operands are in Rm and Rs. The high 32-bits of the result are returned in RdHi and the low 32-bits in RdLo, the N flag shows the MSB (sign) and Z indicates if all bits of the 64-bit result are zero. C and V are unpredictable. The registers RdHi, RdLo and Rm must all be different and r15 must not be used for any register; breaking these rules may produce an assembler error message or might generate an instruction code, behaviour of a program using the code is unpredictable. The multiply-accumulate instructions add the 64-bit result to the previous contents of RdHi and RdLo.

10.5 Division

ARM does not provide a division instruction; even those CPUs that do have a division instruction execute it very slowly compared with the execution of other instructions. Experienced programmers are aware that division using any CPU is slow and they design programs to minimise the extent to which it is used. For example when using systems that allow fractional numbers and the same divisor appears at several points in a program the reciprocal is computed once and saved; whenever the division is required multiplication by the reciprocal is performed. It is possible to devise similar methods for integer division and they are described, together with many other division methods, for ARM systems by Sloss *et.al.* [13].

The division operation has some unusual features. For add, subtract and multiply there is always a single exact result for every possible value of the operands even if not all results are allowed values in the number representation in use. If division is performed with a divisor of zero the result is not a finite value. Secondly when integer division is performed to produce integer results the result consists of two values, the quotient and the remainder. The usual method of avoiding two results is to define two integer division operations. The **divide operation**, often called DIV and represented by the symbol / in many software systems, produces only the quotient. The **modulus operation**, called MOD and sometimes represented by the symbol %, produces the remainder.

There are a number of ways of performing division; the most simple is repeated subtraction as illustrated earlier by Program 8.3. If it is known that the quotient will be small then Program 8.3 is often adequate. However, if there is a possibility that the quotient might be large and the divisor small this method must be avoided as, even on a very fast ARM processor, division could take several seconds. An alternative approach is a looping sequence of shifting the divisor and testing if subtraction is possible. This is the process of long division many people learned when young; it is very simple when performed with binary numbers. Binary long division is illustrated by the example in Figure 10.2 that uses 8-bit unsigned integers because a 32-bit example would not fit on the page; the values chosen are 10110101 divided by 00001001; equivalent to decimal 181 divided by 9.

		Times subtracted
0 0 0 0 0 0 0 0 1 0 1 1 0 1 0 1	dividend with 8 extra leading 0 digits added	
0 0 0 0 1 0 0 1	divisor shifted left 7 places (size of original number less 1)	
0 0 0 0 0 0 0 0 1 0 1 1 0 1 0 1	dividend minus shifted divisor if subtraction possible else unchanged	**0**
0 0 0 0 1 0 0 1	previous divisor shifted right one place	
0 0 0 0 0 0 0 0 1 0 1 1 0 1 0 1	dividend minus shifted divisor if subtraction possible else unchanged	**0**
0 0 0 0 1 0 0 1	previous divisor shifted right one place	
0 0 0 0 0 0 0 0 1 0 1 1 0 1 0 1	dividend minus shifted divisor if subtraction possible else unchanged	**0**
0 0 0 0 1 0 0 1	previous divisor shifted right one place	
0 0 0 0 0 0 0 0 0 0 1 0 0 1 0 1	dividend minus shifted divisor if subtraction possible else unchanged	**1**
0 0 0 0 1 0 0 1	previous divisor shifted right one place	
0 0 0 0 0 0 0 0 0 0 1 0 0 1 0 1	dividend minus shifted divisor if subtraction possible else unchanged	**0**
0 0 0 0 1 0 0 1	previous divisor shifted right one place	
0 0 0 0 0 0 0 0 0 0 0 0 0 0 0 1	dividend minus shifted divisor if subtraction possible else unchanged	**1**
0 0 0 0 1 0 0 1	previous divisor shifted right one place	
0 0 0 0 0 0 0 0 0 0 0 0 0 0 0 1	dividend minus shifted divisor if subtraction possible else unchanged	**0**
0 0 0 0 1 0 0 1	previous divisor shifted right one place	
0 0 0 0 0 0 0 0 0 0 0 0 0 0 0 1	dividend minus shifted divisor if subtraction possible else unchanged This final value of the dividend is the remainder	**0**

Figure 10.2　8-bit subtract and shift division (long division)

To perform binary long division the dividend is extended to double the number of bits by adding additional zeros before the MSB. Initially the divisor is moved left by a number of places one less than the number of bits. In practice it is usually easier to shift it one further position left; the only effects are to slightly slow the program execution and add an extra leading zero to the result.

The shifted divisor is subtracted from the dividend as many times as possible and the number of times that it can be subtracted is noted. Performing this with binary numbers is very simple. The subtraction can either be performed once or not at all so the number of times the subtraction is performed is always 1 or 0, this value is noted. After the subtraction the divisor is shifted one place right and the subtraction process is repeated. The divisor, in the new position, is subtracted from the value of the remainder produced in the previous step if possible and the number of times subtraction is performed is noted. This process continues repeatedly shifting, subtracting if possible, placing the value of the number of times subtracted in a list, and continuing until the divisor has been subtracted, if possible, after it has been shifted to its original position. The value that is left after all the subtractions from the dividend is the remainder. The quotient is the list of values indicating the number of times the shifted divisor could be subtracted at each stage, the first digit produced is the result MSB. For the example the result quotient is 00010100, that is 20 decimal, and the remainder is 1. This process can be converted into a set of rules, an **algorithm**[1], and a program can be developed to implement it. There are many minor variants of the algorithm for this process; Problem 10.4 requires development of a program for this algorithm.

---

[1] An algorithm is a set of rules for the performance of a logical process.

There many other division algorithms, many execute much faster than the process of Figure 10.2, although none is very fast. For example it is not necessary to extend the dividend to double length, the divisor can be left shifted until it has no leading zeros, alternatively it can be left shifted until the most significant one digits of both dividend and divisor are in line. In both cases the number of shifts must be counted. The subtract and shift algorithm is performed with the number of times the divisor is right shifted equal to the number of times it was initially shifted left. The correct number of leading zeros must be added to the quotient. These versions of the algorithm are faster although the speed is variable and the programming is more difficult. Division of signed numbers is more complicated than for unsigned ones; the problem is often avoided by noting the signs of the original operands, converting the operands to same magnitude positive values, performing the division then adjusting the result signs if necessary. Sloss *et.al.*, [13] describe division using ARM processors in detail and describe several fast algorithms.

10.6 Useful techniques

Obscure programming *'tricks'* should be avoided as they greatly increase the risk of creating difficult to find faults. However there are a number of techniques that experienced programmers use to speed program execution or reduce code size. One of the most common is to use shifting in place of multiplication and division whenever possible. For unsigned integers multiplication by 2^N is the same as shift left N places; divide by 2^N is shift right by N places. For almost all types of CPU, not only ARM, shift operations are usually faster than multiply; shifts are always faster than division.

Twos complement integers may be divided by 2^N by using shift right N places provided arithmetic shift right is used. Multiplication of twos complement numbers by 2^N using shift left is possible provided the programmer checks that overflow does not occur, the rule is that all of the bits shifted out and the final result sign bit must be all the same.

The ability of ARM to perform several operations simultaneously provides many of efficient *tricks* for some manipulations, especially multiplication by a constant value. For example

```
ADD  r3, r4, r4, LSL #2
```

sets contents of r3 equal to 5 times the contents of r4. This is multiply by five but, because shift is used, it is quicker than using the multiply instruction. A large range of similar manipulations are possible but are only the concern of the programmer who has to obtain maximum speed for some task.

Another common numeric process is one to change the sign of a twos complement number; numerically this is multiplying it by minus one or subtracting it from zero. For many CPUs the most efficient way is to use two instructions; first invert all the bits of the number then add one to the result. One of the many features that the ARM <shifter_operand> is that small immediate values are automatically extended to 32-bits. Therefore the instruction

```
RSB  <Rd>, <Rn>, #0
```

will subtract the value in Rn from zero and consequently forms the twos complement.

10.7 Summary

The four basic arithmetic operations have been introduced for unsigned integer and twos complement values only. These should be adequate for the majority of programs prepared in assembly language as programs requiring large complex calculations should be developed using a high level language.

It is important to remember that when using assembly language the programmer is responsible for providing code to check the initial values before an arithmetic operation when checks are necessary. The programmer must also provide code to check that results are within the set of allowed values. When a problem is found code to handle the situation must be present. Using high level language the tests and subsequent actions on failure are usually incorporated automatically without any programmer action.

10.8 Problems

10.1 If the code produced by LDR r5, =-54321 is executed determine, without writing a program, the hexadecimal value put into r5.

10.2 If a 32-bit twos complement number is subtracted from a 32-bit unsigned value to produce a twos complement result which input values will cause problems? Design, develop and test a subroutine to perform this operation with all necessary error detection mechanisms.

10.3 Repeat problem 10.2 for the case of an unsigned number subtracted from a twos complement number producing an unsigned result.

10.4 Design, develop and test a subroutine to subtract one 64-bit number from another 64-bit number.

10.5 In Section 10.4 a method was described of converting the input from a sensor providing values from 0 to 255 into values from 0 to 1000 for display as 0.0 to 100.0. Design, develop and thoroughly test a subroutine to implement this function.

10.6 Repeat Problem 10.5 for the case when the sensor provides values from 0 to 255 but these correspond to display values -20 to +60. Don't use twos complement; don't display any decimal places; do produce one value for the magnitude and a second value of 0 for positive and 1 for negative.

10.7 Develop a division subroutine for unsigned 32-bit numbers using the sequence illustrated in Figure 10.2. Note that there are several methods of programming this process. One sequence is test to see if subtraction is possible, subtract if possible, set the bit in quotient to the appropriate value, shift the divisor then repeat the correct number of times. An alternative method is to always subtract, test to see if the result is negative, set the bit in quotient to the appropriate value and if result was negative add back the divisor. After this shift the divisor and repeat the whole subtract, test, etc., process. This second version is known as restoring division and is sometimes considered easier to program. Before preparing the code produce an NS chart for the method you select.

10.8 It was indicated that

```
     ADD  r3, r4, r4, LSL #2
```
performs a fast multiplication of the contents of r4 by five. What action is performed by
```
     RSB  r3, r4, r4, LSL #2
```
Write a list stating which instructions (other than multiply ones) will perform multiplication by the constant value 2, by 3, by 4, by 5 and so on using ARM shift capability (to avoid using multiply instructions).

Which is the first value of constant that cannot be used as the multiplier for this method?

11 Input and Output (IO)

The methods of supplying inputs and using output values depend on the input and output, IO, devices connected to the CPU. ARM systems are embedded in a wide range of products so they are used with many different IO hardware systems. Consequently it is not possible to give a general description of programming methods to implement input and output; only a few typical examples can be described. Operation of any IO device, **peripheral**, depends on the design of the hardware circuits and often involves ensuring that the sequences of CPU actions controlling them have a precise form. To meet hardware requirements the sections of a program that handle IO are often prepared in assembly language.

In previous chapters input and output operations were ignored. It was assumed that the software development system would supply any input data required and that program results, outputs, would be in registers or memory and inspected using the development system test facilities. At some stage in the software development process the modules implementing the IO functions for the application have to be developed, tested and integrated to produce the complete program.

Small target boards are available for initial studies of ARM systems; they use microcontrollers that incorporate IO devices. Evaluator-7T is no longer manufactured but is still widely used in education establishments. Many other boards are available including the Unique ML67Q4000 which has an OKI microcontroller and a large range from Keil Elektronik GmbH that use microcontrollers from NXP (previously Philips) and from STMicroelectronics. The simulator provided with the Keil software tools emulates the input and output systems of many microcontrollers and is adequate for initial programming exercises. However any program for commercial use must be fully tested using the complete production hardware system.

Some development target boards include features that assume that ARM assembler will be used, others are supplied with tools developed by the board manufacturer or require the GNU tools, Appendix F. Assemblers from other manufacturers often differ from the ARM assemblers; usually the mnemonics and general program form are the same but the syntax, directives and other features differ.

11.1 Simple IO

For simple hardware systems each output device, port, appears to be either one byte or one word of memory to which values are written. The values written to an output appear directly as electrical signals at the output connection points with a separate signal connection for each bit. Input values are obtained in a similar manner by reading from a single specified location; electrical signals from the input device supply a signal for each input bit. A read operation from an output port usually returns an unpredictable value unless the hardware includes an input port at the same address. A write to an input port has no effect but should be avoided as some hardware systems may behave in an unpredictable manner.

The Unique ML67Q40000 development board uses the OKI ML67Q4000 microcontroller which has an ARM7TDMI as the CPU and several integrated IO modules. One IO module is a simple output port connected to a seven segment display with a decimal point. The value written to the 8-bit memory at address 0xf0000000 determines which segments of the display are illuminated. Writing a 1 to a particular bit turns on the associated segment while writing a 0 ensures that the segment is off. Consequently writing suitable values to the memory byte at address 0xf0000000 will illuminate segments to show representations of the digits 0 to 9. Figure 11.1 shows the allocation of output port bits to the display segments; Program 11.1 is a subroutine that causes the Unique board to display representations of the digits 0 to 9 when the value of the parameter passed to the subroutine in r0 is any value from 0 to 9. This subroutine also provides an example of one method of performing the task of obtaining the value of a list or array element using an index value with the index of the first list member zero. List members are in order in successive memory locations; in this example one byte is required for each list member.

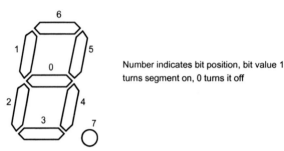

Number indicates bit position, bit value 1 turns segment on, 0 turns it off

Figure 11.1 Unique ML67Q4000 development board 7-segment display

In Program 11.1 the addressing mode used by LDRB r4, [r4, r0] accesses the correct value in the list; the address used is the list start address, loaded into r4, plus the offset. As list entries are single bytes the offset is the number of the list member required and is the parameter value passed to the routine in r0. A more complicated addressing mode described in Appendix D is available for situations where list members require more than one byte of memory.

```
; Note:-  The following equate statement should be one of a block that define
;         hardware features. This is usually near the program start.
LED_Buff  EQU    0xf0000000       ; define address of 7 segment display
; Display digits 0 to 9 on a Unique ML67Q40000 development board 7-segment
; display and turn the decimal point on or off.
; Input values:-   digit value in r0, r1=0 for point off, otherwise point on
; Output values:-  error in r0, 0=successful, 1 shows digit was not 0 to 9
LED_Dig   STMFD  sp!, {r4,r5,lr} ; save work registers and return address
          CMP    r0,#10          ; test for valid digit value
          MOVMI  r0, #1          ; set to indicate error occurred
          BMI    exit            ; exit after error found
          LDR    r4, =pattern    ; point to look-up data start
          LDRB   r4, [r4, r0]    ; get the pattern at start + offset
          MOVS   r1, r1          ; test if point is to be on
          ORRNE  r4, r4, #0x80   ; bit 7 to 1 if point to be on
          LDR    r5, =LED_buff   ; pointer to display memory
          STRB   r4, [r5]        ; send the digit pattern to display memory
          MOV    r0, #0          ; return value for no error
exit      LDMFD  sp!, {r4,r5,pc} ; restore work registers and return
; List of patterns corresponding to segments on in digit order
pattern   DCB    2_1111110, 2_0110000, 2_1101101, 2_1111001, 2_0110011
          DCB    2_1011011, 2_1011111, 2_1110000, 2_1111111, 2_1111011
```

Program 11.1 Decimal display subroutine for ML67Q4000 development board

11.2 More complicated microcontroller IO systems

The IO systems of most microcontrollers are very complicated and often consist of several very flexible multi-purpose IO sub-systems. The flexibility is provided by registers called **special function registers, SFRs**. The SFRs behave as memory words which are usually at addresses that are fixed by the microcontroller manufacturer. Some of the SFRs are loaded with values that determine how the IO sub-systems behave; the programmer configures each IO sub-system to behave as required for the application. Other SFRs are buffer registers which are used to transfer values to or from the connection pins of the microcontroller.

The ARM7TDMI based Samsung KS32C50100 of Evaluator-7T and the NXP devices used by many Keil boards have large numbers of SFRs. Before using a particular IO sub-system the program must execute code to configure the sub-system to function in the required manner. Although the mechanism of providing flexible IO systems using SFRs is a common technique each microcontroller type has its own unique set of SFRs and configuration requirements. The programmer must use the device data to determine how to set the IO as required; frequently data sheets are not very clearly presented.

11.2.1 Simple IO using Evaluator-7T

The most simple IO sub-system of the KS32C50100 provides a number of separate single input or output connections. The function of an individual port bit, connection pin, of the device is selected by writing a specified value to the corresponding bit in a control register. The contents of the IO port mode control register, acronym IOPMOD, determine the behaviour of the IO port and the signals at the connection pins are manipulated using the IO port data register, IOPDATA. Both registers are 32-bit ones although only bits 0 to 17 are used. The addresses of the registers may be changed by the program but are usually left at the addresses set automatically at power on or reset; IOPMOD is at address 0x03ff5000 and IOPDATA is at 0x03ff5008. Before using IOPDATA the program must write a value to IOPMOD. Each bit of IOPMOD controls the behaviour of the corresponding bit of IOPDAT; when 0 is written to a bit in IOPMOD the bit of IOPDAT is an input while writing a 1 makes it an output; any unused bits of IOPDAT should be 0. Table 11.1 defines the use of the IOPDAT bits by Evaluator-7T.

Bit number	Use	Bit number	Use
0	Switch 1 input	9	Unused
1	Switch 2 input	10	Display segment A
2	Switch 3 input	11	Display segment B
3	Switch 4 input	12	Display segment C
4	LED 4 output	13	Display segment D
5	LED 3 output	14	Display segment E
6	LED 2 output	15	Display segment G
7	LED 1 output	16	Display segment F
8	Unused	17 to 31	unused

Table 11.1 Evaluator-7T IOPDAT connections

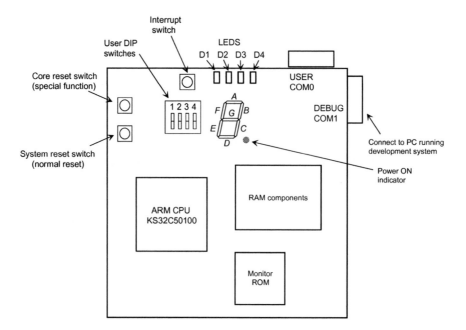

Figure 11.2   Layout of Evaluator-7T

Figure 11.2 shows the layout of Evaluator-7T; the 7-segment display is not connected in the same manner as that of the OKI board; also the decimal point is always illuminated as it is the power on indicator. Most devices with configurable IO, such as the KS32C50100, start at power on with the control register initialised so that all connections are inputs. This reduces the risk of external circuits being damaged by the microcontroller sending output signals to circuits that supply inputs. A program for Evaluator-7T that uses the IO ports usually includes a start up sequence similar to Program 11.2. It is common practice for microcontroller programs to include a section near the start that configures all IO devices; usually once configured the mode of operation of IO devices is not changed as the program is executed although there are exceptions.

```
; IO port initialisation sequence for Evaluator-7T programs
IOPMOD     EQU     0x03ff5000    ; address of control register
IOPDATA    EQU     0x03ff5008    ; address of output port
IO_SET     EQU     0x0001fcf0    ; value for port bit directions in Table 11.1

           AREA    Eval7,  CODE,  READONLY  ; code module definition
           ENTRY
           LDR     sp, =0x10000   ; set up the stack
           LDR     r0, =IOPMOD    ; a pointer to the IO port control register
           LDR     r1, =IO_SET    ; get required control register contents
           STR     r1, [r0]       ; load the port control register
           LDR     r0, =IOPDATA   ; point to the IO data register (the outputs)
           MOV     r1, #0         ; initial value for outputs (all off)
           STR     r1, [r0]       ; set all outputs off
           LDR     r0, =last_out  ; point to copy of output
           STR     r1, [r0]       ; set copy to value sent to output
; the DATA segment must include space to store a 32-bit value whose address
; is defined by a label last_out
```

Program 11.2   Typical section of program to initialise Evaluator-7T IO port bits

In Program 11.2 a variable *last_out* holds a copy of the most recent output to IOPDAT because it is unlikely that all outputs will be changed simultaneously. To perform an output the bits to be changed are altered in the copy and the new value is sent to IOPDAT. A subroutine to perform the same function as Program 11.1 is more complicated; both because of the need to change the output by changing bits in a copy and writing it to IOPDAT, and because the bits changed are not in the least significant positions

11.2.2 Simple IO using LPC2xxx microcontrollers

Some other microcontrollers operate in a manner similar to the Samsung KS32C50100. For example the NXP LPC2102 has a multi-function thirty two bit IO port with connections controlled by two SFRs called PINSEL0 and PINSEL1. Two pin select register bits are required for each port pin because each can perform four different functions. An SFR called IODIR sets each pin as input or output when they are simple IO connections; IOPIN is written to for output operations and read from for inputs. The Keil tools emulate the IO sub-systems of the LPC2102 with screen displays showing the behaviour of the port pins. Program 11.3 performs a simple sequence of changes at the output port.

```
; Simple example of a simple output port using LPC2102 in Prog11_3.s
; Project MUST INCLUDE modified Keil startup.s file, details in Appendix E
; Date:-      10th July 2007
; Revision:-  None
; Author:-    J.R. Gibson
; Define special function register addresses and patterns for some simple tasks

PINSEL0      EQU    0xE002C000         ; controls function of IO pins
IOPIN        EQU    0xE0028000         ; IO actual output register address
off_DIR      EQU    0x8                ; offset of IODIR  (pin direction
                                       ; register) from IOPIN address
             AREA   Serial, CODE, READONLY

             EXPORT __main             ; modified startup.s branches to __main
__main       LDR    sp, = 0x40001000   ; stack at RAM top
             LDR    r1, =PINSEL0        ; point to pin control register
             MOV    r0, #0              ; set P0.0 to P0.15 as general. . .
             STR    r0, [r1]            ; . . . purpose IO (GPIO) pins
             LDR    r1, =IOPIN          ; point to IOPIN
             LDR    r0, =0xffff         ; set P0.0 to P0.15 as outputs. . .
             STR    r0, [r1, #off_DIR]  ; . . . using IODIR register
             MOV    r0, #0              ; initial output value
next         STR    r0, [r1]            ; send to output pins
             ADD    r0, r0, #1          ; increment output value
             LDR    r2, =0x4000         ; simple delay count value
delay        SUBS   r2, r2, #1          ; count down delay
             BNE    delay               ; loop until counted down delay
             B      next                ; loop to do next output
;    program loops for ever so no ending required
             END
```

Program 11.3 Simple pattern output using the LPC2102

The LPC2xxx series contains many devices, all have very complicated IO systems and the systems are sometimes significantly different for different members of the series. Many of the LPC2xxx series devices must have many of their SFRs configured correctly for correct operation; until all the requirements are understood the reader should include the Keil start up code of file startup.s for the specific LPC2xxx device used in any project. Because startup.s is devised for use when programs are written in the high level language C it must be modified for use with assembly language programs; also the assembly language entry point is now defined by the label _*main* (two underscores) instead of by *Reset_Handler*. Appendix E briefly outlines how to modify startup.s for use with assembly language programs and also describes the use of the Keil tools to emulate microcontroller IO devices.

As indicated the IO systems of LPC2xxx series devices are not all the same; for most applications the form illustrated in Program 11.3 would require the technique using a variable of the form of *last_out* required by the Program 11.2 for the KS32C50100 device. Many LPC21xx devices provide SFRs to control the values at output pins using an alternative method; Program 11.4 illustrates this, it displays a sequence on the LEDs on the LPC2129 target board supplied by Keil.

```
; Simple output port using LPC2129 in Prog11_4.s
; Project MUST INCLUDE modified Keil startup.s file, details in Appendix E
; Date:-      11th July 2007
; Revision:-  None
; Author:-    J.R. Gibson
; Define special function register addresses for some simple tasks
IODIR       EQU    0xE0028018       ; IO actual output register address
IOSET       EQU    0xE0028014       ; IO pin setting register address
IOCLR       EQU    0xE002801C       ; IO pin clearing register address
            AREA   Serial, CODE, READONLY

            EXPORT __main            ; modified startup.s branches to __main

__main      LDR    sp, = 0x40004000  ; stack at RAM top
            LDR    r1, =IODIR         ; point to pin control register
            LDR    r0, =0x00FF0000    ; set P1.16 to P1.23 as . . .
            STR    r0, [r1]           ; . . . output pins
            LDR    r2, =IOSET         ; pointer to pin set control register
            LDR    r3, =IOCLR         ; pointer to pin clear control register
rept        MOV    r4, #0x10000       ; mask of 1 for p1.16
next        STR    r4, [r2]           ; turn selected pin on
            LDR    r5, =0x100000      ; simple delay count value
delay       SUBS   r5, r5, #1         ; count down delay
            BNE    delay              ; loop until counted down delay
            STR    r4, [r3]           ; turn pin off
            MOV    r4, r4, LSL #1     ; change mask to next pin
            CMP    r4, #0x01, 8       ; check for done p1.23
            BNE    next               ; if not p1.23 do next pin
            B      rept               ; loop to repeat whole sequence
;     program loops for ever so no ending required
            END
```

Program 11.4 Alternative pattern output method using the LPC2129

Unlike the LPC2102 the LPC2129 does not require definition of pin functions; only the pin direction must be set by loading the SFR called IODIR. The values at output pins are controlled by two SFRs. When a value is written to register IOSET any bits in IOSET that are 1 cause the corresponding output pins to be set to 1; any bits in IOSET which are 0 leave the output pins unchanged. Similarly when a value is written to register IOCLR any bits in IOCLR that are 1 cause the corresponding output pins to be cleared to 0; any bits in IOCLR which are 0 leave the pin unchanged. Note that a 1 in IOCLR clears the pin to 0; a 0 in IOCLR has no effect on the pin. That is the value 0 **is not used** to clear pins.

11.3 Semihosting

ARM development systems ADS and RealView include a feature called **semihosting.** This allows a program under development to use the computer running the development system as a terminal providing input and output for the target while performing debugging tasks. If the target is a hardware system it must have a monitor program that supports semihosting; for example the Angel monitor. If the target is a simulator it must behave as if it has such a monitor; the ARMulator supports all semihosting features.

Using semihosting an extra window appears in the IDE display and shows program output; the host computer keyboard provides program input. Semihosting uses the instruction SWI, to be described fully later; it behaves as a special subroutine call with the semihosting action selected by parameters passed in r0 and r1. Only r0 is corrupted, no other registers are changed. For example the sequence

```
MOV     r0, #0x03
LDR     r1, =address
SWI     0x123456
```

causes the 8-bit value stored in the memory location at *address* to be sent to the host, the value is assumed to be an ASCII code and the corresponding character is shown in the display window. For input

```
MOV     r0, #0x07
LDR     r1, =0x0        ;   MUST BE ZERO
SWI     0x123456
```

causes the ARM program to wait until the semihosting window is active and a key is pressed on the host keyboard. The ASCII code corresponding to the key is returned in r0. For some complex function keys on computer keyboards the host returns two characters and the semihosting function must be used twice.

All the complete program examples introduced end with the semihosting sequence

```
MOV     r0, #0x18
LDR     r1, =0x20026
SWI     0x123456
```

This function is provided so that after a program under test has completed all the instructions to perform the required task it can indicate that it has finished running to the host computer running the development software. Usually when this end is detected the host computer stops debugging and other test actions then waits for the user to indicate which development system task is required next.

One reason this end sequence is required is that ARM does not have an instruction to stop running. Microcontrollers are designed for use in embedded systems which perform some function as soon as power is connected and continue until power is removed. When developing programs testing often requires that a program runs once then waits until the user indicates the next action. Without the semihosting function, or an alternative, the CPU must be prevented from using the random contents of the memory following the last program instruction as further instructions. The general method, as suggested for the Keil simulator, is to end the program with a simple one instruction loop of the form

```
complete   BAL   complete
```

Some complex hardware systems provide a method allowing a program to stop the clock; they also provide a method of an external system restarting it when necessary. Such systems are special designs and each one is different.

11.4 Serial IO

Connecting a processor system to an IO device using one electrical circuit for every bit of input or output data is simple but inconvenient and expensive if the device is some distance from the CPU. An alternative is to send the data bits one after another using a single circuit. This is **serial communication**, the bits are in series in time. There are many serial systems and one of the most easily implemented is that built to the CCITT[1] standards V24 and V28. Systems to these standards are often called RS-232 or EIA-232 ones as they were developed from the single EIA[2] standard. Although this standard is no longer commonly used in consumer products it is still used in industrial systems. The standards were developed to make connections between computer systems and remote terminals using the telephone system; **modems** (modulator-demodulator units) provide the necessary conversion between the digital systems and the analogue telephone line. The full standard is large and complex but for simple systems it is often adapted in a non-standard manner to provide an IO function to transfer one 8-bit value at a time. Figure 11.3 outlines the full connection using two RS-232 links, two modems and the land line based telephone system. The figure shows the standard form; the computer and the terminal are both data terminal equipment devices, DTE, and the modem is the data communication equipment, DCE. Omitting both modems and the telephone network and directly joining the terminal and computer is satisfactory provided the cables are modified and the distance between them is not great; the distance limit depends on the data transfer speed.

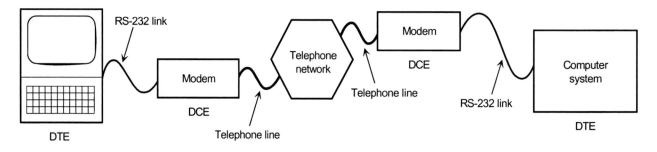

Figure 11.3 Connection of a terminal to a computer via the telephone network

When this type of link is used to directly connect two systems that are not terminal to computer links problems may arise because it is not always clear which is the DTE unit and which the DCE unit. In some cases both units may be DTE units or both may be DCE units. For full communication links all connection wires of the specification must be used between the DTE and DCE units; for very simple tasks reduced connection systems are often used.

---

[1] CCITT - Comité Consultatif International Téléphonique et Télégraphique
[2] EIA - Electronic Industries Alliance (USA)

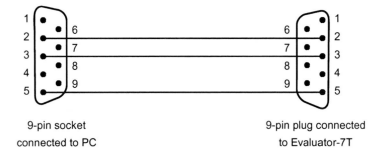

Figure 11.4 Simple serial connection from a PC to Evaluator-7T

Many new PCs do not have an RS232 connector, those that do have a 9-pin DTE connector whereas the full specification uses a 25-pin connector. Evaluator-7T has two 9-pin DCE connectors. Links between a PC and Evaluator-7T may be made using the very simple cable shown in Figure 11.4 provided the PC serial connection is set to require no hardware or software handshakes. When a link requires a cable with sockets on both ends or plugs on both ends, because both units are DTE or both are DCE, the lead must have pin 2 of one connector linked to pin 3 of the other (cross-over). Some systems also have a hardware handshake system activated and can be made to ignore this by deliberate incorrect connections. The required connections vary but typically each connector should have its own pins 7 and 8 linked together; in some cases pins 1, 4 and 6 should also be linked together. That is pins 1, 4, 6, 7 and 8 have no links between the connectors at opposite ends of the cable in this incorrect form.

Microcontrollers, for example the OKI ML67Q4000, Samsung KS32C50100 and NXP LPC2xxx series, usually have at least one IO unit called a universal asynchronous receiver transmitter, UART, to implement serial connections. A UART performs all the tasks to convert an 8-bit value to a serial data stream. Because UARTs are universal they can operate in many different modes and the user must configure them to behave as required. This is similar to setting IOPMOD for the KS32C50100 described in Section 11.1 but is more complicated. Unfortunately every manufacturer has their own UART design and the configuration process is different for each. To develop IO program modules using UARTs the programmer must understand the manufacturer's data; this is often complex and not clearly written.

Register	Access	Purpose
Line control	Write only	Set line operation (e.g. bits, parity, etc)
Modem control	Write only	Set handshakes, etc.
Clock divider	Write only	Set serial data rate
Status register	Read only	Indicate data received, ready to send, errors
Transmit buffer	Write only	Load with data value to be sent
Receive buffer	Read only	Hold data value received
Transmit shift	Not accessible	Outputs formatted data one bit at a time
Receive shift	Not accessible	Receives formatted data one bit at a time

Table 11.2 Typical UART registers (this list does not refer to any specific UART)

A UART has a number of registers; for ARM systems these usually appear as single byte memory locations in a sequence at addresses spaced at four byte intervals with the two LSBs of the address both zero. Table 11.2 outlines a typical general set of UART registers; it does not correspond to any particular real UART. There are a number of control registers which are written to define how the UART must operate, one or more status registers whose contents are read to determine the UART status, and data registers which hold the input and output values. Depending on their function the UART registers may appear to be memory locations that are read only, or are write only, or are read and write.

UARTs have many features; for simple applications many may be ignored and the UART can be set to transmit whenever required and to obtain any values that arrive. For Evaluator-7T a cable wired as in Figure 11.4 can be used from the connector *'USER COM0'* to a spare serial connector on the host PC; if there is no spare connector an extra serial communications card must be fitted. A terminal emulator program, Hyperterm, is included with Windows (usually found from *Start → Programs → Accessories → Communications*). If it is configured to use the port to which the extra serial link has been connected the PC becomes an IO device for Evaluator-7T. Every time an ARM program outputs a character code to UART0 it is displayed in the Hyperterm window. Provided Hyperterm is the active window when a key is pressed on the PC keyboard the corresponding character code is sent to UART0. The ARM programmer must include instructions to configure the UART and to perform the transmit and receive operations.

Program 11.5 continually outputs the letters of the alphabet to the serial port *'USER COM0'* of Evaluator-7T. If this is connected to a PC set to use eight data bits, one stop bit, no parity and a speed of 1200 baud and Hyperterm is running the Evaluator-7T output appears in the Hyperterm window.

The Keil tools can simulate UART operation of some microcontrollers. The tools may be set so the UART input and output use an extra PC window in a similar manner to character input and output using semihosting on ARM development systems. A complicated feature of the LPC2xxx series UART used in many Keil examples, and also in IO systems of other microcontrollers, is that several SFRs appear at the same address. The different SFRs are accessed by performing a sequence of transfers; the IO system automatically uses them in a set order.

11.5 Input from switches and external events

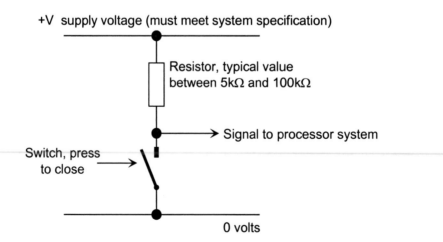

Figure 11.5 Simple switch input circuit

A keyboard is a set of spring loaded switches that close when pressed and spring open when released. When a switch is connected directly to a simple input port, Figure 11.5, a program can determine the switch position by reading the input; the two switch positions correspond to 0 and 1 inputs. The values

```
; Continually output the letters of the alphabet on Evaluator-7T serial port
; Program in file Prog11_5.s
; Date:- 12th July 2007
; Revisions:- none;
; Author:- J.R. Gibson
; The following EQU statements define the UART 0 register addresses required
Sys_Bas     EQU     0x3ff0000
; Sys_Bas = default base address of on-chip peripherals of Evaluator_7 target
Cm0_Bas     EQU     Sys_Bas + 0xd000    ; Offset for UART 0 registers
ULCON0      EQU     Cm0_Bas             ; Line control register address
UCON0       EQU     Cm0_Bas + 4         ; UART control register address
USTAT0      EQU     Cm0_Bas + 8         ; UART status register address
UTXBUF0     EQU     Cm0_Bas + 12        ; UART transmit buffer address
URXBUF0     EQU     Cm0_Bas + 16        ; UART receive buffer address
UBRDIV0     EQU     Cm0_Bas + 20        ; UART baud rate divider address

            AREA    SerialOut,  CODE,   READONLY
            ENTRY                       ; indicate run start position
            LDR     sp, =0x10000        ; initialise stack pointer
            LDR     r1, =ULCON0         ; point to first control register
            MOV     r0, #7              ;= 8 data bits, 2 stop bits, no parity..
            STR     r0, [r1], #4        ;= ..and internal (on chip) clock source
            MOV     r0, #9              ;+ set simple operation with no handshakes
            STR     r0, [r1], #16       ;+
            LDR     r0, =0x5150         ;= set for 1200 baud when using on board..
            STR     r0, [r1]            ;= ..clock
            MOV     r0, #'A'            ; initial output letter A
        ; start of character output loop
cloop       BL      charout             ; output character via serial port
            ADD     r0, r0, #1          ; advance to next letter
            CMP     r0, #'Z'            ; check against last letter
            BLE     cloop               ; loop if not done Z yet
            MOV     r0, #'A'            ; reset to initial output letter
            BAL     cloop               ; go to output starting from A again

; Serial output routine using UART0
; Inputs:-   value to output in low 8-bits of r0 (high not checked)
; Outputs:-  None

charout     STMFD   sp!, {r5,r6,lr} ; save used registers and return address
            LDR     r5, = USTAT0        ; point to status register
ch_rdy      LDR     r6, [r5]            ; get UART status
            ANDS    r6, r6, #0x40       ; extract transmit buffer state
            BEQ     ch_rdy              ; loop waiting if buffer not empty
            LDR     r5, = UTXBUF0       ; point to transmit buffer
            STR     r0, [r5]            ; send value to transmitter
            LDMFD   sp!, {r5,r6,pc} ; restore and return
            END
```

Program 11.5 Continuous output using UART0

for the open and closed positions depend on the circuit construction; for Figure 11.5 the open position provides a 1 and the closed position a 0. This description ignores the switch construction which creates a problem known as *'switch bounce'*. To ensure that switch contacts are pressed together when closed they are made of flexible metal. When the contacts join on closure or break on opening they do so many times for a period of a few thousandths of a second. The contacts *'bounce'* and the signal at the input is similar to that in Figure 11.6 for the input circuit of Figure 11.5.

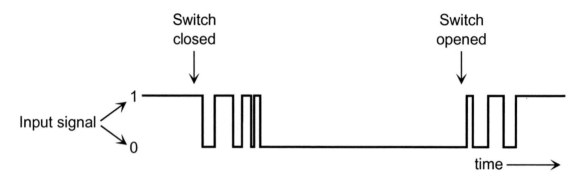

Figure 11.6 Example of a switch input signal; the *'bounce'* typically lasts about 5ms

It is possible to construct circuits to remove switch bounce but most microcontroller systems remove it using software as this is a lower cost method. For the circuit of Figure 11.5 the flowchart of Figure 11.7 shows the sequence required to remove the effects of switch bounce; the delay is usually provided by a software count down loop such as Program 8.1. The delay count is selected to produce a delay of about 5 ms, slightly longer if low quality switches are used. An important feature of the sequence of Figure 11.7 is that it ensures that the switch is not pressed and any *'switch bounce'* when it was released from the previous operation has ended before it starts the process to detect that it is pressed. **Strictly** Figure 11.7 is the sequence to detect a change in input corresponding to pressing a key; the key press is detected as a change from 1 to 0, not simply as a 0 value. If the test was only for 0 and a user held the key down a program that required the user to press several keys would detect a held down key as several key presses.

A flowchart, Figure 11.7, is used to indicate the sequence of events detected. To design a program this is converted to a structure chart. This is not as simple as it first appears; for example to ensure that delays are executed at least once repeat loops are required. This is an unusual example; correct behaviour requires a repeat loop. Figure 11.8 is an NS chart that meets the requirements.

Keyboards with many keys are connected in a more complex manner to reduce the number of wires and inputs. This does not remove *'switch bounce'* and a de-bounce process is still required.

11.6 Timing of IO actions

A feature of all the examples requiring input to a program has been that the input has been obtained when the program requires the value, this is **program controlled** input. When inputs are obtained in this manner the programmer assumes that the input value is available whenever the program requires it.

There are situations when an external system requires that the input value is received by a processor at a time chosen by the source of input rather than by program execution. A typical example is a control system which requires a rapid action when a problem situation arises; for example the control system of an internal combustion engine must react quickly if sensors detect that the oil pressure suddenly

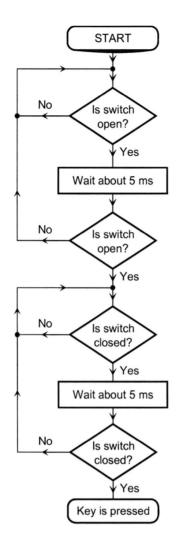

Figure 11.7 Flowchart of the sequence to detect a keyboard switch press

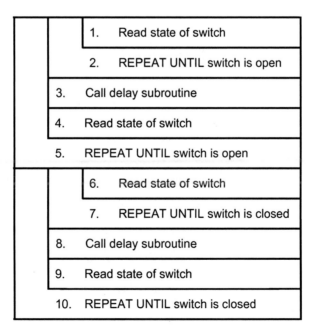

Figure 11.8 NS chart for key press detection

falls or that coolant temperature suddenly rises. In these, and many other cases, a very rapid response is required; the system cannot wait until the program reaches a point at which it performs an input to read and check a sensor reading.

In such cases it is necessary to break the von Neumann fetch-decode-execute sequence. The break is called an **interrupt;** most CPUs provide interrupt facilities but each different CPU type has its own unique form, a brief introduction to ARM interrupts is included in Chapter 13. A general feature of programs that include interrupts is that the rules for well structured programs are broken; it is extremely difficult to construct reliable programs and full proof of correct operation is impossible for any system other than simple laboratory models.

11.7 Summary

IO systems vary greatly and the programmer must understand the operation of the IO hardware to develop IO program modules. The brief examples that have been described illustrate some very simple cases but a much greater range of situations occur in practice. The very important situation of external input signals initiating CPU actions, interrupt inputs, is considered in Chapter 13.

11.8 Problems

11.1 Based on Program 11.1 develop a subroutine for Evaluator-7T, or other development board with a seven segment display, to display the digits 0 to 9 on the display. The subroutine receives a single parameter from the calling program which should be the value 0 to 9; the subroutine specification should state what it does if the parameter is out of range.

Note that if Evaluator-7T is used the decimal point cannot be controlled by the program, it is always on if the system has power applied.

11.2 Using the subroutine from Problem 11.1 and the one second time delay subroutine of Problem 8.1 develop a program that shows the sequence 0, 1, 2, etc., up to 9 then repeats for ever. There must be a one second delay after each new value is shown to enable the sequence to be easily observed.

11.3 Using either semihosting or a UART output to display a single character develop subroutines to

a)   perform a string display operation that outputs any text string with the address of the first character of the string passed to the subroutine as a parameter.

b)   output an unsigned integer (32-bits maximum) as a decimal number.

11.4 Develop a serial input routine for semihosting or UART input. Test it by creating a program loop which receives any serial information sent by Hyperterm or similar terminal program and uses the serial output routine to send the value back to the terminal for display (reflected the input).

Develop a program which outputs a message asking the user to press the Y key if they require the program to run again or the N key if it is to end. The program should behave as requested; if the user presses any key other than Y or N it should output a message stating that the wrong key was pressed and request that a correct key is pressed.

11.5 Using either the semihosting functions or a UART input and output system convert the design of an unsigned integer input program prepared as solutions to the problems of Chapter 2 into a subroutine that obtains a multiple digit unsigned decimal number and returns it as a 32-bit value.

When the routine has been fully tested develop a program which asks for two such numbers in turn then forms their sum and displays this using the subroutine from Problem 11.3(b).

11.6 For any development board available construct a hierarchy chart, NS charts and the corresponding program modules for a program that has a switch input and a seven segment display. Each time the switch is pressed the display moves to the next position in a 0, 1, 2, etc., sequence that loops for ever. The switch input routine should behave as indicated by the sequence of Figure 11.7.

11.7 Many keyboard input systems are programmed to operate in a more complicated manner than Figure 11.7. If a key is pressed for only a short time they behave as Figure 11.7; short usually means a specified time of between two and ten seconds. If the key is held down for longer the system behaves as if the key is repeatedly pressed and released at an interval of about one or two seconds. Design and test a keyboard input routine that behaves in this manner.

12 Utilising ARM Specific Features

Methods of implementing common tasks using assembly language have been described. Although examples use the ARM instruction set and the syntax of the ASD assembler general techniques have been adopted as far as possible and are easily adapted for use with other types of CPU. However, the instruction set of every type of CPU has some unique features; some create problems for the programmer while others provide opportunities for creation of efficient programming techniques.

The restrictions of the RISC structure create some difficulties when devising ARM assembly language programs. For example constant numeric values built into instruction codes, immediate values, must have significantly fewer than 32-bits. However the ability to include several tasks within one instruction code allows one instruction to perform actions that require at least two instructions using some other CPUs. This simultaneous execution of two or more tasks can lead to reduced program size and increased execution speed although the many possibilities can make it difficult to determine the best instruction sequence.

The restricted size of immediate operands with ARM instructions is the main reason for the provision of pseudo instructions. They enable the assembler, instead of the programmer, to determine the most efficient method of loading a register with a value that can be determined before the program is run.

12.1 Use of the mnemonic LDR

When there is more than one method of performing a task in assembly language pseudo instructions determine the most efficient method. The most frequently used pseudo instruction is LDR; it uses many features of the instruction set, the ALU operations, and the shifter capabilities to determine the best method of loading a register with a constant value.

Use of `MOV <Rd>, #<immediate>` only allows values 0 to 255 to be loaded into Rd so MOV cannot be used to load the binary value 11111111111111111111111101001001, hexadecimal 0xffffff49, into a register. However this value is produced by inverting all bits of 0x000000b6. When the LDR pseudo instruction is used the assembler detects this and converts `LDR <Rd>,=0xffffff49` into the code for `MVN <Rd>, #0xb6`. When all the possibilities of selecting MOV or MVN with any immediate value from 0 to 255 combined with rotation by an immediate value are examined many numbers larger than 255 can be loaded using MOV or MVN. Except for small numbers use LDR instead of MOV when an immediate operand is required and let the assembler work out the best method of loading the value. For example it is unlikely that a programmer preparing the instruction sequence to load the negative value –12353 into a register would determine that this can be achieved using MVN with the value 193 rotated 26 places. The assembler converts `LDR r5, =-12353` into the code for the instruction `MVN r5, #0xc1, 26`.

MOV or MVN are the most efficient methods of loading constant values into registers. The assembler determines all possible cases where the LDR pseudo mnemonic can be replaced by either MOV or MVN with an immediate operand that is rotated if necessary. If MOV or MVN cannot be used the assembler stores the required value at the end of the program module in a section of constant data called a **literal pool**. An address is formed using the program counter contents plus an offset value and the value in the literal pool is copied using the instruction `LDR <Rn>, [pc, #±offset]`. The assembler computes the necessary offset taking into account that the pipeline means the program counter changes between the instruction fetch and execution. As the offset range is only ±4095 the programmer may have to force the assembler to create several literal pools for a large program. The assembler produces an error message if the offset is out of range and the directive LTORG is used to create the extra literal pools. Generally if the program has been divided into modules the LTORG directive can be placed at the end of each module when multiple literal pools are necessary; additional guidance is in the ARM assembly language manuals.

The use of the mnemonic LDR for both the real instruction and the pseudo instruction leads to a high risk of errors and great care is required in its use. The risk of error is further increased because there is another form of the real LDR instruction which was not introduced earlier. The pseudo instruction LDR <Rd>,=<user name> causes the assembler to generate an instruction to load register Rd with the numeric value corresponding to the value of <user name>. When the user name is a label the numeric value is the address of the label; in most cases the assembler will put a copy of the address into a literal pool using extra memory and the memory read operation slows program execution. For these cases the alternative pseudo instructions ADR or ADRL, Section 12.2, should be used when possible.

In some situations the best method of loading a register is with another form of the real LDR instruction. This form is LDR <Rd>,<user name> which only differs from the pseudo instruction by the absence of an equals sign. Without the equals sign the instruction loads the value held in memory at the address defined by the user name. Thus LDR <Rd>,=<user name> loads the value of <user name>; when <user name> is a label this is an address. The form LDR <Rd>,<user name> loads the contents of the memory at the location <user name>. A **very small difference in syntax** produces instruction actions which differ greatly. The risk of errors arising because a minor typing mistake is made is high; the programmer must be very careful to type the equals sign when required and omit it when not required.

An important use of this version of LDR is creation of long branches that cannot be performed by the standard branch instruction. Program 12.1 illustrates the best method of creating a long branch; the assembler converts LDR <Rd>,<user name> into the real instruction LDR <Rn>, [pc, #±offset] with the assembler determining the required offset. ARM suggest that the form LDR <Rd>,<user name> should also be the method used in all cases when the instruction LDR <Rn>, [pc, #±offset] is required to load the program counter with a value held in memory at an address defined by a label. For clarity the DCD directive defining the required value should be positioned close to the LDR instruction; for a single branch it should be immediately after it as in Program 12.1.

```
;   perform a branch to label  far_point  where it is too far away for branch
;   or is the result of a calculation not suitable for other forms

            LDR     pc, addr     ; load pc with address held at addr

addr        DCD     far_point    ; required destination set by label or other
                                 ; user value far_point
```

Program 12.1 Partial program using the alternative syntax for LDR

12.2 Other pseudo instructions

The most simple pseudo instruction is NOP; it is a clear short method of writing MOV r0, r0 and provides an obvious method of slowing program execution. Another use is to provide clearly defined positions at which to place breakpoints during development and multiple NOP instructions may be used to leave space for insertion of code still to be prepared or which requires hardware not yet constructed.

The other pseudo instructions are ADR and ADRL which appear to provide a facility available using the LDR pseudo instruction. ADR and ADRL are more efficient than LDR. If a program requires that the address of a position in a program or constant data is loaded into a register a label, for example *xyz*, is placed at the required position then the address can be loaded using LDR <Rn>,=*xyz*. However this is inefficient, the value of the address is put into a literal pool using additional memory locations and the instruction executed reads from memory which is a slow. Using the pseudo instruction ADR *xyz* the assembler determines the amount to add to the present value of the program counter and replaces ADR with either ADD <Rn>, pc, #value,4 or SUB <Rn>, pc, #value,4. ADR is restricted to cases of labels whose addresses are within ±1020 of the program counter. ADRL allows addresses within ±64k to be used although it is unusual as it inserts two instructions into the code sequence. Unlike LDR both ADR and ADRL may only be used with labels in the same code section; that is there must not be an AREA directive between the pseudo mnemonic and the label. Section 12.7 includes examples using ADR.

12.3 ARM assembler behaviour

Assemblers from ARM Holdings plc are very powerful but have a number of unusual features. Those such as the provision of pseudo instructions are very useful although the programmer should be aware that a pseudo instruction may be converted into any one of several different CPU instructions.

A less obvious feature that is not clearly documented is that the assembler sometimes changes one mnemonic into another. This is unusual and removes protection against accidental programmer errors. Such a change by an assembler is usually regarded as dangerous as one reason for using assembly language is that the programmer specifies exactly the instructions to be used. Most assemblers from other suppliers only produce code that corresponds exactly to the mnemonics used by the programmer.

The ARM assembler assumes that the programmer intended to perform the action implied by the instruction plus operands. When the value of <shifter_operand> is not allowed it changes the instruction if possible. Replacement often occurs if immediate operands are outside the range 0 to 255; for example MOV <Rn>, #-5 or ADD <Rn>, <Rm>, #-18. Instead of reporting errors the ARM assembler assumes that the programmer was attempting to perform the action suggested and operands; it converts the two examples into the instructions MVN <Rn>, #4 and SUB <Rn>, <Rm>, #18 respectively.

The assembler also detects cases when the rotate immediate operand may be used to overcome the limitations of the maximum size of a simple immediate operand; it changes an instruction such as ADD <Rn>, <Rm>, #1024 into ADD <Rn>, <Rm>, #1, 22.

There are other many cases where an immediate operand is changed from a simple value into a rotated immediate value or an operation is converted to an inverse one. In addition to changing addition to subtraction, and *vice versa*, the assembler may change OR operations to AND or change AND to OR. The ARM assembler assumes that the programmer's intention is as suggested by the text; **no warning messages are produced** by the ARM assembler when it makes these changes.

12.4 Condition testing

A major feature of almost all computer programs is that programs make decisions that lead to execution of different sections of the program. Usually this process involves determining if some condition is true or false then using the result to select which of two possible sequences of actions to execute next. In many situations conditional execution requires that flag values are set then a conditional instruction is executed.

The logical operations provide a means of setting flags to test for values of single bits or groups of bits as described in Chapter 9. Similarly arithmetic can be used to set flags to for test the size of numbers, for example to find if number *B* is greater than number *A* the programmer may use the instruction SUBS to determine the value of *A* - *B*. As the *'set flags'* suffix is included the flags are set according to the result and can be examined to determine if *B* is greater than *A*; the flag test required depends on the type of numbers represented by *A* and *B*.

There are many test situations where only the flag conditions are required and the numeric result of an operation, such as *A* - *B*, that sets the flags is of no interest. For example when a program plan includes the requirement "IF *X* > *Y* THEN actions" the code produced must perform a subtraction of *X* from *Y* or of *Y* from *X* using an instruction mnemonic that has the *'sets flags'* suffix. A check of the flag states after the subtraction allows the required actions to be performed if the flags indicate that the condition is met. Chapter 6 described use of the compare instruction, CMP, instead of subtract when the numeric result of subtraction is not required. The compare instruction is one of several that assist in creating conditional test structures.

While it does not increase execution time for an ARM processor to put the result of an arithmetic or logic operation into a register it does require that a register is available; that is at least one register is not being used to hold a useful value. Although most ARM registers are not reserved for special purposes the programmer is often using all the registers; the use of a SUBS to set the flags requires that a register is made available for the result. Extra code must save the contents of the chosen register in memory before performing the test then more code restores the register contents. The extra code slows program execution and uses additional memory locations. Most CPUs, including ARM, provide instructions that allow test operations to be performed to set the flags but do not put the numeric result into a register. Although not essential, such instructions are useful and ARM has four test instructions,

```
CMP{<cond>}   <Rn>, <shifter_operand>
CMN{<cond>}   <Rn>, <shifter_operand>
TST{<cond>}   <Rn>, <shifter_operand>
TEQ{<cond>}   <Rn>, <shifter_operand>
```

The test instructions do not have the optional *'set flags'* {S} field as the flags are always updated; the instructions would do nothing if the flags were not changed. There is no destination register, Rd, because there is no result to store. CMP behaves exactly as SUBS except that the numeric result is discarded; similarly CMN is a test version of ADDS, TST is the test form of ANDS and TEQ is the test corresponding to EORS. It is obvious that the CMP instruction could be used instead of SUBS in several earlier programs. For example Program 6.2 earlier is a partial program to implement "IF *X* >= *Y* output *X* ELSE output *Y*"; Program 12.2 is a modified version using CMP instead of SUBS.

```
        . . . .
;   X is in r2 and Y is in r5 (X and Y  are unsigned integers)
          CMP     r2, r5      ; compute X-Y so carry is 0 if Y > X
          BCC     Y_larger    ; skip setting X as output if Y larger
          MOV     r0, r2      ; put X in output register r0
          B       loaded      ; branch to output X
Y_larger  MOV     r0, r5      ; put Y in output register r0
loaded                        ; insert instruction(s) to send contents of r0
                              ; to the display
```

Program 12.2 Revised partial program to implement "IF *X* >= *Y* output *X* ELSE output *Y*"

12.5 Conditional execution

After the flags have been set to indicate some condition the action performed is set by instructions whose behaviour depends on the flag states. The only conditional instructions available for most CPUs are those for conditional branches and conditional structures are implemented in the manner described in Chapter 6. The ARM ability to execute all instructions conditionally allows the creation of efficient code in some situations. This feature is powerful but must be used with care; it can reduce program size and, more importantly, it can reduce the number of branch instructions executed. For a pipelined processor, of RISC or CISC form, a reduction in the number of branch instructions executed increases program execution speed; often the increase is large.

Program 12.2 can be changed to Program 12.3 using conditional forms of MOV instead of conditional branches. The label *loaded* is not required but is retained to allow the forms to be compared.

```
;   X is in r2 and Y is in r5 (X and Y  are unsigned integers)
            CMP     r2, r5         ; compute X - Y so carry is 0 if Y > X
            MOVCS   r0, r2         ; if X >= Y put X in output register r0
            MOVCC   r0, r5         ; otherwise put Y in output register r0
loaded      ****                   ; insert instruction(s) to send contents of r0
                                   ; to the display
```

Program 12.3 Revised Program 12.2 using conditional execution of MOV

The revised version, Program 12.3, requires fewer instructions than the original form and therefore uses less memory to hold the instruction codes. Fewer instructions are executed whenever $X >= Y$ so execution speed is faster; for the alternative $X < Y$ case the number of instructions executed does not change but even in this case execution is faster because no branch instructions are executed.

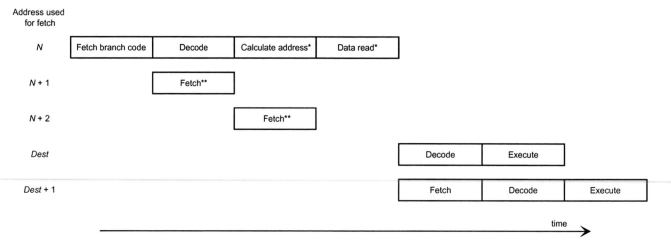

*Calculate branch destination address *Dest* and read data from this address, i.e. fetch instruction at *Dest*
**Codes fetched are discarded

Figure 12.1 ARM7TDMI execution of a branch instruction (simplified)

Whenever it is possible to a program to reduce the number of branch instructions executed any pipelined CPU will execute the program more quickly unless the changes require a large increase in the number of other types of instruction executed. The speed increase arises because after a pipelined CPU executes a branch instruction it has to wait while the pipeline is refilled; the overlapped fetch decode and execute behaviour shown in Figure 3.5 does not apply to branch instructions. Figure 12.1 is a simplified outline of the behaviour of an ARM7TDMI processor executing a branch instruction at address *N*; for simplicity the figure assumes that instructions at all other addresses shown are not multiply, branch or memory data transfer ones. The figure shows that two fetch cycles are performed for which the instructions fetched are discarded and therefore the time to execute a branch is three times that to execute instructions such as arithmetic, logic or MOV that only involve data transfer to and from registers.

Using the conditional forms of MOV in Program 12.3 one of the two actions of the conditional structure executes fewer instructions than Program 12.2; the alternative action executes the same number of instructions. However in the revised version neither action includes any branch instructions so the execution of both branches of the conditional statement is faster than Program 12.2. Another feature is that the amount of memory required for the program code has been reduced by over one third. In applications where the program is permanently fixed in the memory of a product this reduces the amount of memory required which decreases manufacturing cost and power consumption.

The use of conditional forms of instructions instead of creating branches is particularly effective for implementation of the structures

IF   *condition true*   EXECUTE   *actions*

and

IF   *condition true*   EXECUTE   *actions 1*   ELSE   *actions 2*

when all the actions performed conditionally may be executed **using only one or two instructions**.

Optimisation, such as that using conditional execution, which produces more efficient but less obviously structured code must be performed with great care as obscure and difficult to find problems can be created. In particular it might appear that the use of BL*cond   actions1* followed immediately by BL*inverse_cond   actions2* provides a neat method of performing alternative actions but this form is extremely dangerous. There is a high probability that *actions1* will alter the flags so that the condition tested by BL*inverse_cond* is not the expected one. Further BL is a branch instruction so its use does not produce the benefit of avoiding execution of branch instructions.

Optimised code can become particularly obscure when a compound expression has to be evaluated to determine which set of actions must be executed. All examples so far consider simple conditional requirements such as

IF $x > y$ THEN *do actions* 1 ELSE *do actions* 2

whereas in many programs the requirement may be complex; for example

IF $(w > 0)$ AND $(x > y)$ AND $(z = 0)$ THEN *do actions* 1 ELSE *do actions* 2

Brackets are used here to avoid ambiguity in the definition of the condition to be met; even more complex conditions than this example often occur. To fully understand the meaning of expressions defining conditional requirements knowledge of the rules of Boolean algebra and methods of manipulation of Boolean quantities is essential.

There are many ways to develop a program to determine if complex conditions are true or false. The most reliable method for the example of three conditions combined by AND functions is to evaluate all of the terms in brackets as true or false. After this evaluation the results for all three terms are combined using the rules of Boolean algebra to produce a final true or false result which is used to determine which action is to be performed. This is called **complete Boolean evaluation** as every part of the compound conditional expression is evaluated. In some situations, usually for safety critical or financial applications, complete Boolean evaluation is required as part of the specification.

Programs that use an alternative form of evaluation, incomplete Boolean evaluation, are difficult to test rigorously and may contain faults that are not detected during testing. The disadvantage of complete Boolean evaluation is that it usually requires more instructions than incomplete evaluation and the execution time is longer. Highly optimised programs without restrictions in specification usually use incomplete evaluation; the terms in the condition are evaluated systematically and as soon as the value of one term determines the overall result no further terms are evaluated. Figure 12.2 outlines possible sequences of steps to evaluate the $(w > 0)$ AND $(x > y)$ AND $(z = 0)$ for both complete and incomplete evaluation; other sequences are possible in both cases. For complete evaluation temporary Boolean variables $b1$, $b2$ and $b3$ are required to indicate the values of each of the terms in brackets; they represent false by 0 and true by 1. The flowchart for the incomplete case cannot be converted to an NS chart illustrating its poor structural form. Use of a single Boolean variable initially set true and addition of an extra test does allow an NS chart to be drawn.

This example only illustrates evaluation of conditions containing AND operations; it is also necessary to consider OR and inversion operations and all possible combinations of the three operations for expressions containing any number of terms. Such consideration of Boolean evaluation is an important advanced software engineering topic but is beyond the level required for programs examined here.

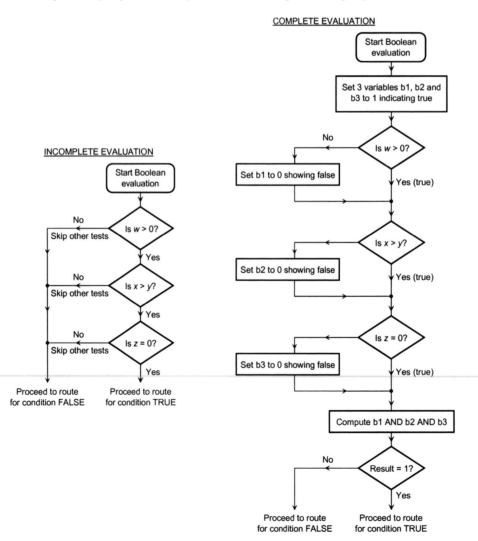

Figure 12.2 Evaluation of IF $(w > 0)$ AND $(x > y)$ AND $(z = 0)$

Using 32-bit words to hold Boolean variables is common even although it is wasteful. The choice of 0 and 1 for false and true respectively matches the convention defined in Chapter 5 with a single bit value 0, clear, representing false and a single bit value 1, set, representing true. Obviously the inverse is possible but as this is the less common approach it should be avoided to reduce the risk of errors.

Programs 12.4 and 12.5 are examples matching the incomplete and complete Boolean evaluation sequences of Figure 12.2; the reader should **attempt** to prepare NS charts for both programs. A small amount of optimisation has been performed using knowledge of the relative addresses of the variables. *addr_w* is used to indicate that a label *addr_w* is the address of variable *w* in the data section. It is assumed that adjacent locations are used for the variables in the order *w*, *x*, *y* and *z* but, provided that they are close together, a similar approach of address incrementing can be used if they are not adjacent. This is not the best method and better techniques to access variables with ARM instructions are described in Section 12.6. For the complete Boolean evaluation of Program 12.5 use of conditional MOV instructions reduces the extent to which this is slower than the incomplete evaluation.

```
; incomplete Boolean evaluation of condition (w > 0) AND (x > y) AND (z = 0)
; to implement  IF condition true DO actions1 ELSE do actions2
; It is assumed w, x, y, z are signed integers in adjacent memory locations
        LDR     r4,=addr_w          ; point to w
        LDR     r5, [r4],#4         ; obtain w and advance pointer to x
        CMP     r5, #1              ; if w - 1 is positive w > 0
        BMI     actions2            ; when w <= 0 branch to ELSE
        LDR     r5, [r4],#4         ; obtain x and advance pointer to y
        LDR     r6, [r4],#4         ; obtain y and advance pointer to z
        CMP     r5, r6              ; if x - y negative x <= y
        BMI     actions2            ; if x <= y branch to ELSE
        LDR     r5, [r4]            ; obtain z
        MOVS    r5, r5              ; find if z = 0
        BNE     actions2            ; if z not 0 branch to ELSE
    ; code for actions1 must follow here
        BAL     endif               ; exit when all actions1 done
actions2
    ; code for actions2, the ELSE actions, must follow here
endif
    ; program continues
```

Program 12.4 Incomplete evaluation of (*w* > 0) AND (*x* > *y*) AND (*z* = 0)

It has been stressed that adequate testing of all programs is essential; the minimum tests of conditional structures were described in Chapter 5. The tests should examine the values of quantities on which a decision is based just before the decision is made, check that the correct value of true or false is found for a wide range of test values, then check that the program follows the correct decision path for every case. It is essential to choose test values so both paths are followed in the testing process. For a complex condition the testing process must ensure that the evaluation of the condition is checked for a wide range of situations. For a condition such as (*w* > 0) AND (*x* > *y*) AND (*z* = 0) the evaluation of each term in brackets should be tested separately using choices of each variable as suggested in Chapter 5. After testing each individual term the combination process should be tested; for this example three Boolean quantities are combined, there are eight, 2^3, different cases shown in Table 12.1.

```
; Partial program for complete evaluation of (w > 0) AND (x > y) AND (z = 0)
; to implement  IF condition true DO actions1 ELSE do actions2
; It is assumed w, x, y, z are signed integers in adjacent memory locations
; Registers r7, r8 and r9 hold temporary Boolean variables b1, b2 and b3
          MOV    r7, #1           ; set b1 to true
          MOV    r8, #1           ; set b2 to true
          MOV    r9, #1           ; set b3 to true
          LDR    r4,=addr_w       ; point to w
          LDR    r5, [r4],#4      ; obtain w and advance pointer to x
          CMP    r5, #1           ; if w - 1 is positive w > 0
          MOVMI  r7, #0           ; if w <= 0 set b1 to false
          LDR    r5, [r4],#4      ; obtain x and advance pointer to y
          LDR    r6, [r4],#4      ; obtain y and advance pointer to z
          CMP    r5, r6           ; if x - y negative x <= y
          MOVPL  r8, #0           ; if x <= y set b2 to false
          LDR    r5, [r4]         ; obtain z
          MOVS   r5, r5           ; find if z = 0
          MOVNE  r9, #0           ; if z not 0 set b3 to false
          AND    r7, r7, r8       ; first AND of full expression
          AND    r7, r7, r9       ; second AND of full expression
          BEQ    actions2         ; full AND evaluates false branch to ELSE
    ; code for actions1 must follow here
          BAL    endif            ; exit when all actions1 done
actions2
    ; code for actions2, the ELSE actions, follows here
    ; all actions2 completed
endif
    ; program continues
```

Program 12.5 Complete evaluation of (*w* > 0) AND (*x* > *y*) AND (*z* = 0)

Using incomplete Boolean evaluation the AND combination of all terms is not always performed; it is still possible to create all eight situations and check that the correct path is followed for every case. For complete Boolean evaluation testing must check that the combination of the three terms produces the correct result in all cases.

w > 0	*x* > *y*	*z* = 0	(*w* > 0) AND (*x* > *y*) AND (*z* = 0)
false	false	false	false
false	false	true	false
false	true	false	false
false	true	true	false
true	false	false	false
true	false	true	false
true	true	false	false
true	true	true	true

Table 12.1 All possible cases of (*w* > 0) AND (*x* > *y*) AND (*z* = 0)

When optimising a program for maximum execution speed using incomplete Boolean evaluation the programmer should determine if any particular term is the one that most often determines the final decision. In such cases the order of evaluation should be adjusted so that this term is the first evaluated.

12.6 ARM memory addressing modes

Manipulation of large data structures should be performed using a high level language; most data handling tasks required in assembly language programs are easily performed using the available ARM addressing modes. The obvious absence for those familiar with CISC systems is a direct addressing mode; there is no instruction allowing the programmer to load a register from a memory address whose complete value is part of the instruction. To perform such a task the programmer must first load another register with the required address, for example with the LDR pseudo instruction, then use LDR Rd, [Rn] to perform the memory transfer. In most embedded system programs the data used within a program module, or the complete program, is located in a single relatively small block of memory locations; efficient programs are often produced if one register is reserved as a base pointer and loaded with the first address of this block.

Once a pointer to the start of a data block is in a register the address of any variable can be determined as an offset added to the pointer. The ability of all ARM memory addressing modes to compute addresses with no additional execution times means that access to variables is relatively fast. However, although as memory transfers for any type of CPU are slower than most other instructions, a well designed program should keep the number of transfers to a minimum.

Manipulation of memory addresses of variables will depend on the particular program requirements. The ability to increment and decrement addresses at the same time as reading memory provides several efficient methods of changing an index or a pointer simultaneously with the memory access. Provision of shift operations as part of the increment process allows pointers to be changed by 2^n which encourages the programmer to make data items 1, 2, 4, 8, 16, *etc.*, bytes in size.

In general the programmer should avoid attempting to compute addresses or rely on knowledge of the address of individual data items within a data set as such actions are prone to error. Instead the assembler should be used to compute addresses. Programs 12.4 and 12.5 have a poor feature; they rely on the programmer knowing that the variables were held in adjacent memory locations. These also continually adjust the pointer used to access memory so the programmer has to keep track of where it is. A better method is to allocate one register, Rp, as a pointer to the start of the data area used within a module and never change this within the module. If the start of the data area is defined by a label, for example *dat_start*, then a variable *x* stored at address *addr_x* is read using the line

```
        LDR     Rd, [Rp, addr_x - dat_start]
```

The assembler and linker together compute *addr_x - dat_start* and build this into the instruction code. At execution time the CPU computes the sum of Rp and the fixed value *addr_x - dat_start*. As the value in Rp is never changed any variable whose address is defined by a label may be accessed in this way. Future program modifications correctly adjust all values. Program 12.6 is a revised version of Program 12.4 using this method; it uses exactly the same number of instructions and is executed in the same time.

In a large program if terms such as *addr_x - dat_start* are used several times it is neater to include a block of definitions in the program heading each with the form

```
off_x           EQU     addr_x - dat_start      ; offset of x from start of data
```

In this brief discussion methods of manipulation of complex data structures have been ignored. The ARM addressing modes allow the programmer to develop several methods of manipulating these efficiently.

```
; Partial program for incomplete evaluation of (w > 0) AND (x > y) AND (z = 0)
; to implement  IF condition true DO actions1 ELSE do actions2
; It is NOT assumed that signed integers w, x, y, z are in adjacent memory
; locations, only that they are in memory starting at dat_start and each is
; defined by a label such as addr_w

        LDR     r4,= dat_start              ; point to start of variables
        LDR     r5, [r4,addr_w - dat_start] ; obtain w
        CMP     r5, #1                      ; if w - 1 positive w > 0
        BMI     actions2                    ; when w <= 0 branch to ELSE
        LDR     r5, [r4,addr_x - dat_start] ; obtain x
        LDR     r5, [r4,addr_y - dat_start] ; obtain y
        CMP     r5, r6                      ; if x - y negative x <= y
        BMI     actions2                    ; if x <= y branch to ELSE
        LDR     r5, [r4,addr_z - dat_start] ; obtain z
        MOVS    r5, r5                      ; find if z = 0
        BNE     actions2                    ; if z not 0 branch to ELSE
    ; code for actions1 must follow here
        BAL     endif               ; exit when all actions1 done

actions2
    ; code for actions2, the ELSE actions, must follow here
    ; all actions2 completed

endif
    ; program continues
```

Program 12.6 Revised incomplete evaluation of ($w > 0$) AND ($x > y$) AND ($z = 0$)

12.7 Selection using case structures

Conditional branch instructions are the ones usually used by any type of CPU to implement conditional selection structures with the form

> IF *condition* THEN *do actions* 1 ELSE *do actions* 2

The ARM ability to conditionally execute any instruction can be used to create very efficient programs when the two alternative actions required are very simple ones. When a multiple selection is required the use of the *'IF'* structure leads to a form such as

> IF $x = value\ 1$ THEN *do actions* 1
> ELSE IF $x = value2$ THEN *do actions* 2
> ELSE IF $x = value3$ THEN *do actions* 3
> ELSE IF $x = value4$ THEN *do actions* 4
> ......and so on.....

For a small number of values of x the most efficient program is one that follows this multiple *'IF'* structure. However, even for a small number of selections this structure is not very clear and when the number of alternatives is large the program is difficult to follow and is inefficient. Instead of multiple *'IF'* statements most formal design methods include a *'case'* or *'switch'* structure; the most simple case structure is one which behaves as Figure 12.3. This defines conditional execution with the actions performed depending on a numeric value rather than the state of some flags. This form of conditional execution does not use the flags to determine which actions are to be performed; instead it uses a numerical value, a case selector also called a case index.

---

case selector *x* has been set. Branch to the block of actions corresponding to the value of *x*.

    Case *x* = 0   Do actions for this case then leave the case structure.

    Case *x* = 1   Do actions for this case then leave the case structure.

    Case *x* = 2   Do actions for this case then leave the case structure.

    Case *x* = 3   Do actions for this case then leave the case structure.

    etc. - actions for all required cases of *x* values.

    ELSE   Do actions, if any, when *x* is not one of the required values.

end of case structure, continue from here for all values of *x*.

Figure 12.3 Organisation of a simple case structure

The minimum number of alternative actions for which a case structure is more efficient than multiple *'IF'* statements varies according to the CPU type, its instruction set, and the detailed program requirements. It is not possible to give a fixed rule that the case structure will be the better form when the number of alternative actions exceeds a specific fixed value, each situation must be examined if the highest speed is essential. However for more than three alternative actions the case structure is usually the best choice as the program behaviour is more easily determined and the risk of faults is lower.

Figure 12.3 implies that only one set of the possible actions is performed for each value of the case selector. Programmers familiar with the C language will find this form unfamiliar; the form used by C is such that after completing actions of one case execution *'falls'* into the next case unless deliberately prevented. A fall into the next case should be avoided; it is a poor structure and leads to programs that are difficult to test and which may have faults that are not detected during testing. In well structured versions of a case statement an ELSE, also called OTHERWISE or DEFAULT, option is always included even if the actions are *'do nothing'*.

There are methods of showing cases in structure charts although many forms are difficult to draw for a large number of options; Figure 12.4 is an example of an NS chart for a case structure when the case selector is an integer *x* with the values illustrated leading to the allowed cases.

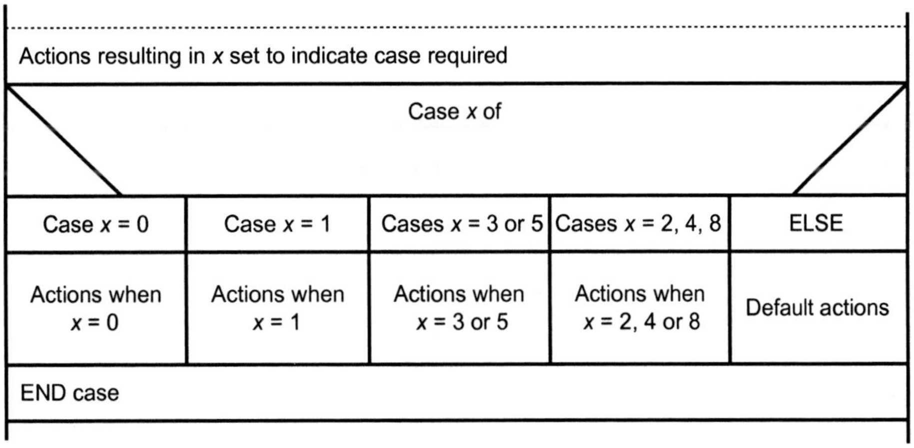

Actions resulting in *x* set to indicate case required				
Case *x* of				
Case *x* = 0	Case *x* = 1	Cases *x* = 3 or 5	Cases *x* = 2, 4, 8	ELSE
Actions when *x* = 0	Actions when *x* = 1	Actions when *x* = 3 or 5	Actions when *x* = 2, 4 or 8	Default actions
END case				

Figure 12.4 NS chart representation of a case structure

Implementation of case structures in an assembly language depends strongly on the type of CPU being used. For some CPUs the general form of the program is similar to that used for ARM but other CPUs have significantly different forms. The case structure requires that a new value is loaded into the program counter by a method other than a branch instruction. The value loaded depends upon the case selector and is the address of the block of instructions that perform the actions that correspond to the case selector value.

For ARM this address load is simple because load operations using the program counter are almost identical to those using any of the general purpose registers. The program counter may be directly loaded with a value using any of the normal register load instructions except that the *'set flags'* behaviour differs. For many other types of CPU a special instruction is provided to copy a value to the program counter. Implementation of a case structure is one of the few situations where the programmer deliberately alters the contents of the program counter.

The case selector can be any variable quantity which has a restricted set of discrete values. The most frequently used forms of selector are unsigned integers or the codes for alphabetic characters. The most simple form is one with the case selector, x, an unsigned integer with the first block of actions corresponding to $x = 0$, the second block to $x = 1$, the third to $x = 2$, and so on. In the program each block of actions is given a label corresponding to the value of x which selects the block; here *actions0*, *actions1*, *actions2*, etc., are used as the labels for the blocks. A well documented program either uses labels that identify the case index or describe the purpose of the block. An unsigned integer was chosen as the selector therefore it cannot be less than 0 and as 0 is used as an index value it is only necessary to provide a check that the index is not greater than the largest allowed value.

Program 12.7 is a framework of the code for one method of implementing this case structure; it is assumed that x is less than 256 as it would be very unusual for an assembly language program to select from more cases. The program uses a branch table to list the addresses of all the action blocks in order by the case selector value. It is then straightforward to use the value of the case selector x determined during execution to obtain the address of the required action block.

The sequence of actions that must be performed to implement this simple case structure is

- Check that case selector is in the allowed range. If it is not branch to the default actions.
- Obtain the address of the start of the branch table.
- Compute the address of entry number x in the branch table.
- Obtain entry number x from the branch table.
- Load the value obtained from the branch table into the program counter, that is set the program counter to the start address of the required block of actions.
- Perform the required block of actions then branch to the exit point of the case structure.

Program 12.7 illustrates the use of the ADR pseudo instruction described in Section 12.1 to transfer the start address of the branch table to a register.

This example also demonstrates the use of the EQU directive to determine the number of values for which actions are defined. Two labels are used to determine how many memory locations are used; as each label value is an address requiring four bytes the number of memory locations used is divided by four to give the number of branch destinations. Again it is good practice to use the assembler, rather than the programmer, to determine a numeric quantity. If the number of branches is modified in the future the assembler will automatically change the number of branches calculated reducing the risk of errors being introduced when such changes are made.

```
; case selector x is in register r2 and is less than 256
        CMP     r2, #num_vals       ; check for x greater than allowed
        BPL     default             ; go to actions if x too large
        ADR     r1, table           ; get start of branch table
        ADD     r1, r1, r2, LSL#2   ; add four times x to branch table
                                    ; start (each entry requires 4 bytes)
        LDR     pc, [r1]            ; copy address from branch table to pc
; branch table, shows address of each set of actions
table   DCD     actions0
        DCD     actions1
        DCD     actions2
        ---- include as many branch addresses as necessary
table_end                           ; set a label just after the table

num_vals EQU    (table_end - table)/4   ; work out how many values

; next are the instructions for each set of actions (it is sensible - but
; not essential to put them in order of the case selector value)
actions0
        ; include all instructions for actions0
        B       case_exit           ; rejoin main sequence at structure end

actions1
        ; include all instructions for actions1
        B       case_exit           ; rejoin main sequence
; -- continue with blocks of actions for each case

default
        ; include all instructions for default (x too large)
        B       case_exit           ; not necessary if case_exit next

case_exit       ; continue main program sequence
```

Program 12.7 Framework of a simple case structure

A further improvement can be made by using one of the memory addressing modes described in Appendix D. The instructions

```
        ADD     r1, r1, r2, LSL#2   ; add four times x to branch table
                                    ; start (each entry requires 4 bytes)
        LDR     pc, [r1]            ; copy address from branch table to pc
```

may be replaced by the single instruction

```
        LDR     pc, [r1, r2, LSL#2] ;****
        ; **** add four times x to branch table start (each entry requires 4
        ;      bytes) and use as address to copy value from branch table to pc
```

Several further minor modifications can be easily made. For example when the default case action is to do nothing the branch to the label *default* can be replaced by branch to label *case_exit* and the default block removed. For documentation purposes the label *default* may be retained with no mnemonics between this label and label *case_exit*; the assembler allows two or more labels to be placed so they define the same address.

The case selector in Program 12.7 is an unsigned integer which may take every value from 0 to the maximum used; this is the most simple form. A slightly more complicated situation occurs when the range of values is continuous but does not start at 0 or when the case selector is a signed integer. For these the initial check of the selector value, x, must ensure that it is not below the minimum allowed as well that it is not too large. This check may be combined with instructions that calculate x minus the start value; four times the result of this subtraction is added to the table start address instead of four times x.

Further complications arise when the list of allowed case selector values is random in nature. Simple situations, such as that shown by the NS chart of Figure 12.4, where some selector values are not used and other actions are the same for more than one value can be handled with a slightly more complicated branch table. When two action blocks are identical only one need be created and the label for the block is put at both positions in the branch table. When a value is not used the table entry is the same address as that used for the default case of the selector not being in the allowed range. For the example case condition of Figure 12.4 the branch table would be that shown as Program 12.8.

```
table    DCD      actions0
         DCD      actions1
         DCD      actions2
         DCD      actions3
         DCD      actions2     ; case 4 same as 2
         DCD      actions3     ; case 5 same as 3
         DCD      default      ; case 6 is not used
         DCD      default      ; case 7 is not used
         DCD      actions2     ; case 8 same as 2
```

Program 12.8 Branch table for Figure 12.4 requirements

When the case selector values are more randomly spaced over a large range an alternative approach is required. For example a simple program may require the user to press a key on a keyboard to select some action to be performed and only a few keys of all those available may be allowed. Often the letters chosen correspond to the initial letters of the action names as this assists the user. A simple communication device might use A for answer, G for go, H for help, Q for quit or end, and S for save. Assuming that only upper case letters are allowed and are represented by ASCII codes the corresponding case statement would have to act on code values 65, 71, 72, 81 and 83; even subtracting the smallest value of 65 from all the values does not produce a useful set of values.

The method of overcoming the rather random, dis-ordered, list of values is to convert the random list to a simple one producing all the values 0, 1, 2, *etc.*, up to the maximum required and then acting as Program 12.7; this method of converting a dis-ordered list into an ordered one has many other programming applications. The conversion requires an extra list; the allowed case selector items are themselves put into a list which is searched; the case selector is converted to the numeric position of the value in the list. Program 12.9 is a framework of a program for allowed case selector values of the ASCII codes for A, G, H, Q and S.

It is possible to *'improve'* this framework although generally this increases complexity which makes the program more difficult to understand and increases the risk of errors. Counting down a fixed number of times is easier to program than count up because the Z flag provides a simple test for the end of the count. However when a match is found either the list position determined by the count has to be corrected to give the correct position in the branch table or, alternatively, one of the lists, but not both, must be written in the reverse order.

```
                . . . .
;  case selector x is in register r0 and is an ASCII code
            ADR     r1, keys            ; point to list of valid keys
            MOV     r2, #0              ; initialise a counter
            MOV     r3, #0xff          ; code to show no match found
        ; *** repeat until all checked (more simple than exit when match found)
repeat      LDR     r4,[r1],#1         ; get key from list and advance pointer
            CMP     r0, r4             ; check x against code just obtained
            MOVEQ   r3, r2             ; if a match list position into r3
            ADDS    r2,r2,#1           ; increment loop counter
            CMP     r2,#num_vals       ; check if done correct times
            BMI     repeat             ; loop if still more to do
        ; *** end of repeat loop
            CMP     r3, #num_vals      ; check for no match code
            BPL     default            ; actions if x too large
            ADR     r1, table          ; get start of branch table
            LDR     pc, [r1, r3, LSL#2] ; table entry from branch table to pc
;  branch table, shows address of each set of actions
table       DCD     actionsA
            DCD     actionsG
            DCD     actionsH
            DCD     actionsQ
            DCD     actionsS
table_end                              ; set a label just after the table
num_vals    EQU     (table_end - table)/4 ; determine how many values

keys        DCB     "AGHQS"
;  follow the table with each set of actions (it is sensible - but not
;  necessary to put them in order
actionsA        ; include all instructions for case when key was 'A'
            B       case_exit          ; rejoin main sequence after all blocks

actionsG        ; include all instructions for case when key was 'G'
            B       case_exit          ; rejoin main sequence after all blocks

            ; -- continue for all other case actions

default         ; include all instructions for default which could be to
                ; indicate that the wrong key was pressed
            B       case_exit          ; not necessary if case_exit next
case_exit       ; continue main program sequence
```

Program 12.9 Framework of a case structure for a random list of case selectors

An alternative to finding the list end by the count value is to place a terminator at the list end; the search ends either when a match is found or when the terminator is reached. The count value is still required to indicate the position of the required entry if found; a count value one higher than the last entry indicates that the search was not successful.

List searching is a common task which is required in many data processing tasks as well as for implementation of a case structure. Most applications that manipulate large amounts of data perform list searches. If the list is short a simple search is adequate and the most simple program structure is when all list entries are checked as in Program 12.9. However for longer lists it is worth ending the search when a match is found even although this is slightly more complex. For searches of very long lists more advanced software techniques are required as a simple search from the start would be extremely slow.

When multiple conditions are unrelated, for example as

IF $w > 5$ THEN *do actions* 1
ELSE IF $x = y$ THEN *do actions* 2
ELSE IF $z = 24$ THEN *do actions* 3
ELSE IF $a + b > c$ THEN *do actions* 4
......and so on.....

a case structure is not the most obvious method of creating the program. A first comment is that a structure of multiple decisions based on unrelated variables is usually the result of poor program design. If possible the design should be revised, a program following this sequence will be difficult to understand and test. However there are circumstances were multiple nested IF statements are essential. If the sections of program required for each action are large a program will not be easy to understand and will probably contain errors. One solution is to make each block of actions a subroutine; an alternative is to create a new unsigned integer variable k and set it for each statement as

Set k = default value when no condition is true.
IF $w > 5$ THEN $k = 0$
ELSE IF $x = y$ THEN $k = 1$
ELSE IF $z = 24$ THEN $k = 2$
ELSE IF $a + b > c$ THEN $k = 3$
......and so on.....

The program then is constructed as a multiple set of IF statements with a single action setting k followed by the simple case structure. Setting a default value is essential for reliable program behaviour, also it is important to note that the behaviour of the version

Set k = default value when no condition is true.
IF $w > 5$ THEN $k = 0$
IF $x = y$ THEN $k = 1$
IF $z = 24$ THEN $k = 2$
IF $a + b > c$ THEN $k = 3$
......and so on.....

is not the same as the version with ELSE. The behaviour of the form without ELSE is not as obvious and **should be avoided**. If only the first four settings are used it behaves in exactly the same manner as

Set k = default value when no condition is true.
IF $a + b > c$ THEN $k = 3$
ELSE IF $z = 24$ THEN $k = 2$
ELSE IF $x = y$ THEN $k = 1$
ELSE IF $w > 5$ THEN $k = 0$

which is easier to understand; note that the order of evaluation is reversed in this situation. The reader should examine the behaviour of all forms of complicated conditional statements and study the possible obscure problems that can arise to ensure that they are avoided.

Processes to test case statements are similar to those for testing other conditional structures; it is essential to check that every possible option is executed and behaves as specified. A wide range of cases with the selector not an allowed value must be checked to ensure that they are correctly identified.

12.8 Further flag handling instructions

In well structured ARM programs it should not be necessary to manipulate the flags by methods other than their automatic setting by execution of instructions with the set flags suffix included or by the four test instructions. In general the requirement for an ARM system to save the flags when only a single program is running should never arise. However for systems which run several tasks or programs *apparently* simultaneously, and in some cases where optimisation is performed, it may be necessary to manipulate the flags. This is an advanced topic usually involving start up and exceptions described briefly in Chapter 13.

ARM7TDMI has four flags and they are the four most significant bits of the register CPSR. The allocation of all bits in CPSR is shown in Figure 12.5.

```
31 30 29 28 27                                              8  7  6  5  4  3  2  1  0
┌──┬──┬──┬──┬──┬──┬──┬──┬──┬──┬──┬──┬──┬──┬──┬──┬──┬──┬──┬──┬──┬──┬──┬──┬──┬──┬──┬──┬──┬──┐
│N │Z │C │V │u │u │u │u │u │u │u │u │u │u │u │u │u │u │u │u │u │u │u │u │ I│ F│ T│ M│ M│ M│ M│ M│
└──┴──┴──┴──┴──┴──┴──┴──┴──┴──┴──┴──┴──┴──┴──┴──┴──┴──┴──┴──┴──┴──┴──┴──┴──┴──┴──┴──┴──┴──┴──┘
```

u - undefined for ARM7TDMI (reserved for use in future architecture versions)

Figure 12.5 The contents of CPSR.

There are two instructions to copy values to and from CPSR; they have several allowed operands and the forms commonly met are

```
MRS{<cond>}    <Rd>, CPSR
MSR{<cond>}    CPSR_<fields>, #<immediate>
MSR{<cond>}    CPSR_<fields>, <Rm>
```

The action of MRS is to copy the contents of the status register to any of the registers r0 to r15; as for most instructions the effect of using r15, the program counter, as the destination is unpredictable.

MSR copies an immediate value or the contents of any register r0 to r15 to the status register although in many situations only the flag bits of CPSR are changed, the values of other bits do not change. CPSR has protection features and in normal operation only the flag bits may be changed. Some assemblers use CPSR alone as the operand with MSR but most assemblers require qualification by the use of fields. In addition to the flags CPSR holds a number of important bits which control CPU behaviour, the use of a field qualifier ensures that only the bits of interest are changed. The contents of CPSR are shown in Figure 12.5, at this time the only the flags are of concern so CPSR_f is used where _f indicates the flag field, bits 24 to 31 (not all used for ARM7TDMI). The only other field used for ARM7TDMI is the control field of bits 0 to 7 identified as _c; in normal use the MSR instruction does not change these bits even if the instruction `MSR{<cond>}   CPSR_c, <Rm>` is executed.

12.9 Programming style and optimisation

Well structured programs that are easily understood by others are an essential requirement of all programs created to control engineering and commercial systems. Ease of understanding can be affected by choices made by the programmer; whenever possible the selection should be the one that most clearly shows the task being performed and the manner in which it is executed.

Examples in this chapter have suggested program modifications to optimise the code. Optimisation is performed either to reduce the amount of memory required to hold a program, optimisation for size; or to improve the speed of execution, optimisation for speed. In some cases optimisation performs both, in others the forms are incompatible and the most appropriate must be selected. While higher speed or smaller code are desirable improvements the first aim of a programmer must be to produce code that fully meets the requirements and has no errors. In some cases optimisation makes the code easier to understand but in many situations the optimised code is difficult to follow increasing the risk of errors; it also makes testing and future modification difficult. Optimisation should only be attempted when it is essential and should be performed after a well structured fully tested program has been produced; the original version should be retained for reference and the optimised version should have comments indicating how it differs from the original.

Care in design of a program produces some optimisation. For example if many operations use a particular variable performing them all close together may reduce the number of times the variable is transferred between registers and memory. Use of fewer transfer instructions reduces the amount of memory for the code; it also improves speed because memory transfer operations are slow.

Generally a reduction in the number of memory transfers produces a greater speed improvement than reduction in the number of simple arithmetic, logic and move instructions. Positioning operations that use a variable close together is good practice as it is easier to understand the program and, in addition to improving speed, it reduces the risk of errors. Chapter 6 illustrated an example of optimisation improving clarity; moving the output actions from both branches of an *'IF-ELSE'* structure to just after the structure showed clearly that output was always performed. It also reduced the number of output instructions required. If an action is present in all routes through a conditional section of program it should be moved into the unconditional part of the program whenever possible.

Programmers of CISC type CPUs will find some ARM programming practices unusual. In general a CISC programmer would not set three registers to the same constant value as in Program 12.5 which has

```
MOV     r7, #1              ; set b1 to true
MOV     r8, #1              ; set b2 to true
MOV     r9, #1              ; set b3 to true
```

This is because fetch of an immediate operand by a CISC processor is often slower than register to register transfer and may also require more memory. An experienced CISC programmer would choose

```
MOV     r7, #1              ; set b1 to true
MOV     r8, r7              ; set b2 to true
MOV     r9, r7              ; set b3 to true
```

As all ARM instructions are exactly 32-bits both methods of loading the same small value into several registers use the same amount of memory and execute in the same time. The first version is probably better because it reduces the risk errors if the program is modified by changing the value loaded into the first register. There is a possibility that during modification the programmer does not detect that this causes an incorrect change to the values put into other registers. However when the pseudo instruction LDR is used the register to register copy should be used to put the same value in several registers. For example, unless the programmer wishes to stress the value loaded the form

```
LDR     r7, =456789
MOV     r8, r7
MOV     r9, r7
```

should be used rather than three separate LDR pseudo instructions. This is because pseudo instructions may use memory to hold constants in a literal pool and generate memory transfer instructions which execute more slowly than the register to register copy. Comments should be included to indicate clearly that copy instructions have been used to load initial values to reduce the possibility of errors being created when future modifications are required

Register contents can be set to zero using any one of the instructions MOV rX, #0 or SUB rX, rX, rX or EOR rX, rX, rX. All three instructions use the same amount of memory and take the same time to execute. For a CISC processor the exclusive-OR instruction often requires less memory, is the fastest, and forces most flags into a known condition. Hence experienced CISC programmers tend to use the exclusive-OR to set register contents to zero and simultaneously set the flags to a known state. Such actions are often required by initialisation sections of a program or program module.

Because the ARM carry flag setting rules are complicated and the overflow flag is not affected for MOVS and EORS the exclusive-OR instruction will not set all the flags to known conditions. The ARM programmer should use the SUBS rX, rX, rX instruction if it is necessary to set a register to zero and force the flags to a known state. When only register contents are to be set to zero with the flags left unchanged the instruction MOV rX, #0 is probably the best choice as the action being performed is immediately apparent.

In general optimisation requires that the programmer has detailed knowledge of how the CPU executes each instruction. For example anyone programming more advanced variants of the ARM core should be aware that the more complex pipeline structures of ARM9 and higher versions are such that some modification to programming style is necessary for high speed, especially when using instructions to load registers from memory. The sequence of LDR Rx, [addr mode] immediately followed by ADD Ra, Rb, Rx is not affected by the pipeline when using ARM7. However on higher versions this is slow because the CPU starts executing the ADD before the value from LDR is in Rx. The CPU recognises this and waits until the value is in Rx before performing the ADD. In many programs it is possible to put the LDR instruction slightly earlier than it is required so that other useful actions are executed between LDR and ADD removing the period the CPU waits doing nothing.

12.10 Summary

All CPUs have their own unique features; the most obvious features of ARM that are unusual are building an instruction from many components and the ability to execute all instructions conditionally. Because an ARM instruction code has many components the most efficient method of performing some tasks is not always easily determined. To assist the assembly language programmer pseudo instructions are provided which enable the programmer to use the assembler to determine the best method of implementing some commonly required tasks.

Evaluation of conditions and conditional execution are essential features that allow computer programs to make decisions. Conditional execution of all instructions by ARM is one reason that it is a very powerful processor. In particular this feature allows some conditional statements to be executed without branch instructions producing a significant increase in speed. Simple use can be made of this in assembly language but full benefit is usually obtained when using highly optimising high level language compilers.

Usually the best method of forming conditional structures that lead to many possible alternative actions is to create a multi-way case selection. This is readily implemented on ARM because the program counter is manipulated as one of the general purpose registers and a value in another register or memory may be transferred directly to the program counter, the value may even be modified before the transfer.

In general good program design will produce some optimisation of programs. Any further optimisation should only be performed if it is essential. A full understanding of the CPU operation and any special features of the memory system are necessary to achieve the best results.

12.11 Problems

12.1　For each of the following pseudo instructions determine (without writing and assembling a program) the ARM instruction that will replace the pseudo instruction. If an offset is required state how this will be determined; do not attempt to compute the value of any offset and assume that the offset is within the allowed range.

```
LDR   r1,=0x56
LDR   r1,=0x54000003
LDR   r4,=0x003c0000
ADR   r3, xyz  ; label xyz is a higher address than this instruction
ADR   r5, abc  ; label abc is a lower address than this instruction
```

12.2　Figure 12.1 outlines the code to execute a conditional branch by an ARM7TDMI. Produce similar figures (more than one sequence can occur) showing the fetch, decode and execute steps for all the instructions up to, and including, the SUB instruction when an ARM7TDMI executes the following code sequence, Branch instruction timing is as in Figure 12.1, all other instructions are simple ones with timing as Figure 3.5.

```
         MOV   r1, #5
         MVN   r4, #3
abc      ADDS  r4, r4, r1
         BCS   abc
         BMI   xyz
         MOV   r1, #0xff
xyz      SUB   r3, r3, r1
         NOP
         NOP
```

12.3　Develop flowcharts similar to Figure 12.2 to show sequences for complete and incomplete Boolean evaluation of the condition $(w > 0)$ OR $(x > y)$ OR $(z = 0)$. Convert the flowcharts into NS charts.

12.4　Develop flowcharts similar to Figure 12.2 to show sequences for complete and incomplete Boolean evaluation of the condition $(w > 0)$ OR $(x > y)$ AND $(z = 0)$. Convert the flowcharts into NS charts. This problem requires knowledge of the precedence of Boolean operators. In a normal algebraic equation, such as $a + b \times c$, it is conventional to perform the multiplication before the addition. The multiply operation is defined as having a higher precedence than the addition one. Similarly in Boolean algebra the AND operation has higher precedence than OR (and inversion has higher precedence than AND) so the condition must be evaluated as $(w > 0)$ OR $((x > y)$ AND $(z = 0))$, that is the AND is always evaluated before the OR unless extra brackets are used to override the precedence.

13 ARM Hardware

Most CPUs, including ARM, have extra hardware to allow the CPU to break out of the conventional von Neumann sequence, Figure 1.4. Most of the additional features support tasks that must be performed at very high speed or they provide mechanisms to detect problems. A common method of breaking the standard sequence is an interrupt; a signal at an interrupt input causes the CPU to respond quickly to an external event. A related feature is the start or reset mechanism which is an extreme form of interrupt.

Special CPU hardware features are complex and are often configured by software in a process similar to that for IO devices, Chapter 11. Hardware configuration is usually the first task of a complete program and is often performed using an assembly language program. Detailed knowledge of the hardware is required to prepare the program and requirements are unique for each CPU type or variant.

Previously configuration was ignored; during initial development tasks associated with power on, reset and interrupts are performed by the development system. However a complete final program requires inclusion of instructions to configure all features. Many applications of ARM processors are in embedded systems and the final software is a single program in read only memory, ROM, that automatically runs when power is connected or the system is reset. Other applications require that the program is loaded into RAM by some mechanism that starts it running after loading. Different mechanisms for loading and running programs require different initialisation code sequences.

13.1 Processor start up

When power is first connected, or when a reset switch is operated, the CPU and some IO systems automatically perform a few essential tasks. These disable complicated hardware features and the program counter is set to a specified value. The flag states, the contents of all registers except the program counter and CPSR_c, and contents of all read and write memory locations settle to random values at power on. Use of register or memory contents before they have well defined values will cause incorrect program behaviour. Such errors are not always obvious; for example ARM development systems set all register contents to zero whereas a CPU running without any development tools will start with random values in the registers. In critical applications tests should be performed using extra initialisation code. After the minimum amount of code essential to configure hardware this initialisation code should be the first executed; it should load all registers, except the program counter, and all memory locations with a set of initial values. Results of program execution with several different sets of initial values should be compared to check that behaviour does not depend on the initial values.

At power on or reset ARM processors force the program counter to zero and disable most special hardware features. The first action is to execute the instruction at address zero; as addresses immediately following are reserved for special purposes the instruction at address zero must load the program counter with a new address. The instruction at address zero may be branch always or may load the program counter using a real LDR instruction or an LDR or ADR pseudo instruction.

Usually the instruction at address zero branches to an initialisation program section that configures the hardware and creates the software environment. The software environment is created by setting pointers and similar items to define areas of memory for specific uses. For a very simple program the only software setting is the stack pointer; more complex programs require additional settings. Hardware configuration is often performed first but if complex IO devices are configured using subroutines the stack pointer must be set before, or part way through, the section of program configuring the hardware.

If necessary the initialisation section also sets contents of some registers and memory locations to specified values. Once the initialisation tasks are complete a simple program then executes its main function or main module.

Preparation of a program to be permanently fixed in a ROM such that it is the only program ever used by the system is straightforward. The hardware is designed with the ROM located at a block of consecutive memory addresses starting at zero. The program has an instruction at address zero that causes execution to move to an area of the ROM above the reserved area; these higher addresses contain the initialisation code, the main program, all other code modules and any constant data. A typical start up code sequence for systems with a simple program in ROM is described in Section 13.5.

For other systems many different situations occur and each requires its own solution to the problem of constructing a complete program. For example many development systems have a mechanism to copy the program code into the RAM and start it running. More complex systems, such as general purpose computer systems, require that there is an operating system program permanently in memory to control the loading and running of all other programs. The range of possible systems is large; any consideration of these is an advanced topic that is not examined.

13.2 ARM modes

ARM has seven operating modes plus a special software mode called THUMB that may be used in any operating mode. The operating modes provide extra features for efficient execution of some tasks and use the extra registers shown in the Programmer's Model, Figure 13.1. In all previous programs only the registers shown as unshaded boxes with a solid border were used; these registers are associated with the normal operating or user mode and with system mode. When running in one of the other modes each user mode register is replaced by the alternative register for the selected mode when there is one, these alternative registers are shown as shaded boxes in Figure 13.1. If there is no alternative register the user mode register is used; in Figure 13.1 a copy of the user registers is drawn with broken lines to stress that the user mode register is used. Symbols with the form _xxx indicate that the name of an alternative mode must be used in place of _xxx; for user mode there is no addition to the register name. The extension _xxx added to the register name is **not used in assembly language**; it is only used in descriptions to show that the actual registers used are set according to the mode. When a program uses several modes the programmer must ensure that the code being executed matches the mode in use.

The programmer always has sixteen registers r0 to r15 and the CPSR register available but the actual registers r8 to r14 used are not always the same physical registers. Sometimes a register SPSR_xxx is also available. For example if a program executes the instruction MOV r14, r1 then in all modes the source operand is the same register r1, there is only one r1 register. However in user and system modes the destination register is r14. If the processor is in FIQ mode the destination register is r14_fiq, in supervisor mode it is r14_svc, and so on. For all modes the same single set of registers r0 to r7, r15 (pc) and CPSR are used. For the mode _fiq all registers r8 to r14 are replaced by r8_fiq to r14_fiq and for all other modes except system mode the user mode registers r8 to r12 are used but r13 and r14 are replaced by the alternatives, r13_xxx and r14_xxx. All modes except user and system have their own special stored program status registers, SPSR_xxx.

user mode	system mode	FIQ mode	supervisor mode	abort mode	IRQ mode	undef mode
r0	r0	r0	r0	r0	r0	r0
r1	r1	r1	r1	r1	r1	r1
r2	r2	r2	r2	r2	r2	r2
r3	r3	r3	r3	r3	r3	r3
r4	r4	r4	r4	r4	r4	r4
r5	r5	r5	r5	r5	r5	r5
r6	r6	r6	r6	r6	r6	r6
r7	r7	r7	r7	r7	r7	r7
r8	r8	r8_fiq	r8	r8	r8	r8
r9	r9	r9_fiq	r9	r9	r9	r9
r10	r10	r10_fiq	r10	r10	r10	r10
r11	r11	r11_fiq	r11	r11	r11	r11
r12	r12	r12_fiq	r12	r12	r12	r12
r13	r13	r13_fiq	r13_svc	r13_abt	r13_irq	r13_und
r14	r14	r14_fiq	r14_svc	r14_abt	r14_irq	r14_und
r15 (pc)	r15 (pc)	r15 (pc)	r15 (pc)	r15 (pc)	r15 (pc)	r15 (pc)
CPSR	CPSR	CPSR	CPSR	CPSR	CPSR	CPSR
		SPSR_fiq	SPSR_svc	SPSR_abt	SPSR_irq	SPSR_und

Figure 13.1 Register use in each mode (broken lines indicate the user mode register is used)

The modes are associated with features required by many applications; additional hardware is necessary in some cases. A common requirement is that some program sections should be protected; the '*user*' cannot alter some important quantities. '*user*' may describe a person using the system or may be another task that is a separate part of the program. Often there is often a requirement to respond quickly to external events indicated by signals applied to interrupt inputs. Other types of event are internal conditions that are a result of actions by the program. All events may be classed together as **exceptions**.

For many microcontroller applications the ability to respond quickly to external events is particularly important; RISC systems are able to react quickly and a fast response is assisted by changing some, or all, of the CPU registers being used. This is register bank switching, it provides fast program context switching. This ensures that values that must be preserved are kept in registers which are not accessible while code associated with the cause of the exception runs; the preserved values are automatically restored when the system reverts to the original mode after completing the exception code.

Mode	Registers	Use	CPSR bits [4..0]
user	user	Normal user programs	10000
FIQ	_fiq	Processing fast interrupts	10001
IRQ	_irq	Processing standard interrupts	10010
supervisor	_svc	Reset (start up) and processing software interrupts, SWI	10011
abort	_abt	Processing memory faults	10111
undef	_und	Handling undefined instructions	11011
system	user	Privileged operating system tasks	11111

Table 13.1 ARM operating modes

Table 13.1 lists the seven ARM operating modes; the mode in which the CPU is operating is defined by the value of the mode bits, bits 0 to 4, in register CPSR. The mode can be changed in several ways; one method is to write a new value to CPSR using the instruction MSR described in Chapter 12. However an important restriction is that when in user mode, the normal operating mode, the instruction MSR cannot write to bits 0 to 4 of CPSR; if the instruction code to write to the bits is executed it will be ignored. This is a protection feature; execution of *'user'* program instructions cannot easily change mode hence it is possible to arrange that features of the hardware and software can only be changed by special tasks which are run in another mode. Modes other than user mode are privileged ones, they can freely change to another mode by changing the mode bits of the CPSR although most mode changes are not made this way. Changing the CPSR mode bits to a value that does not correspond to an allowed mode has unpredictable effects.

A complete description of the modes, their purpose and how to use them is beyond the level of this book. However an introduction is necessary to describe a complete program that includes the start up code and other essential features.

After power on or operation of a reset mechanism the CPU is in supervisor mode; reset is an extreme form of interrupt. Supervisor mode allows the initialisation section of the program to set up some features to restrict the actions of a user program. Implementing the restrictions is complicated and often requires additional hardware. The initialisation code is normally designed to configure software and hardware and usually ends with the instruction MSR to change CPSR bits [4..0], the mode bits, to 10000 causing the CPU to change to run in user mode. This MSR instruction may also be used to set the interrupt enable bits I and F to the required values but an MSR instruction is not the usual method of changing the THUMB control bit T.

Once in user mode the only way to leave it is by an exception; that is by a hardware or software created event. Some exceptions are always accepted but there are mechanisms to prevent the FIQ and IRQ exceptions being accepted while critical sections of a program are being executed. When an exception causes a change to another mode the CPU executes the program code associated with the exception; this code usually ends with a return to the original mode.

The common method of organising a complete ARM program is to arrange that the main function runs in user mode. A change is made from user mode to another mode to perform some special task associated with the exception that caused the mode change; after performing the special task the program returns to user mode. Sometimes another exception may occur while the system is in one of the special modes and this may cause a second mode change. The overall sequence in such cases is usually to change from user mode to some mode A then to another mode B; from mode B back to mode A and finally back to user mode. Obviously more complicated sequences may occur; such sequences are closely related to subroutine nesting and require that the program sections associated with exceptions are constructed in a similar manner to subroutines.

13.3 Exceptions

The ARM7TDMI (architecture version v4T) CPU implements the seven types of exception, these are summarised in Table 13.2. An exception is an event that usually requires the CPU to perform an action which is not part of the normal program sequence. That is an exception causes the CPU to stop executing instructions in the normal von Neumann sequence and perform some other instructions; consequently the use of exceptions results in poorly structured programs that are difficult to test.

Exception type	Mode	Mode name	Vector address (normal)
Reset	supervisor	_svc	0x00000000
Undefined instructions	undefined	_und	0x00000004
Software interrupt – SWI	supervisor	_svc	0x00000008
Prefetch abort (instruction fetch memory abort)	abort	_abt	0x0000000C
Data abort (data access memory abort)	abort	_abt	0x00000010
Not used, vector address reserved for future use	----		0x00000014
IRQ – interrupt	IRQ	_irq	0x00000018
FIQ – fast interrupt	FIQ	_fiq	0x0000001C

Table 13.2 ARM Exceptions

When an exception corresponding to a change to mode _xxx occurs and is accepted the actions that follow are:-

- The execute step of the instruction in progress is completed unless the exception is a reset or data abort. For reset the response is instant; for data abort the instruction completes execution but the data value transferred is indeterminate.

- The register r14_xxx is loaded with a copy of the program counter; that is as for a subroutine the link address is saved but r14_xxx is used instead of the register r14 for the mode that was active when the exception occurred.

- SPSR_xxx is loaded with a copy of the contents of CPSR before these are changed by the exception actions; hence a copy of the current status is retained.

- After a reset the values in r13_svc and r14_svc are undefined.

- Mode bits, CPSR bits 0 to 4, are loaded with the code for the new mode that corresponds to the mode associated with the exception.

- CPSR bits 5, 6 and 7 may be changed; these control the acceptance of FIQ and IRQ interrupts and the operation of THUMB mode.

- If the CPU is in the special THUMB software mode it reverts to normal mode.

- The program counter, r15, is loaded with the exception vector address.

Behaviour when an exception is accepted is similar to that for execution of a subroutine call except that there is no call instruction. The branch destination is the exception vector address. In addition to all the normal actions of a subroutine call the contents of CPSR are copied to SPSR_xxx and the CPSR bits indicating mode are changed. The code that performs the actions required to respond to the exception is called the **exception handler**. Because the CPSR contents are copied to SPSR_xxx the exception handler can restore CPSR, that is the flags, mode, etc., and return to the point in the main program at which the exception occurred after it has performed the tasks required. It is necessary to automatically copy CPSR to SPSR_xxx because, unlike a normal subroutine call, the exception may occur anywhere in a program, not only at fixed points chosen by the program designer.

When the CPU responds to an exception it performs more actions than for a subroutine call; hence a special mechanism is required to return from an exception. The ARM instruction set has a feature which must be used with great care. When the destination register of a move, arithmetic or logic instruction is the program counter, r15, and the S field is used the flags are not changed in the usual way. That is execution of an instruction such as `MOVS pc, <shifter_operand>` performs the normal copy action BUT the flags are not changed according to the result of the operation. Instead the contents of SPSR_xxx are copied to CPSR where _xxx indicates the current mode, the mode before the instruction is executed. For example `MOVS pc, r14` copies r14 to pc and SPSR_xxx to CPSR. The set flags field {S} must never be used with pc as the destination when the CPU is in user or system mode because these modes have no SPSR register; if used in these modes the behaviour is unpredictable. The result of copying SPSR_xxx to CPSR is to change the CPU to the mode it was in before the exception occurred and restore the status flags N, Z, C, and V. The three bits controlling THUMB mode and acceptance of FIQ and IRQ interrupts are also restored to their condition before the exception occurred.

There are some features of ARM exceptions that may be of concern in advanced applications. The gap in vector addresses at 0x00000014 is present because this was used on earlier versions of ARM; it is reserved for future use and no instruction should be placed at this address. Some versions of the CPU allow the vectors to be placed so that they start at a high address instead of at address zero according to the way in which the CPU is connected; this feature is ignored here.

Many problems associated with the use of exceptions apply to all processor systems and require that hardware features are present to resolve them. A major problem arises because, except for reset and data abort, the CPU completes execution of the instruction in progress. It only examines the exception requirements after it completes the execution; if more than one exception occurs during the execution time the CPU detects the exceptions simultaneously. A related problem is that a second exception can occur while one is already being handled. Also there are situations in which the programmer considers the section of program in progress to be more important than certain exceptions. This requires that it is possible to include instructions which enable and disable the CPU response to these exceptions while the section of program is executed.

Problems of simultaneous exception events are solved by giving each exception a priority level. When simultaneous exceptions occur the highest priority exception is processed first; also a higher priority exception is accepted while a lower priority one is running but not *vice versa*. Table 13.3 lists the priorities for ARM exceptions; two exceptions have the same priority as it is impossible for them to occur simultaneously.

Exception type	Priority	
Reset	1	Highest
Data abort (data access memory abort)	2	
FIQ – fast interrupt	3	
IRQ – interrupt	4	
Prefetch abort (instruction fetch memory abort)	5	
Undefined instructions and software interrupt – SWI (impossible to occur together)	6	Lowest

Table 13.3 Exception priorities

Some additional control of interrupt behaviour is provided by bits 5, 6 and 7 in CPSR. Bit 5 controls the THUMB mode briefly described in Chapter 14; when an exception occurs while the CPU is in THUMB mode it automatically switches to the normal ARM mode.

There are situations where a section of the running program is so important that it must not be interrupted by external events. CPSR bit 6 is the F bit, when it is 1 fast interrupts, FIQ, are not accepted; CPSR bit 7 is the I bit, when it is 1 standard interrupts, IRQ, are not accepted. The bits can be adjusted by the running program when in any mode except user mode; they are also changed automatically when an interrupt occurs and is accepted. As soon as an IRQ interrupt is accepted the I bit is set to 1 to prevent repeated interrupts. When a FIQ interrupt occurs both F and I bits are set to 1 because the FIQ interrupt has higher priority than IRQ. As reset is an exception which does not remember the previous mode the processor always starts in ARM mode after a reset, not in THUMB mode, and has F and I set to 1 to disable both interrupts allowing the program to perform all essential configuration actions before any interrupts occur.

13.4 Details of ARM exceptions

13.4.1 Reset

The cause of a reset is obvious; it occurs when power is first connected to the CPU or when a reset switch is operated. Reset causes the program counter to be set to zero, interrupts are disabled and the CPU is in supervisor mode; CPSR bits F and I are set to 1, T is set to 0 indicating ARM mode.

13.4.2 Data and prefetch abort

The two abort exceptions require that extra hardware circuits detect the events. ARM addresses are 32-bits which allows up to 2^{32} bytes of memory to be connected to the CPU. Systems are rarely constructed with 2^{32} bytes of memory so a program with a fault could attempt to use a memory address at which there is no memory or it could attempt to write data to ROM. The additional circuits produce a signal to indicate one of these faults to the CPU. If the circuits are present the data abort exception occurs if instruction execution attempts to read or write data using memory for which the operation is not possible. It has a high priority because any action must occur immediately it is attempted and the programmer must include an exception handler to perform appropriate actions.

Prefetch abort occurs when an instruction fetch is attempted from non-existent memory. This has a lower priority because instructions are in the pipeline and two are still to be executed before the one at the missing location is required. One of the instructions in the pipeline might be a branch instruction with a valid destination address; if so there is no problem otherwise the exception occurs after the valid instructions in the pipeline have been executed.

When there is no hardware to indicate that there is no memory at an address any read access will provide an unknown random value and program behaviour will be indeterminate; a write access will result in loss of the data that is being stored.

13.4.3 FIQ and IRQ

FIQ and IRQ, the fast and standard interrupts, are initiated by signals from external systems requesting immediate action. However each may be blocked by setting the corresponding F or I bits in the CPSR when in one of the privileged modes, this interrupt masking mechanism allows critical sections of program to be protected so that they are completed before an interrupt is accepted.

13.4.4　Undefined instruction

Not all possible 32-bit patterns represent valid ARM instruction codes; this exception occurs if an instruction fetch reads a value that is not a valid instruction code. It can also be used to create blocks of code that behave as the user's own instructions although this is more easily handled by the software interrupt, SWI, instruction. The most common use of invalid instruction codes is to support co-processors, Chapter 14. This exception may be used to activate additional code to emulate, imitate, the actions of a co-processor when it is not fitted.

13.4.5　Software interrupt

A software interrupt occurs when a program executes the software interrupt instruction which has the mnemonic SWI and syntax

```
SWI{<cond>}  <immediate_24>
```

Execution of SWI, or an attempt to execute an undefined instruction code, are the only methods a programmer can use to cause a program to leave user mode. The SWI instruction behaves as an exception; when it is executed the CPU changes to supervisor mode saving CPSR in SPSR_svc and the program counter in r14_svc. The 24-bit immediate value is not used by the CPU; however as r14_svc holds the address four locations ahead of the SWI instruction the value may be determined by memory read using `LDR  Rd,[r14,#-4]`. The programmer may use the 24-bit value to devise a system of multiple software interrupts each leading to a different set of actions.

One use of SWI is to implement the semihosting functions, Chapter 11; this software is complex and may be considered to make a system with two or more programs in memory at the same time and a mechanism for switching between them with transfer of data. A second use of SWI is to support run time fault detection and reporting; including instructions for this always slows program execution but if it is implemented using the SWI instruction the reduction in speed is small. For example if a program includes division operations run time fault detection may be included to detect attempts to divide by zero. Using SWI the exception handler can output a message indicating the fault and where it occurred; the handler may either terminate the program or wait for the user to indicate the next action. A simple method of performing this division by zero detection in a division subroutine is to include the sequence

```
MOVS    rX, rX      ; check divisor held in rX
SWIEQ   <value>     ; if divisor zero cause exception
```

immediately after the STMFD instruction at the start of the division subroutine. The exception handler can determine the position of the fault because the user r14 register will hold the address of the division call instruction. Run time fault detection may be used to detect several problems; the SWI operand value can be used as a code number to identify the problem.

13.5　A complete program framework

At power on an ARM processor will execute the instruction at address zero except when connected to special hardware development systems. A complete program must have instructions at all the exception vector addresses with each one causing execution of the appropriate exception handler. The most general form has instructions of the form `LDR pc, <label>` at every vector addresses and a table of handler addresses; examples by ARM and other writers usually follow this approach. An alternative form of start up code is one with branch instructions `BAL <label>` at each vector address; the programmer must

```
; Start up code framework using LDR instructions and table
        AREA    Vector_Set,  CODE,    READONLY
        LDR    PC,  initial        ; to normal reset start up
        LDR    PC,  undef          ; handle co-processor instructions
        LDR    PC,  soft_int       ; SWI processing
        LDR    PC,  prefetch       ; invalid instruction address
        LDR    PC,  data_abt       ; invalid data address
        DCD    0                   ; fill unused vector location
        LDR    PC,  int_req        ; normal interrupt handler
fiq_handler                        ; label for documentation only
        ; Insert the fast interrupt handler code here.
        SUBS    pc, r14, #4        ; exit handler to instruction after the
                                   ; one completed before FIQ accepted

initial   DCD   ini_handler
undef     DCD   und_handler
soft_int  DCD   swi_handler
prefetch  DCD   pre_handler
data_abt  DCD   abt_handler
int_req   DCD   irq_handler

ini_handler
        ; Put all the hardware and software initialisation code here.
        ; IMPORTANT:- separate stacks should be set for each exception
        ; Usually change to user mode with IRQ and FIQ as required.

main
        ; The main function actions here. Most systems loop for ever.
        BAL    main                ; loop forever if a simple program

und_handler
        ; Insert handler - invalid instruction codes. Emulate a co-processor
        ; if not fitted, detect all other invalid codes and attempt recovery.
        MOVS   pc, r14             ; if sensible return to instruction
                                   ; immediately after the invalid one

swi_handler
        ; Insert handler for SWI instructions here
        MOVS   pc, r14             ; if appropriate return to instruction
                                   ; immediately after SWI

pre_handler
        ; Insert code here to handle fetch from memory which does not exist
        SUBS   pc, r14, #4         ; if sensible (not often true) return to try
                                   ; instruction again else add special code

abt_handler
        ; Insert code here to handle access to memory which does not exist
        SUBS   pc, r14, #8         ; if sensible return to retry data transfer
                                   ; else try to recover.

irq_handler
        ; Insert interrupt IRQ handler here
        SUBS   pc, r14, #4         ; go to instruction after the one
                                   ; completed before IRQ accepted
```

Program 13.1 Start up code framework for a typical system

ensure that all the labels are within the offset range allowed for branch instructions. It is also possible to use LDR pseudo instructions at the vector addresses in some situations.

Whichever form is used each instruction at a vector address must redirect the program to the appropriate exception handler. The reset vector must re-direct to the initialisation code followed by the main program. Each of the other vectors will require its own handler which will be application dependent; obviously for an embedded system the two abort exceptions should never occur unless deliberately used to implement special tasks, any situation in which they arise should have been detected during testing. Usually the undefined instruction exception is used for co-processor emulation.

Program 13.1 is a complete program framework of a typical system including start up with LDR instructions at the interrupt vector addresses. In general every handler should have an STMFD instruction on entry and an LDMFD instruction on exit as every register used by the handler, including r0 to r3, must be saved. There is no branch to the FIQ handler; because it is the last vector and requires fast response the handler is at the vector address. The recommended instructions to return at the end of each handler are shown in the framework. The handlers do not all have the same return instruction because pipeline effects cause the value stored in the link register to vary with exception type. **It is important** to note that each mode must have its own stack area defined by initialising its stack pointer.

In many cases the effects of exceptions are catastrophic; for these alternative exit instructions must be used as the program must not return to the interrupt point. For example if a pre-fetch abort occurs the program counter may point to the end of the memory fitted therefore the next location will also not be a valid one.

Program 13.1 is the framework for a complete program to be held in ROM; it is also suitable for use with a development system that can load programs into RAM at address zero. For small programs where all code is in a memory located between address 0 to address 0x1ffffff branch always instructions branching directly to the handlers may be placed at the vector addresses and the table removed.

```
; Framework to set IRQ vector in RAM at run time, first initialisation task
IRQ_vect   EQU    0x00000018          ; address of IRQ vector
           AREA   Int_Vec, CODE, READONLY  ; section to set vector of IRQ
           ENTRY                       ; run time start position
; Probably change to user mode here (Evaluator-7T is usually left in
; supervisor mode after start up)
           LDR    sp,  =0x10000        ; initialise stack pointer
           LDR    r0,  =IRQ_vect       ; set pointer to interrupt vector
           LDR    r1,  =(IRQ_Hndl - 8) ; handler address adjusted for pipeline
           LDR    r2,  =0xEA000000     ; code for BAL with offset bits zero
           ADD    r1, r1, r2, LSR #2   ; add offset shifted two places to BAL
           STR    r1, [r0]             ; store BAL IRQ_Hdl at vector
       ; program continues
; The handler for the IRQ interrupt, the linker must not place this at an
; address above 0x01000000 - limited by maximum offset
IRQ_hndl
       ; perform required actions and ensure that the cause of the interrupt
       ; is removed before returning
           SUBS  pc, r14, #4           ; return using correct address
```

Program 13.2 Simple method of replacing an interrupt vector in RAM by a running program

More complicated programs are required for general purpose software systems that run multiple programs or for development boards with monitor programs in ROM at address zero. Each system is unique and requires its own special purpose solution. For example the microcontroller of Evaluator-7T has complicated memory interface circuits allowing the addresses of the memory components to be changed by the actions of a program itself. The monitor uses this to place programs in RAM and allow the user to modify the exception vectors; such modification may cause loss of debug facilities. There is support for changing interrupt vectors but use requires knowledge of the monitor construction. An alternative for changing a single vector for an Evaluator-7T program is to create a branch instruction and copy it to the vector address in the initialisation section of the program. This requires a clear understanding of ARM instruction codes and how to calculate an offset; Program 13.2 sets the IRQ vector for Evaluator-7T.

13.6 Exception handlers, program structures and testing

Developing reliable programs that use exceptions is difficult; exceptions break many rules of good program design as the action of exceptions, except the SWI instruction, cause an unstructured program branch, a GOTO. Except for SWI the branch may occur at any point in the program. Any program that includes exceptions, especially interrupts, will be poorly structured; extensive testing is essential and even then the probability of undiscovered faults is high. The following are a few initial guidance notes.

13.6.1 Data and prefetch abort

These exceptions do not lead to poorly structured programs; they provide an additional check of running programs and should never arise. They are useful in the testing phase of development as they provide a clear indication of errors and their positions. A common cause of this exception is a mistake in addressing mode used or a typing error in the operands defining memory location of an LDR or STR instruction; the data abort exception is used by most development systems to detect such problems.

A difficulty when preparing handlers for these exceptions is checking that they function correctly as, if the program is well designed, the exceptions should never occur. Consequently it is necessary to prepare a version of the program containing faults that will generate the exceptions then check that they occur at the correct point and that the exception handlers behave as required.

A second problem is deciding the action to be performed by the exception handlers as they only occur if there is a program fault that was not found during testing. If the equipment including the CPU and program interacts with a user; for example a personal computer, an entertainment device with a display or other device not performing a critical task; then a message to the user requesting that the manufacturer is contacted may be adequate. However if the CPU is built into equipment performing some critical function such as control of an automobile engine, operating an aircraft flight system, *etc.*, such a response is not suitable. Whatever action is decided must be fully specified and included in the detailed specification of the software.

13.6.2 Undefined instruction

A number of instruction codes are instructions for co-processors connected in parallel with the main CPU. If a co-processor is fitted it intercepts the instruction, executes it and informs the main CPU when execution is complete; typical tasks are complicated arithmetic, handling complex IO and other system tasks. Most systems do not include every co-processor and this exception is used to run software that includes co-processor instructions without the co-processor. When the exception handler is activated it determines which co-processor instruction occurred then branches to a program that performs the same actions as the co-processor, this is software emulation of the co-processor. A co-processor performs the action very quickly whereas emulation executes many instructions and takes a relatively long time.

When checking an undefined instruction the handler may find that the code is not that of any expected co-processor instruction. The situation is similar to that when a prefetch abort occurs and similar considerations of defining the action to be performed and providing adequate tests are essential.

13.6.3 Software interrupt

The SWI instruction has many uses; a common one is to handle error situations within a program; typical errors are attempts to divide by zero or to access a data array element with the index larger than the array size. Although such tests can be performed by subroutines the software interrupt with a conditional extension leads to a very simple structure that does cause a large increase in program execution time.

Semi-hosting functions are an example of a second use of SWI instructions. They implement a simple form of system running multiple programs; in this case the user program under development and the monitor program providing test and debug facilities. In a multiprogram situation two, or more, programs are simultaneously present in memory. At any time only one program is being executed but the running program may require that the system switches to another program. Such systems are too complex to examine here but software interrupts assist in performing the switch.

13.6.4 FIQ and IRQ

External signals requiring an almost instant response by the CPU, regardless of the task it is performing, are a frequent feature of embedded control systems. Such signals are applied to the interrupt input pins of the CPU and, provided interrupts are enabled, cause an exception. Many systems have more than two sources of interrupt; additional external circuits combine the signals so that a particular interrupt activates either IRQ or FIQ depending on the response speed required. Preparing interrupt handlers that behave reliably is a difficult programming task for any type of CPU and the necessary testing processes are extremely difficult and time consuming.

The rule *'keep it simple'* is particularly important when creating interrupt handlers. Whenever possible the code executed by the handler itself should be short, simple and not include loops; as much of the task as possible should be in the main program. One method for embedded processors performing critical control tasks is to set up a number of variables as software indicators; one indicator for each possible requirement generated by interrupts. The main program should be a small loop continually executed with the main control task performed once every time around the loop. In addition to the control task the main program checks any indicators and acts if they are set.

An example of the use of indicators to simplify an interrupt handler is a program that uses a UART to transmit a message while continuing with its main task. Because serial transmission is slow the program can execute many instructions while each character of the message is transmitted. This example is simple; it assumes that the system will always complete sending a message before it is required to send another message which removes the need to form a queue of messages. To transmit a message the UART is configured to generate an interrupt every time it completes sending one character. The program has two indicator variables; one variable, *message*, indicates that a message is being transmitted and the second, *TX_rdy*, indicates that the UART is ready to send another character. Figure 13.2 outlines the program structure; the main program performs some control functions and transmits a message using the UART at the same time as performing the control tasks. Minor modifications will be required if the UART is a type that does not automatically reset some of its status indicators after each interrupt.

Figure 13.2 shows that the interrupt handler is very simple; it executes very few instructions so is fast; and it does not have any loops or conditional statements so its behaviour is always the same. The program does not leave the main control loop for long periods of time; all decisions are made in the main program or subroutines called from it and they can be designed in a well structured manner. With a simple handler there is only a low risk of errors in the handler code and there is a low probability of complex situations arising that cause unexpected behaviour. There are many alternatives to this simple messaging system but the example illustrates an approach that leads to systems with reliable interrupt behaviour.

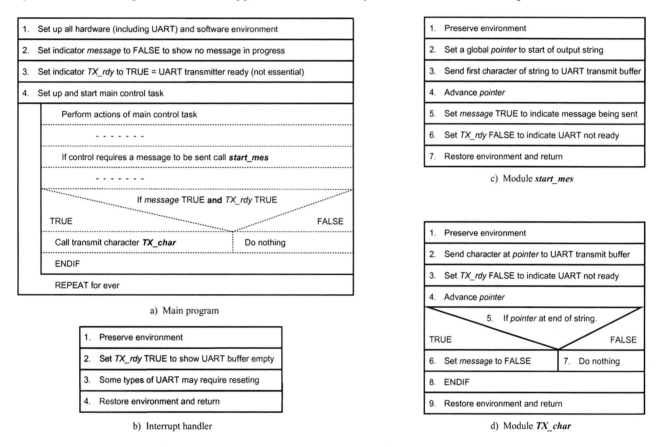

a) Main program

b) Interrupt handler

c) Module *start_mes*

d) Module *TX_char*

Figure 13.2 Structure for serial transmission while performing another task

13.6.5 Other modes

System mode has not been described; it differs from other modes as it does not have special registers and, as it cannot be reached by an exception, it cannot be entered from user mode. The only method of accessing system mode is by changing the CPSR mode bits when in another protected mode.

The main use of system mode is to support operating system software, an advanced task that is not examined here. An operating system such as Unix/Linux, Symbian OS, Windows, etc., allows many programs to appear to run simultaneously. Such a system is a master program that controls all other programs, hardware resources, etc.; part of the operating system program is always present in memory. It is essential that the operating system can set up some software features that cannot be accessed by a user program. System mode provides a mechanism allowing such protection mechanisms to be developed.

The other mode not considered is the software one called THUMB. This is used to improve performance in certain applications, usually low cost embedded ones, and is briefly discussed in Chapter 14. In THUMB mode the CPU runs a modified instruction set and programs are usually prepared in a high level language.

13.7 Summary

Every type of CPU has its own unique hardware that controls the behaviour at power on or reset; ARM start up is simple and for ROM based systems the required section of program is easily prepared. Interrupt mechanisms and other forms of exception which break the standard von Neumann sequence also differ for every CPU type. To develop a complete working system that uses all hardware features the programmer must understand the detailed hardware operation.

Systems that use exceptions are complex and it is usually impossible to fully test them as the number of situations that can arise is very large. To produce programs that use interrupts and have a low probability that any errors are not found during testing the programmer should construct very simple exception handlers using indicators, or other systems, to enable most actions associated with the interrupt to be performed in the main program sequence.

13.8 Problems

If your development system allows you to incorporate your own exception handlers develop and test programs to perform the following tasks.

13.1 Most development systems include LED displays. Prepare a program that is a simple count for ever loop. Whenever the count value is 0xXX000000 where XX are any two hexadecimal digits the program executes a software interrupt instruction. The action of the exception handler changes the state of a LED; if the LED is on it is turned off, if it is off it is turned on.
Alternatively if the system only has a seven segment display use this to indicate 0, 1, 2, 3, etc., changing the value shown each time the exception occurs.

13.2 Prepare a program that tests if your development system implements and reports a data abort exception. If it does and the system allows modification of the handler replace the development system handler with your own and prepare the following program. The program searches all possible memory addresses of the form 0xXXX00000 by reading from every possible address of this form. If no memory is present the program should display a message *'No memory at address 0xXXX00000'* (with XXX the actual value used) then continue to the next address.

13.3 Most ARM microcontrollers used in development system incorporate simple hardware timers. Usually these can be set by software initialisation to count a user programmed number of pulses from a clock then generate a hardware interrupt.
If you have such a system determine how to configure the counter and set it to interrupt once every second. Each time an interrupt occurs make the main program perform some task, for example change the state of a LED.

14 Larger Programs

Most examples in previous chapters, problems, and descriptions of assembler features in manuals are devised to illustrate a single feature of assembly language. That is tutorial examples are small programs that perform a simple task whereas most applications are large programs that perform complex tasks. Most assemblers include features to assist development of large programs and are part of development systems that have additional tools for large program construction. Although many advanced development system features are not the concern of an introductory text the reader should be aware that they exist and study them once familiar with basic techniques. A few topics are introduced to indicate areas for further study.

14.1 Advanced assembler features

ARM assemblers have an unusually large number of directives. Some assist development of large programs; others help to meet the requirements of programs for embedded processors. Many directives provide methods of producing different versions of programs automatically; either for different hardware systems or to meet slightly different specifications. Macros are a common method of producing slightly different sections of program with little programmer effort; they are supported by many assemblers and compilers although each one has its own unique syntax. Assembler macros often confuse the beginner as superficially they appear to behave as subroutines; however macros and subroutines are different.

A subroutine is a section of program whose instruction code sequence occurs only once in the program. The single code section is executed at any position in the program by the use of a call instruction to branch to the subroutine code section which ends with a return instruction that continues execution starting with the instruction immediately following the call. For ARM processors the standard method of performing a call is by the branch with link instruction; the return is performed by retrieving the address saved in the link register when the call was executed and copying it into the program counter.

A **macro** is a set of instructions used to instruct the assembler to insert a specified sequence of assembly language statements, often modified at each insertion, at required positions in a program. The insertion is macro expansion; every expansion inserts the sequence of instructions defined by the macro into the code sequence. Macros are used to include similar sequences of instructions at several points in a program when a subroutine call is not appropriate.

To create a macro the programmer prepares a macro definition; this is usually placed in the heading section that contains other general definitions such as equate statements. If a large number of macros are used they may be placed in a separate file or in a library. The macro definition does not generate any instruction codes. At every point where the code corresponding to the macro definition is required the macro is expanded by using its name as a directive. Every expansion of a macro inserts a new copy of the code it defines; hence using macros instead of subroutine calls leads to programs requiring more memory for the instruction codes. However there is often an increase in execution time when a subroutine is used, especially in a pipelined CPU such as ARM. The use of macros instead of subroutines often produces programs that run faster.

Consider Program 10.4 again; it is a subroutine to add two 64-bit integers held in memory and put their sum into memory in place of one of the numbers. The input parameters are the addresses of the two numbers and must be in specific registers before the call; this may require extra instructions. Execution of the call by branch and link and the return by copy into the program counter both break the pipeline operation. The program will run significantly faster if the code to perform 64-bit addition is inserted whenever it is required instead of using a subroutine call; the disadvantage is that the program code will occupy more memory as all the instructions are inserted every time required. A macro provides an efficient method of inserting similar sequences of instructions at several positions in a program.

```
; Macro for addition of two 64-bit integers stored in memory.
; Requires two work registers $Wrk1 and $Wrk2 which are corrupted.
; Each 64-bit number uses 8 successive memory locations, low 32-bits first.
; The first addresses of the numbers are in registers $ptr1 and $ptr2.
; The result is in place of the number at the position given by $ptr1
; The two pointer values $ptr1 and $ptr2 are not corrupted.

                MACRO
$label          add64   $Wrk1, $Wrk2, $Ptr1, $Ptr2
                ASSERT  $Wrk1 <> $Wrk2      ;= these ASSERT statements ensure
                ASSERT  $Wrk1 <> $Ptr1      ;= that the registers chosen at
                ASSERT  $Wrk1 <> $Ptr2      ;= expansion are different
                ASSERT  $Wrk2 <> $Ptr1      ;=
                ASSERT  $Wrk2 <> $Ptr2      ;=

                LDR     $Wrk1, [$Ptr1]      ; get low 32-bits first operand
                LDR     $Wrk2, [$Ptr2],#4   ; get low 32-bits second operand
                                            ; and advance pointer
                ADDS    $Wrk1, $Wrk1, $Wrk2 ; add low 32-bits producing carry
                STR     $Wrk1, [$Ptr1],#4   ; save result low 32-bits, and
                                            ; advance pointer
                LDR     $Wrk1, [$Ptr1]      ; get high 32-bits first operand
                LDR     $Wrk2, [$Ptr2],#-4  ; get high 32-bits second operand
                                            ; and restore pointer to original
                ADCS    $Wrk1, $Wrk1, $Wrk2 ; add high 32-bits setting carry
                                            ; plus the carry from the low parts
                STR     $Wrk1, [$Ptr1],#-4  ; save result high 32-bits, and
                                            ; restore the pointer
                MEND
```

Program 14.1 Example of a simple macro definition

The ARM assembler macro form is powerful but complicated; it is essential to read the manuals to fully understand the syntax and all the possible uses. A macro definition starts with the directive MACRO and ends with the directive MEND. The line immediately following the MACRO directive assigns the macro a name and defines any parameters. Program 14.1 is the definition of a macro called *add64* that performs 64-bit addition in the same manner as the subroutine of Program 10.3 except that:-

- The pointers to the numbers are in registers chosen when the macro is expanded; therefore different registers may be used on each expansion. The program does not require instructions to move the pointers into specific registers as required by subroutine parameter passing. Macro parameters are not passed to the program running on the target, they are used by the assembler at assembly time.

- The same register may be used for both pointers; this is trivial as the macro would just double the value and this would be an inefficient method of doubling a number.
- The sum is returned in place of the first number, the macro could be modified to return it in either the same or different locations at the point where the macro is expanded.
- Two registers, chosen by the programmer at each point where the macro is expanded, are required for temporary working.

The directive, ASSERT, is introduced and used to test that neither pointer register is used as a temporary register and that the temporary registers are different. If an ASSERT test indicates that the requirement is not met the assembler produces an error message and does not produce code. ASSERT is not restricted to use in macros; it is used wherever the programmer wishes to check that some condition is met when the assembler processes the source file.

Parameters to be replaced at expansion are indicated by the $ character as the first character in the definition. The use of the parameter $label is not necessary for the example but is included to show that a feature is provided allowing a label to be positioned at the start of a macro. A macro may include internal labels to form conditional statements and loops but names must incorporate parameters to prevent the same label appearing more than once if the macro is expanded several times.

The macro definition, Program 14.1, does not generate any code at the point it appears in the program. When it is required at some point it is expanded by typing its name with actual values in place of the parameters. For example at the point where the program requires addition of 64-bit numbers pointed to by the contents of r5 and r8 using registers r2 and r3 as work registers then the following line is used.

```
addn2          add64     r2, r3, r5, r8
```

This line causes the macro to be expanded to produce the equivalent source shown as Program 14.2; this expanded source program is processed by the assembler to produce the code.

```
addn2
          ASSERT   r2 <> r3        ;= these ASSERT statements ensure
          ASSERT   r2 <> r5        ;= that the registers chosen at
          ASSERT   r2 <> r8        ;= expansion are different
          ASSERT   r3 <> r5        ;=
          ASSERT   r3 <> r8        ;=

          LDR      r2, [r5]        ; get low 32-bits first operand
          LDR      r3, [r8],#4     ; get low 32-bits second operand
                                   ; and advance pointer
          ADDS     r2, r2, r3      ; add low 32-bits setting carry
          STR      r2, [r5],#4     ; save result low 32-bits, and
                                   ; advance pointer
          LDR      r2, [r5]        ; get high 32-bits first operand
          LDR      r3, [r8],#-4    ; get high 32-bits second operand
                                   ; and restore pointer to original
          ADCS     r2, r2, r3      ; add high 32-bits setting carry
                                   ; plus the carry from the low parts
          STR      r2, [r5],#-4    ; save result high 32-bits, and
                                   ; restore the pointer
```

Program 14.2 Source program produced by expansion of 64-bit addition macro

It is not possible to give rules defining when subroutines should be used and when macros should be used. If the choice is not obvious a subroutine is probably the appropriate selection. Macros usually, but not always, produce sections of program that run faster than similar sections implemented using subroutines; the disadvantage is that they usually require more memory for the program code. The speed increases because there is no requirement to move variables into the specific registers chosen for parameter passing to and from a subroutine, there are no branches to enter and leave code section, and multiple register storage and retrieval can often be avoided.

The STM and LDM instructions can be used at the start and end of a macro in a similar manner to that for subroutine construction. However as these perform slow memory operations it is probable that if they are required this is a situation where a subroutine should be used.

Another macro use is when a number of separate, but similar, hardware features exist. For example many microcontrollers have two or more UARTs which are identical in construction but applications often require that they are often configured differently and used for different tasks. The code blocks for each of the functions performing UART initialisation, character transmission and character reception are often similar for each UART but are not identical. Generally most UART operations will be implemented by subroutines. A single subroutine could be devised for a particular function when using either UART; this would require passing several parameters to define which UART to use and some of its features every time a UART operation was performed. These parameters would always have the same values when a subroutine was used for one specific UART. In such cases separate subroutines for each UART would be more appropriate; the routines can be created by macro definitions expanded to produce the different subroutines for each UART. That is there are cases where a subroutine is created by expanding a macro.

A feature closely related to macros is the use of conditional assembly; this is another method of inserting sections of program at assembly time according to the programmer's requirements. The directives IF and ENDIF can be used to insert a section of code, possibly that defined by a macro, only if some condition is true at assembly time; an optional ELSE directive allows the insertion of alternatives. A further directive ELIF provides a method of creating multiple alternatives.

```
; select one of the two languages by making one line a comment
lang            SETS      "English"
;lang           SETS      "French"

; constant strings for display messages
                IF        lang = "English"
first           DCB       "Hello", 0
second          DCB       "Please wait", 0
; and other messages
                ELSE
first           DCB       "Bonjour", 0
second          DCB       "Attendez SVP", 0
; and other messages
                ENDIF
```

Program 14.3 Conditional assembly, illustrated for alternative languages.

A typical use is to create versions of a product for different markets; for example where fixed messages are displayed by the program and the product is intended for sale in several countries that have different language requirements. Another use is when equipment must meet different regulatory standards or incorporate different IO hardware for different applications. A value can be defined at the head of the program, or often as part of the software build instructions that combine many components, and whenever the program reaches a point where different sections of code must be inserted the code is bracketed by IF and ENDIF statements. Program 14.3 is the framework outlining the method. The directive SETS gives the user name the value of the string; SETS behaves in the same way as EQU except that instead of setting a user name to a numeric value it sets the user name to a string.

Note that the assembler only produces code for one of the two options hence no problems are created by using the same names for labels in the two possible cases. Also in this example the option was set by making one of two lines a comment; that is the program has to be modified to produce the required version. Most development packages provide a mechanism of passing information to the assembler from the complete software build instructions to indicate the parameter value for the version to be produced.

14.2 Assembler arithmetic

At many points in example programs the assembler has been instructed to perform simple arithmetic operations. For example Program 12.6 includes the line

```
num_vals   EQU   (table_end – table)/4   ; work out how many values
```

Here the program defines a value related to the difference between two labels; that is it depends on two user names that define the addresses of two points in the program or data. This difference divided by four because each address defines the position of an 8-bit value whereas the program requires the number of 32-bit words between the labels. Programmers should avoid computing values themselves whenever possible; instead the source file should be written so that the assembler performs the calculations. There are two reasons; firstly the computer running the assembler is less likely to make a mistake that the human programmer. Secondly if the program is changed at some time in the future the programmer does not have to search the whole program and detect and modify every calculation affected by the change; the risk of creating errors on program modification is greatly reduced.

The assembler is able to perform all the standard operations of addition, subtraction, multiplication and division. Numbers are usually treated as unsigned 32-bit integers but because underflow and overflow do not generate error messages negative results may be regarded as twos complement numbers if necessary. For division the ADS and RealView assemblers provide two operations; the operator / is used to produce the quotient and the operator :MOD: to give the remainder.

Most assemblers also perform bitwise logic operations, shift and rotate actions, and comparative logic operations producing Boolean values. The syntax for these and the exact set of operations available and vary greatly from one assembler to another, for example ADS and RealView use symbols such as :AND: and :OR: for assembler computations of bitwise AND and OR respectively. The manual of the particular assembler being used should be consulted for full details of the form used.

Once a large number of numeric and logic operations are available the order in which they are performed becomes important. This is called the precedence of operators; most readers will be familiar with the convention in arithmetic that to evaluate $A + B \times C$ the multiplication is performed before the addition because multiply has precedence over addition. When many more operators are allowed precedence is more complicated; assembler manuals provide tables showing the precedence of all operators. Brackets may be used to modify precedence rules as in conventional arithmetic; the degree of nesting of brackets allowed varies from one assembler to another. Superfluous brackets do not cause problems, for example $A + (B \times C)$ is exactly the same as $A + B \times C$. Extra brackets should always be used to ensure the required precedence. Brackets also make the programmer's intention obvious to others; they are a good form of documentation and overcome the problem that when using more than one language there may be confusion if each employs a slightly different order of preference.

14.3 High level and mixed language programming

Large software projects often contain components in both high level and assembly language. Frequently the initial section of program to configure the hardware and create the software environment is prepared in assembly language and the main program is in a high level language. Modules that handle hardware features or which must operate very quickly are also written in assembly language and used by the high level language program. Conversely assembly language sections of code may use the functions built into the high level language to perform complex tasks such as floating point arithmetic operations.

Some compilers support in-line assembly language; a compiler directive indicates that the lines following, until a terminating directive is met, are in assembly language. To use such a feature the programmer must study the manuals as all systems tend to be unique to the complier being used and require that a very restricted form of the assembly language is used.

A common form linking assembly language and a high level language is by use of complete subroutines prepared as separate program modules. Most high level languages have components called functions or procedures that the compiler converts into subroutines when generating code; an assembly language program may access these by a subroutine call. Similarly an assembly language subroutine may be accessed from the high level language as if it was a function or procedure in that language. To pass information between the various components the assembly language programmer must know how parameters are passed to routines by the high level language. In general ARM high level language compilers follow the rules of the ARM Architecture Procedure Call Standard, AAPCS; the programmer must determine from the compiler manuals how the parameter representation in the high level language correspond to the AAPCS concept of first parameter, second parameter, etc.

To use a function in high level language the assembly language programmer must arrange that the parameters are in the appropriate registers then include a `BL <label>` instruction where the label is the name of the high level language function. The assembler has no knowledge of the function name as it is not defined in the module; the additional directive EXTERN is used and the line

EXTERN   `<label/user name>`

is included early in the program. ARM assemblers usually accept either EXTERN or IMPORT as the directive. The directive informs the assembler that the label or user name is defined somewhere else and therefore it does not generate an error message. The linker inserts the correct value when all the modules are combined.

If a subroutine in an assembly language program is to be used by another program module that is either in assembly language or high level language then information concerning this must be passed to the linker. To do this the directive EXPORT is used in the assembly language module, the line

EXPORT   `<label/user name>`

is included in the program heading. Again most ARM assemblers accept either of two names, EXPORT or GLOBAL. The directive indicates that the label or user name is defined in this program module and the value must be available to other modules.

A program using a mixture of assembly language and high level language consists of more than one source file. Use of multiple source files is common when developing all but the smallest programs even if all files are in assembly language. Development systems are designed to support multiple source files; the complete group of all the source files, code files, etc., is usually called a project and the development tools automatically assemble all assembly language files, compile all high level language files then link them together. For simple programs the automatic settings are often adequate but for more complex tasks the programmer must create a set of instructions, usually in a text file called a *make file*, that informs the linker which files to use, how to combine them, etc. This is another process that varies greatly from one development system to another.

An additional directive to break a large program into smaller files is INCLUDE; the line

> **INCLUDE**   `<filename>`

with <filename> replaced by the actual name of any text file causes all the text from this file being inserted into the assembly language file at the point where the INCLUDE directive is found. This is a useful method of inserting the same block of text in several source files to ensure that identical changes are made in them all. For example it may be used to implement a method similar to the header files used in the C language; all the EXTERN statements necessary to provide links to a source file that contains commonly used names are placed in a single file which is included in all the individual files that use any of the names.

14.4 Advanced ARM hardware features

The ARM family includes more extensions to the basic von Neumann CPU architecture than are described in Chapter 13. An unusual feature is the provision of a second instruction set called THUMB that overcomes a disadvantage of RISC processors. If a program for the same task is prepared for both RISC and CISC processors the number of instructions for the RISC processor is often greater than for the CISC. As a result RISC systems require more memory to hold the program code and require more time to fetch instructions; however as a RISC executes all instructions quickly the overall speed is often higher. In practice the relative speed of two processors depends on the nature of the task to be performed, the quality of the software, the hardware configuration and other features. A CPU that performs well for one type of task often performs poorly for another.

In THUMB mode an ARM processor uses an alternative set of instruction codes that have only 16-bits. The THUMB instruction set is closely related to the ARM instruction set. A very simple circuit in the CPU translates THUMB codes into ARM codes for execution; Figure 14.1 illustrates conversion of the THUMB instruction ADD `<Rd>,#immediate` into the ARM `ADD <Rd>,<Rn>,#immediate` instruction with Rd and Rn the same register; THUMB arithmetic and logic instruction codes require that one source register is always the same as the destination register. Using THUMB instructions reduces the amount of memory required by the code section of a program. The penalty is that more instructions are executed because a THUMB instruction does not contain as much information as an ARM instruction. The increase in number of instructions varies as it depends on the task performed by the program and the skill of the programmer. On average the number of THUMB instructions is about 40% greater than the number of ARM instructions to perform the same task; the difference can be much larger or much smaller.

As THUMB instructions only use half the memory of an ARM instruction a 40% increase in the number of instructions results in an overall reduction in memory required of 30%. Because 40% more instructions are executed the program will run more slowly. However for many low cost applications an ARM processor is connected to memory with 16-bit words and only 16-bits are transferred at a time.

Using ARM instructions the system has to perform two memory reads to obtain each 32-bit instruction; in THUMB mode only one read is required for each instruction. The resulting speed increase often compensates for the extra number of instructions required in THUMB mode.

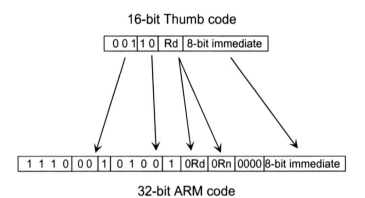

Figure 14.1 Relationship between ARM and THUMB move immediate code

THUMB mode assembly language is modified form of ARM assembly language and is supported by most assemblers. The RealView assembler assumes that instructions are normal ARM instructions and is changed to use THUMB instructions by the directive THUMB immediately after an AREA directive; it reverts to ARM instructions by an ARM directive after another AREA directive. Other assemblers use the older directives CODE32 for ARM mode and CODE16 for THUMB mode. It is important to insert instructions to perform the mode change as well as using the directives when changing mode. Because the assembler assumes that a program uses ARM instructions by default the ARM or CODE32 directive is not required in programs that only use ARM mode. ARM advise that programs in THUMB mode should be prepared in a high level language; development of efficient THUMB programs in assembly language is difficult. As the CPU always starts in ARM mode it must be changed to THUMB mode when required; to do this documentation describing ARM-THUMB interworking must be studied and the process of changing mode must be fully understood.

One feature is that to avoid the problem of knowing if the processor is in ARM or THUMB mode after an exception the processor always switches to ARM mode when an exception occurs. THUMB mode is defined by CPSR bit 5 and the state of the system before the exception is saved in SPSR; at a normal end of an exception handler the previous CPSR is restored. That is when in THUMB mode an exception automatically switches to ARM mode, on completion of the exception handler the standard return method changes to THUMB mode to continue running normally. Other than this automatic change of mode a program should not change to and from THUMB mode by changing CPSR bit 5.

The branch and exchange instructions, BX and BLX, are primarily intended as the mechanisms to switch between ARM and THUMB mode. The action of the instruction

                              BX   <Rs>

is to copy the contents of Rs into the program counter except that the least significant bit, bit 0, has a special use as indicated later and is forced to 0. If the CPU is in ARM mode bit 1 in Rs must be zero. The least significant bit of Rs sets the CPU into ARM mode if it is 0 and into THUMB mode if it is 1. Some ARM assemblers generate a warning if the programmer uses the instruction MOV pc, Rs to return from a subroutine instead of using STM and LDM. Warnings indicate that BX Rs is the preferred instruction that should be used. This preference is to support standard methods of creating large programs that use both ARM and THUMB modes.

The other major hardware feature of ARM, and many other CPUs, is the use of co-processors. A co-processor is a special purpose CPU linked to the bus system in parallel with the normal CPU. It is capable of performing a limited range of special tasks. The hardware designer incorporates any required co-processors into the complete system. Up to sixteen co-processors to be connected to an ARM CPU with typical ones providing floating point, DMA, and hardware control (memory management).

The manner in which co-processors are connected varies with CPU type and is complex; there are significant differences for different ARM versions. For ARM7TDMI co-processors are connected in parallel with the main CPU and they examine all instructions as they are fetched by the ARM processor. Specific ARM instruction codes, usually identified by the values of a small number of bits in the code, are co-processor instruction codes. When a co-processor detects an instruction code for itself it signals this to the ARM processor; instead of the ARM processor generating an undefined instruction exception the ARM processor allows the co-processor to execute the instruction.

Development systems require that they are configured to support the processor system, including co-processors, being used. Provided that the system has been correctly configured the co-processor instructions will be accepted. It is not always apparent to beginners that development systems must be configured; many ARM systems set a default configuration that uses ARM7TDMI without co-processors, this matches the hardware form of many low cost development systems.

14.5 Using other CPUs

Throughout this book features of ARM assembly language that are unusual from the viewpoint of a programmer with experience of other CPUs have been stressed. For the benefit of the reader who first programs in assembly language using an ARM system it is useful to briefly indicate the reverse; what to expect when programming a different type of CPU.

- It is very unusual for all instructions to have conditional forms; for most CPUs the only conditional instructions are conditional branches and the only method for constructing conditional structures and loops is to use conditional branch instructions.
- For many CPUs flag setting is not controlled by the programmer. Such CPUs always set some or all of the flags when they execute arithmetic and logic instructions; the settings used are not always obvious and care is required to ensure that the flags act as expected. In about 50% of CPU designs move instructions do not set the flags, in the other 50% they set some, but not all, flags. Memory transfer instructions rarely affect the flags.
- If there are instructions that copy memory to part of a register (similar to LDRB, LDRRH for ARM) the other register bits may be unchanged whereas ARM clears them.
- Shift and rotate operations are provided by separate instructions.
- Once set the stack takes care of itself as for ARM; however the programmer does not have to handle subroutine nesting. The instruction set has call and return instructions that automatically put the return address on the stack, retrieve the return address when required, and correctly adjust the stack pointer.
- Some CPUs automatically save the flags when executing a subroutine call or provide a simple method of copying them to the stack; this sometimes leads to a different style of programming when implementing multiple conditional statements.
- Some CPUs provide instructions for modifying the flags directly; this may provide alternative methods of implementing compound conditional tests.

- Pseudo instructions are not common for those CPU designs for which immediate values are not restricted in range as instructions can include large immediate values.
- If the programmer chooses operands that are not allowed for an instruction the assembler indicates an error. Often, when an alternative operation could perform the task that is apparently required, ARM assemblers change the instruction to another.
- If a large numeric value can be part of an instruction code there may be instructions which perform direct memory addressing. That is there are memory read and write instructions of the form *load memory or store into memory using absolute address X'*. While not very useful for general data handling it is useful for handling IO in microcontroller applications. It also allows branch instructions to have the form *'branch to or call subroutine at absolute address X'*.
- The method of implementing a case structure is often unique.

14.6 Final comments

This text has provided an introduction to the ARM assembly language with methods of using it to produce programs or program modules with a low risk of obscure faults. The reader is advised that there are many more topics to consider than those presented. The bibliography provides starting points for further study of some topics. Creation of reliable programs requires discipline by the programmer, application of quality assurance procedures and extensive testing. The first task of any programmer is to produce a program that will always function as specified.

Commercial software should be prepared and documented in such a manner that other programmers can readily understand how the program functions so that later modifications are easily, and reliably, made. Good software engineering methods are essential. These are practiced by industries such as the aerospace and nuclear ones but some other industries have been slow to appreciate the need.

14.7 Problems

14.1 For any program you have prepared previously that includes a subroutine used several times modify the program by replacing the subroutine by a macro.

In addition to checking that the program behaves correctly determine the amount of memory required to hold the code for the original program and for the modified program.

14.2 If your test system incorporates a UART revise any program that uses the UART so that it includes conditional assembly. Create a user name and arrange that you can give it any one of the values 1200, 2400 or 4800. Prepare the conditional section of the program so that the UART is set to operate at the baud rate equivalent to the value of the user name.

14.3 For any program you have prepared that includes subroutines convert it into two separate source files, one holding the main program and the other the subroutines. Build the revised program and check that it behaves correctly.

Appendix A
Partial solutions to selected problems

Program writing problems are design exercises with many solutions; any solution for such a problem **is only one of many possible solutions**. Answers to many other problems can be checked by preparing short programs and running them using a simulator or development system. The following are answers to some problems; some are incomplete with answers only to part of the problem. Few answers are given to problems in the later chapters because their solutions depend on the hardware available.

1.1 $2^{16} = 65536$

1.3   a) 182_{10} and $B6_H$

        b) 1110001110001100_2 and 58252_{10}

        c) 100011011_2 and $11B_H$

1.4   a) 1100100_2 b) 10201_3 c) 400_5 d) 144_8 e) 121_9 f) 84_{12} g) 64_H

2.1   List of actions for **Buff_In** only. The list in the buffer requires an end marker, enter is used and is adequate; note that enter is usually a poor choice as it is useful to be able to include it in the string.

      i)   Set a pointer to the start of the buffer used for input.

      ii)   Get one key input code, **Char_In**

      iii)   Echo input code to display, **Char_Out**

      iv)   Store input code in memory at address set by the pointer

      v)   Advance the pointer to the next memory location

      vi)   Repeat from item 2 unless input code was 'Enter'.

2.3   Modified list of actions for **Buff_In**

      i)   Set a pointer to the start of the buffer used for input.

      ii)   Get one key input code, **Char_In**

      iii)   Echo input code to display, **Char_Out**

      iv)   Store input code in memory at address set by the pointer

      v)   Advance the pointer to the next memory location

      vi)   If pointer is past buffer end move back one place (output BEL if specified, **Char_Out**).

      vii) Repeat from (ii) unless input code was 'Enter'.

2.5   This is the top level list. A hierarchy chart, lower level lists and NS charts are also required. The number to be displayed is *NUM*, and the module to convert 0 to 9 to the 7-bit pattern is **Seven**.

      i)   Set a pointer to the start of the display memory (least significant digit position).

      ii)   Set *count* = ten (as largest 32-bit number is 4294967295 which has ten digits).

      iii)   Divide *NUM* by ten, that is *NUM* becomes $NUM \div 10$, and note remainder *REM*.

      iv)   Convert *REM* to 7-bit value, **Seven**.

      v)   Store 7-bit value at position set by pointer.

      vi)   Change pointer to point to the memory location for the next display digit.

      vii) Subtract one from *count*.

      viii) Repeat from (iii) unless *count* is zero.

3.1

Address	Contents
0x00008000	0x5a
0x00008001	0xe4
0x00008002	0x23
0x00008003	0x00
0x00008004	0xc1
0x00008005	0x70

Address	Contents
0x00008006	0xd2
0x00008007	0x90
0x00008008	0x0a
0x00008009	0x13
0x0000800a	0xef
0x0000800b	0x04

Address	Contents
0x0000800c	0x38
0x0000800d	0x6b
0x0000800e	0x01
0x0000800f	0xff

3.3   Use r0 to r11 (or r12) inclusive for general purposes. r13, r14 and r15 have special uses.

Some advanced systems reserve r12; this use is usually selected by the programmer.

4.1   a)   Original value in r3 is lost (over written).

b)   Contents of r3 equal twice contents of r5.

c)   New contents of r3 equal twice old contents of r3.

4.3   One answer is modify Program 4.4 by replacing the three lines starting at the label *mystart* with

```
mystart    LDR    r3, =127             ; load first value
           LDR    r4, =0xe45ad         ; load second value
           LDR    r5, =2_10101110010   ; load third value
           ADD    r2, r3, r4           ; form the sum of first two values
           ADD    r2, r2, r5           ; add third value to previous total
```

The total is 936862 (decimal) = 0xe4b9e

4.5   a)   0xffffff0b

b)   0x00010044

c)   One more than the previous value unless it was 0xffffffff when it is zero.

5.1   Approximately 214 seconds.

5.3   a)   r4 holds 0xf081fb10, N = 1, Z = 0, C = 0, V = 0.

b)   r4 holds 0x6deb32d0, N = 0, Z = 0, C = 0, V = 0.

c)   r4 holds 0x00000000, N = 0, Z = 1, C = 1, V = 0.

5.6   a)   r4 holds 0x3ea98506, N = 0, Z = 0.

b)   r4 holds 0xa307a153, N = 1, Z = 0.

c)   r4 holds 0x2d056399, N = 0, Z = 0.

d)   r4 holds 0xd0d47fe8, N = 1, Z = 0.

6.3   a) 8   b) 1   c) 9   d) 9

6.5   The section of the program that performs the division should be similar to the following

```
;   Preceding instructions put the dividend into r6 and the divisor into r7
           MOVS   r7, r7          ; is divisor zero ?
           BEQ    somewhere       ; suitable action at somewhere if divisor zero
           MOV    r5, #0          ; set a counter
sub_loop   ADD    r5, r5, #1      ; count times subtracted
           SUBS   r6, r6, r7      ; set divisor = divisor - dividend
           BPL    sub_loop        ; loop if divisor still positive
           ADD    r6, r6, r7      ; restore remainder left in r6
           SUB    r5, r5, #1      ; correct quotient
```

0x00001000 divided by 0x00000008 leaves 0x200 in r5 and 0 in r6.

The programmer must decide the actions for 0x0f0f0f0f divided by 0x00000000.

0x0f0f0f0f divided by 0x0000000e leaves 0x01135c81 in r5 and 1 in r6.

7.1   One answer is below. The difference between versions is that more instructions are required for count up than count down. Also an extra register r6 is required for a general solution (it is not essential for special cases restricted to length less than 256).

```
            LDR     r4, =list_start  ; list_start = address of first element
            MOV     r5, #0           ; counter for number of items tested
            LDR     r6, =list_len    ; value of list_len, the number of items
                                     ; in the list (defined elsewhere)
            ; r4 is used as ptr and r5 as count
            MOV     r0, #0           ; r0 holds result, initial value zero is
                                     ; the smallest possible unsigned integer
loop_st     LDR     r7, [r4], #4     ; load memory value at ptr, advance ptr
            CMP     r0, r7           ; test for value > than largest so far
            BCS     small            ; if value was smaller then skip load
            MOV     r0, r7           ; make value new largest result
small       ADD     r5, r5, #1       ; count up number done
            CMP     r5, r6           ; test if all done
            BCC     loop_st          ; continue looping if more to do
```

The while forms are also required but are not illustrated here.

7.3   A simple modified program (modified section from ENTRY to NOP only shown) is

```
;           ENTRY
    ; r3 holds count and r4 holds total, r5 is the pointer to the data, ptr
            MOV     r3, #Numvals     ; initialise count
            MOV     r4, #0           ; initialise total
            LDR     r5, =datstart    ; set ptr to the start of the data
cloop       MOVS    r3, r3           ; check count
            BEQ     end_whi          ; exit loop if all done
            LDR     r6, [r5], #4     ; get value at ptr, advance ptr
            ADD     r4, r4, r6       ; add value to total
            SUB     r3, r3, #1       ; decrement count
            BAL     cloop            ; always loop using while form
end_whi     NOP                      ; NOPs to help testing
```

A minor improvement is MOV r3, #(*Numvals* + 1) to load r3; also replace MOVS r3, r3 by SUBS r3, r3, #1 and remove the later SUB r3, r3, #1.

8.1   The delay subroutine is that in Program 8.1 except that the value 0x234567 must be replaced by one to give a delay of 1 second. The value will depend on the target used, it will probably be between 0x100000 and 0x4000000. A possible *N* second delay subroutine is

```
; N second delay routine using a 1 second delay subroutine delay. N is a value
; from 0 to 0x1e13380 (one year) set to 0x1e13380 if too large. N is destroyed
; Inputs:-   N in r0
; Outputs:-  None
Nsec        STMFD   sp!, {r5, lr}    ; save used registers and return address
            LDR     r5,=0x1e13380    ; load maximum allowed
            CMP     r0, r5           ; test for N above maximum
            BPL     valid            ; branch IF not too large
            MOV     r0, r5           ; ELSE set N to maximum allowed
valid       MOVS    r0, r0           ; check for times to do over zero
            BEQ     end_while        ; end if all times done
            BL      delay            ; 1 second wait
            SUB     r0, r0, #1       ; count down times to do
            B       valid            ; continue WHILE loop
end_while   LDMFD   sp!, {r5,pc}     ; pop and return
```

8.3   One possible subroutine to find the largest value in a list.

```
; Find largest value in a list of 32-bit unsigned integers
; Inputs:-   r0 = pointer to the first list item, r1 = the list length
; Outputs:-  r0 holds largest value
get_max   STMFD  sp!, {r5,r6,lr}  ; save used registers and return address
          MOV    r5, #0           ; r5 holds result, initial value zero is
                                  ; the smallest possible unsigned integer
loop_st   LDR    r6, [r0], #4     ; get value at pointer, advance pointer
          CMP    r5, r6           ; test for value > than largest so far
          BCS    small            ; if value was smaller then skip load
          MOV    r5, r6           ; make value new largest result
small     SUBS   r1, r1, #1       ; count down number to do
          BCS    loop_st          ; continue looping if more to do
          MOV    r0, r5           ; put result into return register
          LDMFD  sp!, {r5,r6,pc}  ; pop and return
```

8.5   The plan selected for the subroutine is Figure A.1 (note it avoids output of the terminator).

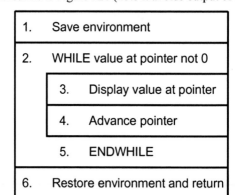

Figure A.1 NS chart for null terminated string output

9.1   a)   0x02090f06   b)   0xcf0faf1f   c)   0xcd06a01a

d)   0xc000a010   e)   0x30f050e0

9.5   A suggested plan is Figure A.2; note that any leading spaces are removed. The ASCII codes for space and all normal punctuation characters have bit 5 set to 1 so forcing bit 5 to 1 will not affect them.

Figure A.2 NS chart to convert text to sentence case

9.7 The specification requires development. For example the suggested plan requires that the number, *value*, and the address of the start of the string, *ptr*, are passed as parameters. One design is the NS chart of Figure A.3.

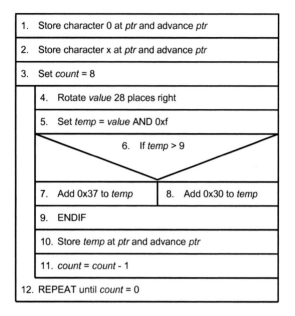

1. Store character 0 at *ptr* and advance *ptr*

2. Store character x at *ptr* and advance *ptr*

3. Set *count* = 8

> 4. Rotate *value* 28 places right
>
> 5. Set *temp = value* AND 0xf
>
> 6. If *temp* > 9
>
> | 7. Add 0x37 to *temp* | 8. Add 0x30 to *temp* |
>
> 9. ENDIF
>
> 10. Store *temp* at *ptr* and advance *ptr*
>
> 11. *count = count* - 1

12. REPEAT until *count* = 0

Figure A.3 NS chart for subroutine to output a hexadecimal string

9.8 Again the specification requires some development. It is suggested that the 32-bit pattern is the only input parameter and the output is a Boolean value for true (yes) or false (no). More generally a pointer to a test pattern could be an input allowing a test for any pattern. Two logic operations will be required in a loop which tests the pattern, shifts the 32-bit pattern (probably easier than shifting the test pattern but the number of instructions are probably the same for ARM unlike some other CPUs) and tests for the match.
The pattern is only found in 0x12345678 and 0xaa998877.

10.1 0x000a7cdf

10.5 The following actions are required
- Always show the decimal point
- Multiply value by 64251 as indicated
- Shift right 14 places
- Use ADC Rd, Rd, #0 to round up if necessary.
- If value > 999 send 100·0 to display
- Otherwise set first digit as blank and determine each in turn.

Except for 100·0 there are only three digits and division is difficult it is easier to find how many times 100_D can be subtracted from the result, if 0 blank the second display digit otherwise show number of times subtracted. Then repeatedly subtract 10_D from the remainder using the number of times subtracted as the third display digit (always shown) and the remainder as the digit after the point.

10.8 Multiply by 2 is by `MOV  Rd, Rn, LSL #1`
Multiply by 3 is by `ADD  Rd, Rn, Rn, LSL #1`
The first multiplication that cannot be performed without a multiply instruction is multiply by 6 (unless someone can see a method of doing it). In general, except for powers of two, even number multipliers are difficult to devise using a single instruction. They can usually be performed with two instructions which will in some cases be faster than multiply for ARM7TDMI.

11.2   The important feature is parameter passing. If the output device is set up by a subroutine called ***Init***, the output routine is called ***Display*** and the delay is ***Delay*** then the program (without the routines and assuming rum on a development system which performs general initialisation) will be

```
; Demonstrate use of display
; Note that the subroutines must be added to the program
; Date:-      13th July 2007
; Revisions:-
; Author:-    J.R. Gibson
maxdis    EQU     9                   ; maximum value displayed
          AREA    Demo,  CODE,  READONLY
          ENTRY
; r4 dval the value to be shown
          LDR     sp, =0x10000        ; initialise stack pointer
          BL      Init                ; set up display system
          MOV     r4, #0              ; initialise dval, the output value
    ; start of loop
loop      MOV     r0, r4              ; pass parameter in r0
          BL      Display             ; show digit value
          BL      Delay               ; wait so digit visible
          ADD     r4, r4, #1          ; increment dval
          CMP     r4, #(maxdis + 1)   ; has last value been displayed?
          MOVEQ   r4, #0              ; if required re-initialise dval
          B       loop                ; loop always so no program end
          END
```

11.4   Figure A.4 shows the hierarchy chart and NS chart for the main program. This requires subroutines ***Str_Out*** for string output, ***Ser_Out*** to display one character and ***Ser_In*** to input one character. Note that the input is forced to upper case so that N, n, Y and y are accepted.

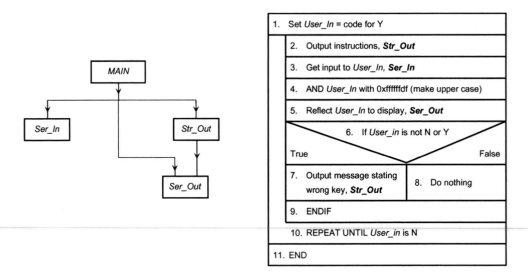

Figure A.4 Hierarchy and NS charts for test of serial input

12.1   LDR   r1,=0x56 becomes MOV   r1, #0x56

LDR   r1,= 0x54000003 becomes MOV   r1, #0xD5, 6

LDR   r4,= 0x003c0000 becomes MOV   r4, #0x3C, 20

ADR   r3, *xyz* becomes ADD   r3, pc, #offset where offset is a positive value

ADR   r5, *abc* becomes SUB   r5, pc, #offset where offset is a positive value

12.3   The flowcharts are Figure A.5; note how all the tests have to be inverted in the incomplete version but only the evaluation of the complete equation is changed in the complete version.

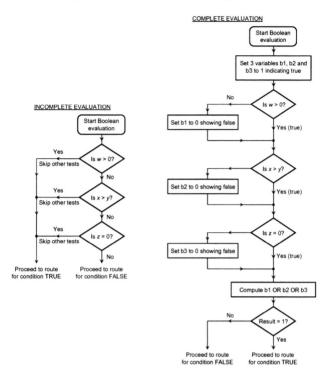

Figure A.5   Evaluation of ($w > 0$) OR ($x > y$) OR ($z = 0$)

The chart for the incomplete evaluation contains one less IF structure but as for the AND case it is impossible to draw an NS chart to exactly follow the chart.

13.2   Figure A.6 shows the NS charts for one design; one chart is the main program and the other the handler. An extra feature, variable *count*, held in a register has been added; this allows the program to indicate how many cases of no memory were detected.

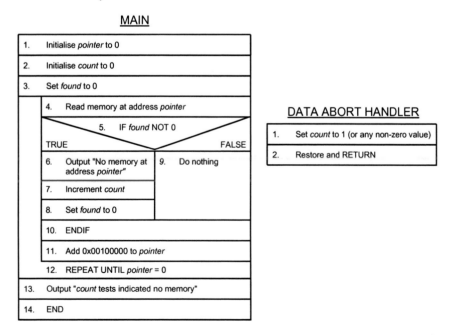

Figure A.6   NS charts for data abort exception testing

Appendix B
ASCII codes

Letters, numeric digits, punctuation symbols, etc., are often represented by code numbers. A common system is the American Standard Code for Information Interchange, ASCII. The codes are 7-bit numbers but are usually used in 8-bit form by adding a leading zero. Table B.1 lists the standard ASCII codes as decimal and hexadecimal values. Quantities SOH, ETX, LF, etc., are control codes. For example LF is line feed, move to next line before output of next character; CR is carriage return, return to start of the line. Two codes are used for output to appear at the start of a new line, both CR and LF are output. Some systems do not work this way; for example those using Unix or Linux.

Character	Hex	Decimal	Character	Hex	Decimal	Character	Hex	Decimal
NUL	00	0	+	2B	43	V	56	86
SOH	01	1	,	2C	44	W	57	87
STX	02	2	-	2D	45	X	58	88
ETX	03	3	.	2E	46	Y	59	89
EOT	04	4	/	2F	47	Z	5A	90
ENQ	05	5	0	30	48	[	5B	91
ACK	06	6	1	31	49	\	5C	92
BEL	07	7	2	32	50	]	5D	93
BS	08	8	3	33	51	↑	5E	94
HT	09	9	4	34	52	←	5F	95
LF	0A	10	5	35	53	`	60	96
VT	0B	11	6	36	54	a	61	97
FF	0C	12	7	37	55	b	62	98
CR	0D	13	8	38	56	c	63	99
SO	0E	14	9	39	57	d	64	100
SI	0F	15	:	3A	58	e	65	101
DLE	10	16	;	3B	59	f	66	102
DC1	11	17	<	3C	60	g	67	103
DC2	12	18	=	3D	61	h	68	104
DC3	13	19	>	3E	62	i	69	105
DC4	14	20	?	3F	63	j	6A	106
NAK	15	21	@	40	64	k	6B	107
SYN	16	22	A	41	65	l	6C	108
ETB	17	23	B	42	66	m	6D	109
CAN	18	24	C	43	67	n	6E	110
EM	19	25	D	44	68	o	6F	111
SUB	1A	26	E	45	69	p	70	112
ESC	1B	27	F	46	70	q	71	113
FS	1C	28	G	47	71	r	72	114
GS	1D	29	H	48	72	s	73	115
RS	1E	30	I	49	73	t	74	116
US	1F	31	J	4A	74	u	75	117
SP	20	32	K	4B	75	v	76	118
!	21	33	L	4C	76	w	77	119
"	22	34	M	4D	77	x	78	120
#	23	35	N	4E	78	y	79	121
$	24	36	O	4F	79	z	7A	122
%	25	37	P	50	80	{	7B	123
&	26	38	Q	51	81			7C	124
'	27	39	R	52	82	}	7D	125
(	28	40	S	53	83	~	7E	126
)	29	41	T	54	84	DEL	7F	127
*	2A	42	U	55	85			

Table B.1 Standard ASCII codes

Appendix C
Numbers, bases and conversions

C.1 Numbers

Arithmetic operations produce a new numeric value by combining existing numeric values. The rule for each operation is defined for initial numbers from the infinite set of all real numbers which extends from an infinitely large magnitude negative value through zero to an infinitely large magnitude positive value. Between any two numbers, no matter how close together they are, there are infinitely many sub-divisions.

Any of the infinite set of all possible numbers may be represented using the general form

$$d_n \times b^n + d_{n-1} \times b^{n-1} + \cdots + d_2 \times b^2 + d_1 \times b^1 + d_0 \times b^0 + d_{-1} \times b^{-1} + d_{-2} \times b^{-2} + \cdots + d_{-m+1} \times b^{-m+1} + d_{-m} \times b^{-m}$$

where each d_x is a **digit** of the number system and b is the **base** or **radix**. Any integer greater than one may be chosen as the base, b. For the chosen base there must be exactly b different digits with the values zero, one, two, up to b - 1. In the familiar decimal system the base is ten and the digits are 0, 1, 2, 3, 4, 5, 6, 7, 8 and 9. The system evolved from counting using fingers, digits, to keep track of the count hence the choice of ten for the base. The printed symbols 0, 1, 2, 3, etc., are graphical devices to represent each of the quantities zero, one, two, three, etc.

Conventionally only the digit symbols are printed; for example 835·29 represents eight hundred and thirty five and twenty nine hundredths using base ten. The decimal point indicates the position of d_0, the digit multiplied by the base to the power zero; it is immediately to the left of the decimal point. The other digit positions are in order of the power to which the base is raised; movement one place left corresponds to increase of one in the power to which the base is raised, movement one place right corresponds to a decrease of one in the power. Absence of a decimal point indicates that the number is an **integer** with the point immediately to the right of the least significant digit.

The general form is extremely powerful as every possible number may be printed in a readily understood manner. Use of a plus or minus sign before the number extends the system to positive and negative values; if there is no sign the number is assumed to be positive. Restricting the numbers allowed to those without digits to the right of the point gives a sub-set in which all the numbers are **integers**; if the set is further restricted to numbers without a sign all values are positive and are **unsigned integers**.

Numbers with base ten are the most familiar but any integer value greater than one may be used as the base provided the choice is clearly stated; if no base is indicated base ten is usually assumed. An important feature is that the number of different digit symbols equals the base. When the base is ten the familiar symbols 0 to 9 are used; however any set of ten symbols may be used provided that everyone using the numbers knows the value allocated to each symbol. Printed symbols are just one method of representing the individual digit values. Another set of symbols is the magnitude of electrical signals such as voltage or current indicating the condition of an electrical circuit. If the circuit is a *'logic circuit'* the input and output signals are only allowed two different values; hence there are only two symbols and the only possible base has $b = 2$. The number system using base two is the **binary number system**. In printed form binary numbers only have the digit symbols 0 and 1 and the general form of binary number is

$$d_n \times 2^n + d_{n-1} \times 2^{n-1} + \cdots + d_2 \times 2^2 + d_1 \times 2^1 + d_0 \times 2^0 + d_{-1} \times 2^{-1} + d_{-2} \times 2^{-2} + \cdots + d_{-m+1} \times 2^{-m+1} + d_{-m} \times 2^{-m}$$

where each d_x may only be either 0 or 1.

Electronic processors manipulate groups of logic signals and programmers use the groups to represent multiple digit binary numbers. In general the number of signals is fixed by the hardware designer so that numbers have a fixed number of binary digits, bits. This fixed number of bits causes problems because not all of the infinite set of numbers may be represented. Situations arise where an arithmetic operation combining two numbers each represented using the fixed number of bits produces a result that requires more bits than are available. The limitations of machine computations must be understood when they are used in critical applications.

A fixed number of bits may be used to represent different types of number. If all the bits represent binary digits with the point to the right of all digits the number is an unsigned integer. Alternatively some bits may be used to indicate a sign and some the position of the decimal point. The number of possibilities is large leading to **signed integers** and **fractional numbers** with many different forms. The most common fractional numbers are **floating point numbers** but other types such as **fixed point numbers** may be used; fractional numbers are not examined in this book.

It is usual to regard a written number as being in base ten unless another base is indicated. For example 1011 normally represents the quantity one thousand and eleven; however it could be a number in base two, or in any other base and if so it would represent a different quantity. Because binary numbers are used frequently the practice adopted in this book is to assume that all numbers that contain only the digits 0 and 1 are binary numbers unless they are deliberately indicated as having another base.

There are a large number of different representations used to indicate the base of a number; a few are shown in Table C.1. Other methods exist and their meanings are usually obvious. Hexadecimal numbers have a base of sixteen and are briefly described in Section C.3.

Base representation	Application	Examples
Suffix	All bases	1011011_2 or 1011011_B binary 133_8 or 133_O or 133_Q octal 91 or 91_{10} or 91_D decimal 77_{12} duodecimal $5B_{16}$ or $5B_H$ hexadecimal
Prefix	Usually bases less than ten	2_1011011 binary 5_331 base five 8_133 octal
Postscript	Usually common bases only	1011011B binary 133O or 133Q octal 91 or 91D decimal 5BH hexadecimal
C language style	Used for hexadecimal only	0x5B

Table C.1 Common forms of indicating the base of a number

Minor variations of the various forms of indicating base are frequently used, for example forms such as 2_1011011 may have an alternative character in place of the underscore between the base and the value. Because hexadecimal representation is common many other prefix forms are used for hexadecimal numbers; common ones use $ or & giving the forms $5B and &5B.

C.2 Conversion

A frequent requirement is to convert a number from its representation in one base to its representation in another base. For example most computer systems work internally in binary but usually present the results in the familiar base ten form. When the initial number representation is in a base with a smaller value than the required new base the conversion is simple for relatively small integer values. All that is necessary is to write the original number in the form

$$d_n \times b^n + d_{n-1} \times b^{n-1} + \cdots + d_2 \times b^2 + d_1 \times b^1 + d_0 \times b^0$$

then replace each b^x by the base raised to the appropriate power x with this quantity evaluated in the new base. For example 1011100110_2 is

$$1 \times 2^9 + 0 \times 2^8 + 1 \times 2^7 + 1 \times 2^6 + 1 \times 2^5 + 0 \times 2^4 + 0 \times 2^3 + 1 \times 2^2 + 1 \times 2^1 + 0 \times 2^0$$

Evaluating the various powers of two in base ten gives

$$1 \times 512 + 0 \times 256 + 1 \times 128 + 1 \times 64 + 1 \times 32 + 0 \times 16 + 0 \times 8 + 1 \times 4 + 1 \times 2 + 0 \times 1$$

which reduces to $\quad 512 + 128 + 64 + 32 + 4 + 2 = 742_{10}$.

The method is obvious but is not suitable for implementation by a computer program. The following general method is simple and may be used for machine conversion from one base to any other base. The algorithm requires that the following steps are performed in sequence working in the original base except where noted.

    i)   Divide the number by the new base and note the remainder produced as a single digit in the new base; a digit of 0 must be noted if there is no remainder. Make the digit noted the first element of a list. The remainder will always be a single digit in the new base as division by the new base can only produce a remainder less than the divisor.

    ii)   Divide the result, the quotient, produced by the previous division by the new base and again note the remainder as a digit in the new base, including digit 0 if the division does not produce a remainder. Add this new digit to the list as the next element.

    iii)   Repeatedly perform step (ii) dividing each new quotient produced by the base and adding the remainders at the end of the list. Only stop when the quotient is zero.

    iv)   Write the list of remainders as the number in the new base with the member of the list that was the last one produced as the most significant digit; the list member that was produced first is the least significant digit.

This calculation is entirely in the initial base, **except** that the remainders are noted as digits in the new base. Figure C.1 illustrates the process for the example of conversion of the number 876_D to binary. The list of remainders, with last one produced written first as the most significant digit, is the number in the new base; 1101101100_2 for the example. Using the previous method of conversion by evaluating the powers of the base, the reverse conversion may be used to confirm that this is the correct value.

$$1 \times 2^9 + 1 \times 2^8 + 0 \times 2^7 + 1 \times 2^6 + 1 \times 2^5 + 0 \times 2^4 + 1 \times 2^3 + 1 \times 2^2 + 0 \times 2^1 + 0 \times 2^0$$
$$= 512 + 256 + 64 + 32 + 8 + 4 = 876_{10}$$

The repeated division process, although slow, is suitable for machine conversion; Figure C.2 is an NS chart of a module to display a number held in binary form as the equivalent in another base. The difficulty with the conversion is that producing each digit of the result requires a division operation. Chapter 10 indicates that division is a difficult arithmetic operation using a processor and programs involving many divisions are slow. The inclusion of a large amount of decimal output in any program significantly reduces the speed with which it runs even using very high power computers.

876	÷	2	=	438	remainder	0
438	÷	2	=	219	remainder	0
219	÷	2	=	109	remainder	1
109	÷	2	=	54	remainder	1
54	÷	2	=	27	remainder	0
27	÷	2	=	13	remainder	1
13	÷	2	=	6	remainder	1
6	÷	2	=	3	remainder	0
3	÷	2	=	1	remainder	1
1	÷	2	=	0	remainder	1

Figure C.1 Conversion of 876_D to base 2.

1.	Set *'quotient'* = initial number
2.	Set *'pointer'* to start of a buffer for a list
3.	Set *'divisor'* = new base
4.	WHILE *'quotient'* > 0
	5. *'quotient'* =*'quotient'* divided by *'divisor'*
	6. *Store 'remainder' at 'pointer'*
	7. Advance *'pointer'*
	8. ENDWHILE
9.	WHILE *'pointer'* not before list start
	10. Decrement *'pointer'*
	11. Convert value at *'pointer'* to code for digit
	12. Send code for digit to display device
	13. ENDWHILE
14.	RETURN

Figure C.2 Process to convert a number from one base to another and display the result

C.3 Hexadecimal and octal numbers

A problem writing binary numbers is that a large number of digits are needed; for example one thousand in binary is 1111101000. This requires ten digits rather than the four for base ten or three for base sixteen. It is convenient to represent numbers in a form that is quickly converted to and from binary but does not use many digits or require division. Generally conversion requires division, is error prone if performed manually and slow using a processor system; however conversion is simple if one base is an integral power of the other. If the base is two the most useful powers of two are three and four giving bases eight, **octal**, and sixteen, **hexadecimal**, respectively. Both are common although hexadecimal versions are most frequently used.

Hexadecimal numbers require sixteen digit symbols. Symbols **0** to **9** are used for digits zero to nine; the other symbols are the first six letters of the alphabet with **A** or **a** for ten, **B** or **b** for eleven and so on to **F** or **f** for fifteen. Each hexadecimal digit can be individually converted to the equivalent four digit binary value, Table C.2.

Value	Hexadecimal digit	Binary	Value	Hexadecimal digit	Binary
zero	0	0000	eight	8	1000
one	1	0001	nine	9	1001
two	2	0010	ten	A or a	1010
three	3	0011	eleven	B or b	1011
four	4	0100	twelve	C or c	1100
five	5	0101	thirteen	D or d	1101
six	6	0110	fourteen	E or e	1110
seven	7	0111	fifteen	F or f	1111

Table C.2 4-bit binary equivalents of the hexadecimal digits

To convert a binary integer into the hexadecimal equivalent divide it into groups of four bits starting at the decimal point, the extreme right hand side, and move left. If the final group has fewer than four digits extra 0 digits are added at the left. Each group is replaced by the corresponding hexadecimal digit. Hence the binary number 11101011100101 is broken into groups as, 11 1010 1110 0101 and two leading zeros are added giving 0011 1010 1110 0101. Replacing each group by the hexadecimal digit gives 0x3ae5 as the hexadecimal equivalent. The reverse conversion is even more simple. Each hexadecimal digit is replaced by the 4-bit equivalent; 0xc3f1 is binary 1100 0011 1111 0001 or 1100001111110001 if the grouping is removed.

The only difference for binary to octal and octal to binary conversions is that groups have three bits, the octal system has only eight digits 0 to 7. Now 11101011100101 becomes 11 101 011 100 101, one leading 0 is added and the octal equivalent is 35345_8. The reverse conversion is also simple, the octal number 3702_8 becomes binary 011111000010.

These conversions are easily performed manually or by software or by hardware. A numeric value requires only a quarter of the number of hexadecimal digits that it does in binary form; consequently hexadecimal form is often used to print numbers held in binary form in processor systems. Octal numbers are also used but only reduce the number of digits to a third although, as letters are not required, display and printing are more easily implemented.

C.4 Signed integers

A processor system is constructed with logic circuits so signals have only two states and only two symbols are available. The states are usually used to represent 0 and 1 leaving no symbols to represent plus and minus signs. This problem is overcome by choosing that bits at different positions in the pattern provide different information; bits in specified positions represent digits and those, usually just one bit, in other positions indicate the sign. Because the position of bits affects their interpretation it is usually essential that **the number of bits in a signed number must be fixed**.

If N bits represent a number with one bit as the sign only N-1 bits remain for the magnitude so the number range is usually $-(2^{N-1}-1)$ through 0 to $+(2^{N-1}-1)$. There are many methods of representing signed numbers, the most common one is twos complement. This has advantages in ease of use and in the construction of circuits to perform arithmetic operations. The mathematical definition of the operation to change the sign of a number X in N-bit twos complement is to subtract the N-bit value as if it is an unsigned integer from 2^N. The most significant bit, MSB, automatically becomes the sign bit with 0 indicating a positive number and 1 a negative number. Most CPUs, including ARM, have features that support the use of twos complement to represent signed numbers.

Printed forms of numbers with thirty two bits are very cumbersome so the properties of twos complement are illustrated here with $N = 8$. The first point is that to change the sign of a number using twos complement the operation **does not** consist of changing the MSB. For example

| 00001100 | represents the positive number twelve |
| 10001100 | represents a negative number but **it is not minus twelve** |

The twos complement of a number is defined as 2^N minus the number. Therefore to find the magnitude of 10001100 it is converted to the positive number with the same magnitude by subtracting it from 2^N, that is 2^8 for this 8-bit example. The subtraction requires nine bits, $N+1$ bits, as 2^8 cannot be represented in eight bits; the subtraction is outlined in Figure C.3.

1 0 0 0 0 0 0 0 0	2^8
1 0 0 0 1 1 0 0	A two's complement negative number
0 0 1 1 1 0 1 0 0	the original negative number multiplied by -1

Figure C.3 Sign change of an 8-bit number by subtraction from 2^8

Ignore the MSB of the nine bit result as there are only eight bits available to hold numeric values; the result is 01110100 which is equivalent to 116_D. Hence 10001100 either represents 140_D as an unsigned integer or -116_D as a twos complement integer in 8-bits. The programmer chooses which of the values the bit pattern represents; when using more than one number representation in a program the programmer must organise and document the data carefully.

There is a simple trick to change the sign of a number in twos complement while keeping the magnitude the same. All bits of the number are inverted and one is added to the result ignoring any carry out from the MSB. Figure C.4 shows this for conversion of $+12_D$ to -12_D in 8-bit twos complement.

0 0 0 0 1 1 0 0	Number, value $+12_D$
1 1 1 1 0 0 1 1	Invert all bits
0 0 0 0 0 0 0 1	Value +1 to be added
1 1 1 1 0 1 0 0	Result representing -12_D

Figure C.4 Sign change of an 8-bit number by inversion and addition of 1

The twos complement representation of -12_D in 8-bits is 11110100. An important feature of any signed arithmetic process is that a double negative should produce no overall effect. Performing the negation process a second time should result in the original number as in Figure C.5.

1 1 1 1 0 1 0 0	-12_D in two's complement
0 0 0 0 1 0 1 1	Invert all bits
0 0 0 0 0 0 0 1	Value +1 to be added
0 0 0 0 1 1 0 0	Result, value $+12_D$

Figure C.5 Second sign change to confirm process action

Why does inversion of all bits followed by addition of one give the value 2^N - X? Subtraction of +12 $_D$ from the 8-bit value that is all ones is shown by Figure C.6.

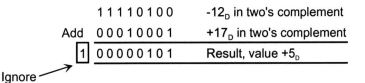

	1 1 1 1 1 1 1 1	Number with all digits 1
Subtract	0 0 0 0 1 1 0 0	Number, value +12$_D$
	1 1 1 1 0 0 1 1	All 1s minus 12$_D$

Figure C.6 Subtraction of +12 $_D$ from the all 1s number

In binary the subtraction in any column is either $1 - 0 = 1$ or $1 - 1 = 0$. There are no cases requiring a borrow from the column to the left; the value at each position is determined independently of all others. Also if the quantity subtracted is 1 the result is 0; if the quantity subtracted is 0 the result is 1; the result in each column is the opposite, inverse, value of the bit subtracted. Hence to subtract an N-bit number from the number which is all 1s all that is necessary is to invert the bits. The value corresponding to all bits 1 is 2^N - 1. Hence inverting all bits of some number X produces 2^N - 1 - X; addition of 1 to this gives 2^N - 1 - X + 1 = 2^N - X, the twos complement.

A reason twos complement is widely used is that if signed numbers represented in N-bit twos complement form are added or subtracted as if they are N-bit unsigned integers and any carry or borrow from the MSB position is ignored the result is correct. The result has the correct sign regardless of the signs of the individual numbers **except when the result magnitude is too large**. Using two obvious small 8-bit values Figure C.7 illustrates that the result is correct.

	1 1 1 1 0 1 0 0	-12$_D$ in two's complement
Add	0 0 0 1 0 0 0 1	+17$_D$ in two's complement
1	0 0 0 0 0 1 0 1	Result, value +5$_D$

Ignore

Figure C.7 Example of twos complement addition

Why is the result correct? The twos complement of X, call it X^*, was defined as 2^N - X. Hence if the subtraction of X from another number Y is performed by computing $Y + X^*$ then $Y + X^* = Y + 2^N$ - X = $2^N + Y$ - X. However the 2^N is in the position of the ignored carry that does not fit into N-bits so the N-bit result is Y - X as required. Consequently addition behaves correctly with twos complement signed numbers and all that is necessary to perform **subtraction** is to invert all bits of the subtrahend, add 1 to it and add the result to the minuend. Implementing subtraction when designing the arithmetic circuit of a CPU is simple; it only requires circuits to invert all the bits of a number and the addition circuit which already exists to perform the additions required.

Problems arise when the result is too large, for example if numbers are in 8-bit twos complement and 120$_D$ is added to 117$_D$. The result should be 237$_D$ but because the largest positive number in 8-bit twos complement is 127$_D$ a problem occurs as illustrated in Figure C.8.

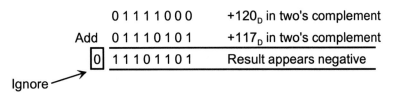

	0 1 1 1 1 0 0 0	+120$_D$ in two's complement
Add	0 1 1 1 0 1 0 1	+117$_D$ in two's complement
0	1 1 1 0 1 1 0 1	Result appears negative

Ignore

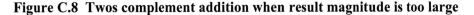

Figure C.8 Twos complement addition when result magnitude is too large

The result appears to be a valid negative number but obviously is not. Using 8-bits twos complement it is only possible to represent values -127_D through 0 to $+127_D$ but the total in this example is 237_D. As 7-bits are for the magnitude the carry from these 7-bits is added into the sign bit causing it to be changed when it should not change, this is called **overflow** rather than carry. Overflow using signed numbers is more difficult to detect than for simple unsigned arithmetic, it occurs when the carry out from the bit position one below the MSB is different from the carry out from MSB position. Processors such as ARM indicate this by the overflow flag, V. When two large magnitude negative numbers are added **underflow** can occur and is also indicated by the V flag. Overflow and underflow can also occur when numbers with different signs are subtracted; again it is indicated by the V flag.

To summarise twos complement is a very effective method of representing signed integers but the user must be aware of the limitations. The number of bits used to represent numbers must be fixed and cases of overflow must be detected.

Appendix D
Data memory transfer

Only some versions of the LDR and STR instructions and associated memory addressing modes were described in Chapter 7. Brief descriptions of all the addressing modes of LDR and STR for ARM7TDMI are here; full details are in the ARM Architecture Reference Manual [12]. Addressing modes for LDR and STR can be divided into two groups; the first are regarded as the main memory addressing modes called *"Addressing Mode 2 - Load and Store Word or Unsigned Byte"*. The second group are special cases with restrictions on their use and are referred to as *"Addressing Mode 3 - Miscellaneous Loads and Stores"*.

"Addressing Mode 1" refers to all the addressing modes that do not use memory to obtain their operands, that is instructions such as MOV and ADD that use register and immediate operands.

D.1 Memory Addressing Mode 2

The main methods of load and store operations using Addressing Mode 2 apply to the versions of LDR and STR listed in Table D.1

Mnemonic	Dest Reg'r	Memory location
LDR{<cond>}	<Rd>,	<addressing_mode>
LDR{<cond>}B	<Rd>,	<addressing_mode>
LDR{<cond>}T	<Rd>,	<addressing_mode>
LDR{<cond>}BT	<Rd>,	<addressing_mode>
STR{<cond>}	<Rd>,	<addressing_mode>
STR{<cond>}B	<Rd>,	<addressing_mode>
STR{<cond>}T	<Rd>,	<addressing_mode>
STR{<cond>}BT	<Rd>,	<addressing_mode>

Table D.1 Versions of LDR and STR used with Addressing Mode 2

The versions of the LDR and STR mnemonics with the additional letter T are associated with memory systems that use the CPU modes introduced in Chapter 13; this is an advanced topic which is not described here. When the mnemonic does not include the letter B the memory transfer is a 32-bit word; when the additional letter B is appended only a single byte is transferred.

It is important to note that the optional condition suffix is positioned between the mnemonic and the extra mode letter B or T. ARM have recently changed the assembler definition and the preferred form has the mode letter before the optional condition; for example the revised form of LDRB is LDRB{<cond>} <Rd>,<addressing_mode>. However only the RealView assembler accepts this form; it also accepts the older form so use of the older version causes fewer difficulties.

For all the mnemonic forms in Table D.1 the field <addressing_mode> may be any of the Addressing Mode 2 forms in Table D.2. Mode 1 in Table D.2 is the basic addressing mode described in Chapter 7. The address used for the transfer is formed by adding the signed 12-bit offset value to the contents of the register Rn; it is not essential to type the plus sign when the value is positive. When an offset of zero is used the printed form is reduced to [<Rn>]. Mode 2 is similar to mode 1; it differs because instead of adding a constant offset known when the program is written a computed offset held in register Rm is added to, or subtracted from, the contents of the base register Rn. It is very important to remember that for these modes the **contents of Rn are not changed**; the computed value is used as the memory address and then discarded. A simple use of these modes is to access elements of an array of words or bytes. Mode 1 is used when the programmer knows which element is required at the time when the program is written, mode 2 is used when the program actions determine which element is to be used.

Mode	Base Reg'r	Offset
1.	[<Rn>,	#+/-<offset_12>]
2.	[<Rn>,	+/-<Rm>]
3.	[<Rn>,	+/-<Rm>, <shift> #<shift_imm>]
4.	[<Rn>,	#+/-<offset_12>]!
5.	[<Rn>,	+/-<Rm>]!
6.	[<Rn>,	+/-<Rm>, <shift> #<shift_imm>]!
7.	[<Rn>],	#+/-<offset_12>
8.	[<Rn>],	+/-<Rm>
9.	[<Rn>],	+/-<Rm>, <shift> #<shift_imm>

Table D.2   Forms of <addressing_mode> for Addressing Mode 2

Mode 3 is complicated; the quantity <shift> is replaced by one of the shift operations LSL, LSR, ASR, ROR or RRX described in Chapter 9. <shift_imm> is replaced by the number of places to be shifted or rotated; the value used should be restricted to the range 1 to 31 to avoid problems and no shift value must be used with RRX. The shift or rotate is performed on the contents of register Rm in the same manner as described in Chapter 9 except that no flags are changed. The result after the shift operation is added to, or subtracted from, the contents of Rn; again the contents of Rn are not changed.

One use of mode 3 is manipulation of array and structure data when the number of memory locations used to hold an item is 2^N. Availability of this feature suggests that programmers should attempt to create data structures with elements with size 2^N bytes. The mode is also useful in creating a case structure as described in Chapter 12.

Modes 4, 5 and 6 are related to the corresponding modes 1, 2 and 3 but differ in the effect they have on the contents of Rn. This is indicated by the use of an exclamation mark after the closing square bracket. The memory address used for the read or write with these modes is exactly the same as that for the corresponding modes without the exclamation mark. The difference in behaviour is that the address calculated is put into register Rn. The mode is called **pre-indexed** because the new address is calculated and used **before** being stored in Rn. These modes can be used for array processing operations; they are most useful for complex data structures. Note that [<Rn>]! must not be used; when no offset is required the form [<Rn>] without the exclamation mark is used. In large programs the exclamation mark is not obvious and accidental errors arising from its inclusion or omission can arise and are difficult to detect.

The final three modes are also similar to the corresponding versions of the first three modes; the only difference in the printed form is the position of the closing square bracket. These modes are **post-indexed** addressing modes. They are very similar to the pre-indexed modes but behave in a significantly different manner. The address used for the memory transfer is given by the contents of Rn before the new address is computed. After the memory transfer is performed the new address is computed in the manner corresponding to the addressing mode and this new value is put into Rn.

While pre-indexed is the term used by ARM to describe the modes 4, 5 and 6 it may also be called pre-increment when the offset is positive and pre-decrement when it is negative. Similarly post-indexed may also be called post-increment or post-decrement.

D.2 Memory Addressing Mode 3

These additional miscellaneous addressing modes apply to the special versions of LDR and STR in Table D.3. As the versions of LDR and STR with the suffix D are not implemented on ARM7 versions of the CPU they are ignored here.

Mnemonic	Dest Reg'r	Memory location
LDR{<cond>}H	<Rd>,	<addressing_mode>
LDR{<cond>}SH	<Rd>,	<addressing_mode>
LDR{<cond>}SB	<Rd>,	<addressing_mode>
LDR{<cond>}D	<Rd>,	<addressing_mode>
STR{<cond>}H	<Rd>,	<addressing_mode>
STR{<cond>}D	<Rd>,	<addressing_mode>

Table D.3 Versions of LDR and STR used with Addressing Mode 3

The addition of the letter H to the mnemonic is the mode to transfer a half word of 16-bits starting at the address set by <addressing_mode>. The addition of S indicates a signed number, an 8-bit or 16-bit value is automatically sign extended to 32-bits for LDR instructions; there are no corresponding STR instructions as there cannot be a storage operation requiring sign extension. These versions cannot use all the addressing modes in Table D.2. Modes 3, 6 and 9 which perform a shift of register contents when computing the address are not allowed; also the immediate offset values, shown as #<offset_12>, for modes 1, 4 and 7 are limited to 8-bit values #<offset_8> instead of 12-bit ones.

D.3 Complicated effects and restrictions

Several complicated situations arise in memory transfer operations. For all forms of <addressing_mode> except the most simple form [Rn] an address is computed; the computation is a normal 32-bit unsigned integer addition or subtraction. There is no indication when the result exceeds 32-bits or is less than zero;

the 32-bit value produced is used as the address even if the computation produced a carry or required a borrow. No flags are affected by the computation of the address.

When LDR or STR are used to access a 32-bit word in memory the address computed should be aligned, that is the two LSBs of the address should both be zero. If the address is not aligned the behaviour is complicated and the **behaviour differs for LDR and STR.** For STR the two LSBs are both forced to zero; that is the address is always aligned regardless of the value calculated. For LDR the memory access obtains the 32-bit value starting at the address which has the two LSBs both zero but the value loaded into the destination register is adjusted if the two LSBs of the computed address are not both zero. The two LSBs are treated as a numeric value; that is they represent the values 0, 1, 2 or 3. As the value is read from memory it is automatically rotated by the 0, 8, 16 or 24 places, the amount is determined by multiplying the value of the two LSBs by eight. The effect produced by the rotation depends on the CPU organisation as it differs for big-endian and little-endian systems.

Half word transfers in either direction must use an address with the LSB zero; that is addresses must be half word aligned. Unlike 32-bit transfers the effect of non-alignment is unpredictable.

Finally there are restrictions on the registers that may be used for Rd, Rn and Rm. In cases where the addressing mode computes a value and changes the contents of Rn the use of the same register for Rn and Rm is often unpredictable; all such uses should be avoided. However the form `LDR Rx, [Rx]` where there is no address computation is very useful. This replaces an address in a register by the contents of the memory at that address.

In general the use of r15 for Rm is unpredictable; if r15 is used as Rn the value used in address computation is the address of the instruction plus eight. r15 may be used as Rd; this use is demonstrated as a method of creating case structures in Chapter 12. Instructions to change the contents of r15 must always be used with great care and should only be used for standard techniques such as subroutine return and case structure implementation.

Appendix E
The Keil tools

This is a brief introduction to the very powerful Keil tools. Documentation and examples with the tools assume programs use a combination of assembly language and C/C++ whereas this book examines program development using assembly language only. A simple method of working with assembly language programs is outlined in this appendix.

E.1 Installing the software

At the time of writing the Keil tools are in the self extracting file *mdk311.exe* downloaded from *'ARM Evaluation Software'* at *http://www.keil.com/demo/*. Details here assume this version; other versions differ; examples are in different locations and command sequences vary slightly. Download the file and double click it to install. Unless there is a conflict install in the default directory *C:\Keil*; after installation check all options. Download the GNU assembler at the same time to ensure compatible versions. The file is *gccARM331.exe* also from *http://www.keil.com/demo/*; install to the default folder *C:\Cygnus*.

To avoid problems create a separate new folder for each of your projects (programs). For simple assembly language exercises each project has a single source file but the tools add other files to the project folder; if separate folders are not used conflicts may arise. To match examples create and use a folder *MyProjects* in *C:\Keil\ARM* so the full path for project folders is *C:\Keil\ARM\MyProjects*.

The installation sets the tools to use a RealView example. Double click the Keil µVision3 icon and select *Project → Rebuild all target files*. Messages in the output window; the lower section of the screen, should end indicating no errors or warnings. Select *Debug → Start/Stop Debug Session* to run the program using the simulator. For the evaluation version indicating *'security key not found'* appears; click *OK*. Select *Debug → Start/Stop Debug Session* and choose further commands to run. Some examples require that other windows are opened (tabs below program window) and may initially require removal of breakpoints. To end simulation stop the program if running by *Debug → Stop running* then *Debug → Start/Stop Debug Session* to return to the main window. Most Keil examples use Atmel or NXP microcontrollers with programs in C. A simple method for assembly language only is suggested later.

E.2 Possible problems

The download sets the package to run an example loaded at start up. There are three different tool sets; the initial example loaded should be one using the RealView tools. If there are problems:-
- Check that the project is from *C:\Keil\ARM\Examples\xxxx* where *xxxx* is replaced by example name. There are examples for each tool set and the paths only differ slightly.
- If the wrong example project is loaded close the project by *Project → Close Project*.
- Next ensure that RealView is in use; select *Project → Manage → Components, Environment and Books*. Under tab *Folders/Extensions* and check *RealView compiler*.
- Use *Projects → Open Project* to find and load *C:\Keil\ARM\Examples\xxxx\xxxx.UV2*.

E.3 Constraints, etc.

The assembler included is the full ARM RealView assembler with minor adjustments to match the Keil tools. For example the directive ENTRY is not always required but causes no problems if present.

Most programs are tested initially using the Keil simulator. This is excellent but it simulates real hardware so must imitate a specific microcontroller selected from the library of models supplied with the tools. Program memory use is restricted because microcontroller designers fix many features; simulator restrictions add further limits. Often memory addresses cannot be set to those used by ARM development systems. Consequently program code, data and stacks cannot be placed in locations used by examples for these systems and such examples require minor modifications to run with the Keil tools.

Keil assume that users will create complete programs for a permanently programmed system. This is reasonable but means that, unlike the ARMulator or Evaluator-7 with built in monitor programs, the correct start-up code is required. However developers can build and test the complete final program including all exception handlers, *etc*. Also most microcontrollers cannot stop running unless power is removed or the clock is stopped; programs that do not run for ever require a mechanism to handle this.

The evaluation version of the tools has several not unreasonable restrictions; the main ones are:

- The size of the code plus constant data (material that is in ROM in a real application) is limited to 16kbytes maximum. For initial exercises this limit is unlikely to be reached.
- The base address used for code and constants is restricted to values of 0xXX000000, 0xXX800000, or 0x00080000. This causes minor difficulties as the address 0x8000 used by many ARM examples and development systems is not one of these.

E.4 Creating a first simple program using the RealView assembler

If after starting μVision3 a project is opened by default close it with *Project → Close Project*. Then select *Project → Manage → Components, Environment, Books*...and the *Folders/Extension* tab; ensure that the box against *Use RealView Compiler* is checked, if not check it and click *OK*. Next create a new project; select *Project → New μVision Project* and change the folder in the *Save in* box to the one created; that is *C:\Keil\ARM\MyProjects* to match these notes. Click the *NewFolder* icon; the icon is a folder with a set of rays coming from the top right corner and is usually two to the right of the *Save in* box. Give the new folder a name identifying your project; for each program you write create a new folder in this way. Double click the folder just created, it becomes the name in the *Save in* box.

Type a name for the project without an extension in the *File name* box and click *Save*; .UV2 is added automatically. A new window requires CPU selection; to match examples expand the tree for *NXP* and select *LPC2102* then click *OK*. When asked if you want to copy start up code click *No*; **this is the opposite choice to that suggested.**

Next select *File → New* which will open a text file. Select *File → Save as* and save the new empty file with a name for your program; **make sure** it has an extension which must be *.s*

At this point select *Project→ Options for Target 'Target 1'* then select tab *Target* if not already selected. The tab has many edit boxes with only seven filled. The values should show Xtal (MHz) 12.0, ARM-Mode, no operating system, IROM1 at 0x0 size 0x4000 and IRAM1 at 0x40000000 size 0x4000 (possibly add a check *NoInit* against *IRAM1*). If there are fewer boxes filled the wrong tools selection was in use when the target was chosen; close this project, set the tools for RealView (as in Section E.2) and create **another** new project; once corrected delete the first unused project folder.

Check the *listing* tab; all options should be checked. List files of assembly language programs have long lines; if you can print in landscape mode set a longer line length, shorter page length and always print list files in landscape mode. Finally select the *Linker* tab; the *R/O base* and *R/W base* should be set at *R/O base* 0 (zero) and *R/W base* 0x40000000; these match the *Start* values in the *IROM1* and *IRAM1* sections under the *Target* tab. These settings cause the linker to put the program components in the correct sections of the microcontroller memory. **There is no warning** if the settings are not correct but when the program is simulated error messages are generated and results are wrong.

In the *Project Workspace* window, usually a narrow column on the left of the screen, expand the tree *Target 1* and right click *Source Group 1* then choose *Add Files to Group 'Source Group 1'*. In the new window change *files of type* to either *Asm source file* or to *All*. Select the file with extension **.s** saved previously and click *Add*. Then close this window (it stays open to allow addition of multiple files). Expand the *Source Group 1* tree to show the files of your project (only one in this instance).

Type the program into the edit window of the source file, the editor accepts cut and paste from other documents if an existing program is available. The program must have at least one CODE section; if it has a DATA section this should be defined by a second AREA directive.

```
; Simple Keil tools demonstration program in file demo.s in project Proj1
; Date:-      14th July 2007
; Revision:-  None
; Author:-    J.R. Gibson

              AREA    Demo1,  CODE,  READONLY   ; the only code module name Demo1
              ENTRY                             ; indicate first instruction

              EXPORT      Reset_Handler
Reset_Handler
mystart       MOV     r3, #25             ; load a first value
              MOV     r7, #204            ; load a second value
              ADD     r2, r3, r7          ; form the sum of the two values
; a never ending loop because the processor continues to fetch instructions
stop          BAL stop
              END                 ; END directive to show nothing more
```

Program E.1 A very simple example

The very simple program *demo.s* listed as Program E.1 is adequate to check that the system is set correctly. The lines with the directive EXPORT and the label *Reset_Handler* are essential in any simple assembly language program that does not use the start up code provided by Keil. They replace the ENTRY directive which is not necessary but is ignored if present and indicate where the program starts. The lines at the end using SWI for ARM systems are replaced by the single never ending loop at the label *stop*. The Keil tools assume the program is a complete free standing one that will never stop running until deliberately stopped by the using the tools *Stop Running* command. To prevent the program executing the random values in memory after the instruction codes a never ending loop is been placed at the end.

Once the program has been input it can be assembled by selecting *Project → Build target* or *Project → Rebuild all target files*; the second version is provided for programs with many source files and forces all files to be processed, not just the one currently selected. Provided there are no typing errors the following sequence of messages will appear in the output window.

```
Build target 'Target 1'
assembling demo.s...
linking...
Program Size: Code=16 RO-data=0 RW-data=0 ZI-data=0
"proj1.axf" - 0 Error(s), 0 Warning(s).
```

Provided that the listing controls were set as suggested a detailed listing file is produced as *C:\Keil\ARM\MyProjects\proj1\demo.lst*

To run the program on the simulator select *Debug → Start/Stop Debug Session*. For evaluation tools a message indicating *'security key not found'* appears; click *OK* to continue. This program is so simple that the only way to examine it is by executing one instruction at a time. Initially two suitable commands are available, *Debug → Step* and *Debug → Step Over*, they are used frequently so they have icons on the toolbar. Users familiar with other development systems may prefer to regard *Debug → Step* as *Debug → Step Into*. Step executes one instruction each time it is used; if the instruction is a subroutine call the system steps into the routine showing execution of the subroutine instructions. Step over behaves as step for normal instructions but for a subroutine call the complete subroutine is executed without any details of each execution step being displayed. That is execution runs until the instruction immediately after the subroutine call.

When running the simulator the project window shows the register contents in the project workspace. If this is not displayed click its icon on the toolbar to cause it to appear; if necessary select the register tab at the bottom of the workspace to change to register display. Other windows can be added to show memory contents, disassembly, and other features. For those familiar with ARM development systems the CPSR and SPSR registers are shown in different manner; expand the tree for each of them to see details of their contents.

Single step through the program using the register contents display to see the effects of executing each instruction. For larger programs there are additional execution commands; for example to **run at full speed.** Breakpoints can be inserted in the program and when it is run at full speed it will stop at any breakpoint it reaches allowing registers and memory to be inspected; the program run can be continued at full speed or in single step mode. These features assist in finding faults in programs. Another aid is the trace facility, if tracing is enabled a record is kept of the most recent instructions executed and the file holding the record can be examined to determine the route the program followed.

To return from debug mode to the program development mode ensure any running program is stopped by *Debug → Stop running* (this command is only available if a program is running); select *Debug → Start/Stop Debug Session* to return to the programming environment. **Note** that if you do not stop a running program any selection of *Start/Stop Debug Session* to end debugging will be ignored and no message will be given that this has happened.

E.5 Start up code

The simulator or a Keil target board assume that a complete microcontroller program will be prepared. Therefore there must be an appropriate instruction at the reset address (0x00000000) and in some cases the vector table at addresses which immediately follow must be set correctly. Also most microcontrollers include hardware features such as input and output ports, serial communications devices, *etc.*, on the same integrated circuit as the CPU. The usual methods of controlling and using these extra features are by writing to and reading from special function registers, SFRs. Unfortunately every different type of microcontroller has its own unique set of SFRs that require their own setting that must be determined from the device data. Usually the initial section of code for a microcontroller sets contents of some SFRs so that the extra hardware behaves as required for the application.

Keil provide start up code for each microcontroller, Section E.7. At the stage when a particular device is selected, for example *LPC2102*, the system asks if it should copy start up code. If *Yes* is selected an extra file *startup.s* is added to the project. This is usually quite a complicated file but can be useful as it will correctly set values in many of the SFRs for the particular microcontroller.

For simple use the start up file is not required; Program E.1 will run with no problems but it is better to set the simulator to more closely follow a complete program. Instead of the simple form of Program E.1 include all lines of Program E.2 between the AREA directive line and the line with the ENTRY directive of example programs in the main text.

```
              LDR     pc, Reset_Addr  ; load reset handler address
; the next line is not essential but it leaves room for addition of the other
; vectors when extending this framework to a full version start up code
              SPACE   0x1c            ; remove when vectors added here
; Full start up has a table of all exception handlers here, not only one

Reset_Addr  DCD     Reset_Handler
              SPACE   0xdc            ; not essential but sets main program code
                                      ; to start at 0x100 which is easy to find

              EXPORT  Reset_Handler
Reset_Handler                         ; a label at the ENTRY point
; Set stack pointers for all used modes and change to user mode
```

Program E.2 Simple start up program sequence

The `LDR PC, Reset_Addr` instruction is not the pseudo instruction but is the preferred method of writing `MOV pc, [pc, #offset]`. The assembler creates an instruction to load PC with the value stored at the address which has the label *Reset_Addr*. Hardware and software initialisation tasks follow the label *Reset_Handler*; usually the final task sets the mode so the main program runs in user mode. For very simple programs without exception handlers the change to user mode is not essential.

E.6 Memory and related matters

The selection of a particular microcontroller determines the addresses for ROM and for RAM. The linker settings must match those for the microcontroller selected; it will place program code and constant data in ROM starting at the R/O base address given in the linker settings. Any data sections will be placed in the RAM starting at the R/W base address. In general if there are multiple AREA statements, for example when a project has several source files, the linker places them in successive memory locations without space between them. It places them in the order found; usually the file order in the source group window. If required the programmer can specify the order in which sections of code and data are placed in memory.

For all but the most trivial task a program will call subroutines. Consequently the program must **set the stack pointer** to point at a usable area of RAM. The normal place to put this when using a stack in the full descending mode is at the address one above the highest address of the RAM available. Hence for the *LPC2102* with the 0x1000 bytes of RAM starting at 0x40000000 the instruction

```
LDR   sp, = 0x40001000      ; initialise stack
```

should follow the ENTRY directive. For other microcontrollers a different address is required.

If your program requires the use of RAM for data then for the *LPC2102* with these memory settings use 0x40000000 upwards but do not use so many locations that your program affects the stack.

E.7 Other features

The Keil tools are very powerful and can simulate many of the peripheral devices built in to a microcontroller; for example the UART or USART of most devices may be used to provide a serial communication link between the microcontroller and a window that makes the PC simulate a terminal. The tools also allow programs to be built that combine a mixture of assembly language, C and C++.

It is often convenient to include the complete start up code supplied by Keil in the file *startup.s* which is added to the project when the option to include it is selected. Your own program should be in a separate file; if you write it in C it will link correctly to the start up code. If your program is in assembly language **DO NOT INCLUDE** the extra lines of Program E.2; instead put a label __main (two underscore characters followed by the text main) after the AREA statement and before the first instruction. The label __main should be exported by the line

    EXPORT   *__main*

This is required so that the linker can correctly combine the start up code (*startup.s* includes *Reset_Handler*) and your program. Using two underscore characters is a common method of naming program features included by tools packages; it is assumed that the programmer using the tools will not create labels starting with two underscores. For projects in which all source files are in assembly language *startup.s* will set the stack pointers for all modes so a further LDR sp instruction is not required.

The file *startup.s* is for programs written in the C language; to use with a program that is assembly language only it must be modified. Find the line near the end of *startup.s* with the instruction BX   R0; keep this line but remove all those that follow **except** the final END directive. For many microcontrollers removal of these lines is also necessary because they add a feature that requires further code and the linker will generate an error message if the lines are not removed.

Another feature of the simulator that may surprise users arises because several ARM instructions have more than one mnemonic; for example STMFD and STMDB both describe the same instruction. When disassembly is shown by the simulator it may produce either mnemonic so the disassembly mnemonics may not be identical to those used in the original program. Similarly when pseudo mnemonics are used in the source program the disassembly will show the mnemonic for the actual instruction used instead of the pseudo instruction.

Programmers familiar with the ADS assembler may find some new mnemonics in the disassembly listing and new duplicate names; a list is in Section 2.11 of the RealView Assembler Guide [15].

E.8 Using simulated peripherals in assembly language programs

The simulated peripherals are very powerful but setting them up can be difficult. The following is a quick method for some simple peripherals using the Keil *startup.s* file for one particular microcontroller. In addition to setting up CPU features the start up file includes a large number of commands for the Keil Configuration Wizard to set up the simulated clock, memory and other items. Only make the alterations described and no others to *startup.s*. The example sets a simple serial link for one microcontroller so the PC behaves as a terminal with the PC keyboard used to provide input to the ARM program with an extra window as a display.

The microcontroller selected is the NXP LPC2102. Start a new project in the usual way. When asked if you wish to include start up code answer *Yes*; the file *startup.s* is added to the project. As in Section E.6 delete all lines after `BX R0` except the final END directive. Choose *Project→ Options for Target 'Target 1'* and make the same settings under the *Target* and *Linker* tabs as in Section E.3.

Program E.3 at the end of this Appendix (because it is long) is an example that shows how to set up UART0 and UART1 on the LPC2102 microcontroller provided *startup.s* is included in the project. It also provides subroutines to input the key code value when one key of the PC is pressed and displays one character in a window on the PC. Finally it shows very simple simulation of parallel port output.

To use the serial input and output you must open window *UART #0* by selecting *View → Serial Window → UART #0* and window *UART #1* by selecting *View → Serial Window → UART #1* as soon as you select *Start/Stop debug sessions* for the first time.

One peculiarity, a feature of Windows not the Keil tools, is that whenever a simulated ARM program outputs a character it appears in the window *UART #0* or *UART #1* immediately but the keyboard only works as an input for the relevant UART when the window is active. That is you must click anywhere on a *UART #X* window so the title bar at the top changes to the colour of the active window.

Program E.3 also shows very simple simulation of an output port. Select *Peripherals → GPIO → Slow GPIO* to obtain a window showing the logic levels in certain SFRs and at the output pins (background greyed because these are actual pins not SFRs). A check in the box indicates that the bit is at logic 1, no check indicates logic 0. Other options under *Peripherals* allow the values of other SFRs to be inspected; for example there are windows to show the SFRs of UART0 and UART1.

Note that with the settings made the ROM holding the program starts at address zero and if these instructions are followed exactly the label __main is at address 0x0110. The RAM is at address 0x40000000 and although *startup.s* sets the stack the program changes it to the RAM top at 0x40001000.

E.9 The GNU tools

The Keil tools download includes the examples provided for RealView modified for GNU. Check that one example works before attempting to develop your own programs. The GNU tools are not restricted to programs with a maximum size of 16k bytes as they are supplied by the Free Software Foundation; see their Internet site for license conditions.

After starting µVision3 close any project currently open with *Project → Close Project* then select *Project → Manager → Components, Environment, Books...* to set the tools for GNU. Under *Select ARM Development Tools* the box against *Use GNU Compiler* should be checked. The *GNU-TOOL-Prefix* should be set as *arm-uclibc-* and the *Cygnus Folder* should be *C:\Cygnus*. Click *OK* to close the window. Note that changing after starting a project and selecting the processor results in inclusion of the wrong start up code and an incorrect processor model.

Load an example from *C:\Keil\ARM\GNU\Examples* and as for the RealView tools select *Project → Rebuild all target files* to create the program code. Messages concerning success or otherwise appear in the output window and should indicate no errors or warnings for example programs. Select *Debug → Start/Stop Debug Session* to run the program in the simulator exactly as for the RealView example. After running select *Project* → *Close project* to remove the example and to prepare to start developing your own programs.

To create programs with the GNU tools proceed as for use of the RealView tools. Perform all set up tasks as in *Section E.3*. In *Options for Target 'Target 1'* the window showing the target settings **will not** be the same as when using the RealView tools; very few details will be shown. Most details are set using the linker which is not set in the same manner as for RealView. For the LPC2102 set the linker selections as *Text Start* to 0x0 and *Data Start* to 0x40000000. Also the default listing settings are usually set so no listing is produced; change using the *Listing* tab to produce listings.

Because the GNU assembler is general purpose it can be set to operate in a very simple manner; the example here is created so that the linker has to do very little as the assembler may be instructed to produce code at a fixed address. Once the settings have been made and the source file created put the test of Program E.4 into the source file, assemble it and run it.

```
# Simple example program in file demo.s in project GNU1
# Date:-      15th July 2007
# Revision:-  revised for GNU tools
# Author:-    J.R. Gibson
# Performs simple addition to illustrate Keil tools


        .arm                        /* not essential but a useful reminder */
        .org    0x0
        MOV     r3, #25     /* load a first value */
        MoV     r7, #204    /* load a second value    */
        ADD     r2, r3, r7  /* form the sum of the two values */
# a never ending loop because the processor continues to fetch instructions
    Stop:   BAL Stop
        .EnD                        /* demonstrates that mixed case is allowed */
```

Program E.4. A very simple example using the GNU assembler

Note the large number of syntax differences between the ARM assembler and the GNU assembler, a brief outline is in Appendix F. Also note that it is not necessary to inform the tools of the program start position with an exported label.

E.10 Program E.3, an example to illustrate simulated peripherals

Although still small compared to real applications this program is much longer than previous examples. To preserve layout the program starts on the next page, to reduce length subroutines that are almost identical are not listed.

```
; File  IO_demo.s to demonstrate peripheral simulation in project IO_Sim

; Example uses simulated serial IO and a simple output port, actions are:-

; First:-  UART0 outputs character > to Serial#1 then get user keyboard input.
;          Values typed are reflected. Type * to end using UART0, < is shown.
; Second:- Repeats whole sequence using UART1 to Serial#2
; Third:-  Sends simple counter display to GPIO port for ever
; Subroutines are in the main file after the end of the main program. LDM/STM
; are used although a simple method could be used for these routines
; Date:-   15th July 2007
; Author:-   J.R. Gibson


; *** Define device SFR addresses and some patterns for simple tasks only ***
PINSEL0     EQU     0xE002C000      ; controls function of IO pins
IOPIN       EQU     0xE0028000      ; IO actual output register address
off_DIR     EQU     0x8             ; offset of IODIR (pin direction reg)
En_RxTx0    EQU     0x5             ; sets P0.0 as Tx0 and P0.1 as Rx0
En_RxTx1    EQU     0x50000         ; sets P0.8 as Tx1 and P0.9 as Rx1
U0_bas      EQU     0xE000C000      ; UART0 base, also buffers & a ctrl reg
U1_bas      EQU     0xE0010000      ; UART1 base, also buffers & a ctrl reg
Off_LCR     EQU     0x0C            ; line control offset from base
Off_LSR     EQU     0x14            ; line status register offset from base
S_fmt       EQU     0x83            ; for 8 bits, no Parity, 1 Stop bit
S_fmt2      EQU     0x3             ; keep format but set control DLAB = 0
Speed       EQU     97              ; to set 9600 Baud @ 15MHz VPB Clock


            AREA    Serial, CODE, READONLY    ; the only code module
            ENTRY                       ; indicate first instruction

            EXPORT    __main            ; startup.s will branch to here

__main      ; NOTE - user mode and sp have already been set by startup.s


            BL      set_U0          ; set up all SFRs for USART0 operation
            BL      set_U1          ; set up all SFRs for USART1 operation


            ; *** sequence to demonstrate UART0 on Serial#1
            MOV     r0, #'>'        ; load ASCII code of > ...
            BL      Char_Out0       ; ...and display on Serial#1
next_ch0    BL      Char_In0        ; get serial input from Serial#1
            MOV     r4, r0          ; put in safe place (BPCS used)
            BL      Char_Out0       ; echo input to display on Serial#1
            CMP     r4, #'*'        ; check if input was *
            BNE     next_ch0        ; repeat loop unless input was *
            MOV     r0, #'<'        ; load ASCII code of < ...
            BL      Char_Out0       ; ...and display on Serial#1
```

```
                   ; *** sequence to demonstrate UART1 on Serial#2
                   MOV    r0, #'>'           ; load ASCII code of > ...
                   BL     Char_Out1         ; ...and display on Serial#2
next_ch1           BL     Char_In1          ; get serial input from Serial#2
                   MOV    r4, r0            ; put in safe place (BPCS used)
                   BL     Char_Out1         ; echo input to display on Serial#2
                   CMP    r4, #'*'          ; check if input was *
                   BNE    next_ch1          ; repeat loop unless input was *
                   MOV    r0, #'<'          ; load ASCII code of < ...
                   BL     Char_Out1         ; ...and display on Serial#2
                   ; reset PINSEL0 occurs before UART output completes so add delay
                   LDR    r2, =0x8000       ; simple delay count value
delay              SUBS   r2, r2, #1        ; count down delay
                   BNE    delay             ; loop until counted down delay

                   ; *** next demonstrate simple parallel output
                   LDR    r1, =PINSEL0      ; point to pin control register
                   MOV    r0, #0            ; set P0.0 to P0.15 as general IO. . .
                   STR    r0, [r1]          ; . . .GPIO pins (UART settings lost)
                   LDR    r1, =IOPIN        ; point to IOPIN
                   LDR    r0, =0xffff       ; set P0.0 to P0.15 as outputs. . .
                   STR    r0, [r1, #off_DIR] ; . . . using IODIR register
                   MOV    r0, #0            ; initial output value
lp1                STR    r0, [r1]          ; send to output pins
                   ADD    r0, r0, #1        ; increment output value
                   LDR    r2, =0x8000       ; simple delay count value
lp2                SUBS   r2, r2, #1        ; count down delay
                   BNE    lp2               ; loop until counted down delay
                   B      lp1               ; loop to do next output
; program loops for ever so no ending required

; Set up all the SFRs for UART0 requirements only
; Corrupts r0, r1 and r2 as allowed by the BPCS
; Inputs:-  none
; Outputs:- none
set_U0             STMFD  sp!, {lr}         ; not strictly needed but be consistent
                   LDR    r2, =En_RxTx0     ; pattern to enable RxD0 and TxD0
                   LDR    r1, =PINSEL0      ; point to pin control register
                   LDR    r0, [r1]          ; get existing pin control pattern
                   ORR    r0, r0, r2        ; mask in enable Tx0 and Rx0
                   STR    r0, [r1]          ; set pins as Tx0 and Rx0
                   LDR    r1, =U0_bas       ; UART base address
                   MOV    r0, #S_fmt        ; for 8 bits, no Parity, 1 Stop bit
                   STRB   r0, [r1, #Off_LCR] ; set format in LCR
                   MOV    r0, #97           ; for 9600 Baud Rate @ 15MHz VPB Clock
                   STRB   r0, [r1]          ; set baud rate
                   MOV    r0, #S_fmt2       ; set DLAB = 0 so addresses are . . .
                   STRB   r0, [r1, #Off_LCR] ; . . .now TX/RX buffers
                   LDMFD  sp!, {pc}         ; return (could use MOV pc,lr)
```

```
; Output one character using serial port 0
; Corrupts r1 and r2 as allowed by the BPCS
; Inputs:-  character code for transmission in r0
; Outputs:- none


Char_Out0   STMFD   sp!, {lr}         ; not strictly needed here
            LDR     r1, =U0_bas       ; UART base address
wt_rdy0     LDRB    r2, [r1, #Off_LSR] ; get UART status
            TST     r2, #0x20         ; check for transmit buffer empty
            BEQ     wt_rdy0           ; loop until TX buffer empty
            AND     r0, r0, #0xFF     ; ensure callee has only set byte value
            STRB    r0, [r1]          ; load transmit buffer
            LDMFD   sp!, {pc}         ; return (could use MOV pc,lr)


; Wait for input of one character at serial port 0 then read it
; Corrupts r0, r1 and r2 as allowed by the BPCS
; Inputs:-  none
; Outputs:- received character code in r0


Char_In0    STMFD   sp!, {lr}         ; not strictly needed here
            LDR     r1, =U0_bas       ; UART base address
wt_rcd0     LDRB    r2, [r1, #Off_LSR] ; get UART status
            TST     r2, #0x1          ; check if receive buffer has something
            BEQ     wt_rcd0           ; loop until RX buffer has value
            LDRB    r0, [r1]          ; get received value
            LDMFD   sp!, {pc}         ; could use MOV pc,lr


; Subroutines set_U1, Char_Out1 and Char_In1 only differ in that values for
; UART1 are used instead of for UART0 so the routines are not listed. To
; create them copy set_U0, Char_Out0 and Char_In0. Rename the copies changing
; all names, values, etc., relating to UART0 to values for UART1, for example
; Char_In1 starts
Char_In1    STMFD   sp!, {lr}         ; not strictly needed here
            LDR     r1, =U1_bas       ; UART base address
wt_rcd1     LDRB    r2, [r1, #Off_LSR] ; get UART status
            TST     r2, #0x1          ; check if receive buffer has something
            BEQ     wt_rcd1           ; loop until RX buffer has value



            END
```

Program E.3 Use of the simulated peripherals

Appendix F
Comments on using the GNU assembler

The GNU assembler configured for ARM processors may be downloaded from several Internet sites and is often supplied with small low cost development systems. It is straightforward to set GNU tools to perform simple assembly tasks but configuration to download code to a target, to run debug tools and simulators is sometimes difficult. The Keil evaluation tools can be used with GNU and the download for this is described in Appendix E; the combined packages work immediately with few problems.

GNU tools are written in a generic form allowing the same tools to be used to prepare programs for many different CPUs; over forty are supported at the present time. As a result many assembly language features are common to all the GNU tools and differ from those of tools from ARM Holdings. The main feature of the GNU tools that will cause some difficulty for the reader of this book is that the GNU syntax rules and directives differ significantly from the standard ARM assemblers. Full details of the assembler are in the rather complex documentation provided.

F.1 General syntax

The GNU tools do not use the syntax rules for assembly language that have been described in this book; one reason is that they can be configured for any CPU so must allow the mnemonics, registers and similar features of any processor to be used. The assembler cannot assume that any group of letters it uses for a directive or other quantity will not be that of a mnemonic or other feature of a particular CPU.

As for all software packages the rules for use of upper and lower case letters are very important. For the GNU assembler user names such as labels, those defined by equate statements, *etc.*, are case sensitive. That is the user name *'Abc'* is not the same as *'abc'* or *'aBC'* or any other combinations of case; this is the same as for ARM assemblers. However for mnemonics, directives and register names the GNU assembler is not case sensitive. For example the mnemonic MOV may be written as Mov, mOv, MOv or any other combination. Examples in GNU manuals tend to be written in lower case as GNU tools are often used with the LINUX operating system by programmers who tend to work entirely in lower case.

F.2 Comments and labels

There are two methods of including comments in GNU assembly language; both require more care in use than those for ADS and RealView. Any line starting with the # character at the first position on the line is entirely a comment; there must not be any spaces before the # character.

The other form of comment precedes the comment with the two characters /* with no space between them. This is not restricted to starting at any position on a line nor to a single line. All text after the character pair /* is a comment until the closing pair */ is found. This is a very useful form but a minor typing error such as one of the characters being mis-typed or a space between the characters can result in a large number of errors being reported or in a section of program being removed as it has become a comment..

The rules for user names, such as labels, introduced in Chapter 4 should be followed when using the GNU assembler. Additional characters are allowed in user names but to avoid problems follow rules that are common to as many systems as possible; this makes it relatively easy to transfer software from one system to another and reduces the risk of errors when a programmer uses several systems.

A major difference of the GNU assembler compared with the ARM ones is that when a user name is defined in the label field, **but not when used as an operand**, it must be followed by a colon with no spaces between the last character of the label and the colon. It is no longer essential that the first character of the label is in the first column of a line although it is usual to put it there as the program has a clear layout. The colon removes the problem of an error if there is space before a label. However if the programmer forgets to type the colon this produces obscure error messages because the assembler considers the label to be a mnemonic and any mnemonic following to be an operand.

F.3 Directives

The GNU assembler does not use the same directives as ARM Holdings and in addition all directives **must have** a full stop immediately before the directive name. The full stop solves a problem for any general purpose assembler; it is possible that a CPU manufacturer may select a mnemonic name that is the same as one selected for a directive. The full stop allows a mnemonic and a directive to have the same name.

For most tasks the GNU assembler has directives to perform the same function as the ARM directive, Table F.1 lists the important ARM directives with their GNU equivalents and some comments. Examples in Programs E.4 (earlier) and F.1 illustrate most common GNU directives.

ARM ADS/RealView	GNU Assembler
AREA used with parameters	Simple programs may use .ORG followed by an address, most use .TEXT and .DATA with or without parameters.
ASSERT followed by test	Similar actions can be performed but in a different manner.
DCB {*parameter list*} DCW { *parameter list* } DCD { *parameter list* }	.BYTE { *parameter list* } .HWORD { *parameter list* } .WORD { *parameter list* }
name EQU *expression*	.EQU *name, expression*
END	.END
ENTRY	No equivalent, not required
EXPORT *symbol* or GLOBAL *symbol*	.GLOBAL *symbol*
EXTERN *symbol* or IMPORT *symbol*	.EXTERN *symbol*
INCLUDE filename	.INCLUDE "*filename*"
LTORG	.LTORG
MACRO, MEND	.MACRO and .MEND Structure and use differs significantly.
SPACE *size*	.SPACE *size, fill*

Table F.1 Comparison of common GNU and ARM directives

Two types of directive differ significantly in use and syntax between GNU and ARM. These are the defining directives such as equate, and the program section heading directives such as AREA in ARM systems. There are also large differences in the definition and use of macros and in the syntax for conditional assembly. The ARM syntax for an equate statement is

```
name           EQU          expression evaluated to value
```

whereas the GNU version is

```
               .EQU          name, expression evaluated to value
```

The AREA directive with parameters is replaced by selection of one of several different methods of defining the program structure; these generally require the use of one or more of the directives .ORG, .TEXT and .DATA. Simple forms are illustrated in Programs E.4 and F.1.

F.4 GNU programs and the Keil simulator

There are two main methods of constructing GNU assembly language programs to run on the Keil simulator; one assumes that the program is modular and put together by the GNU linker. A simple alternative is that all the information about how the code and data fits into memory is included in the assembly language using the origin directive. The second form uses .ORG as in Program E.4 which is Program 4.3 modified for the GNU assembler. The code section starts at address zero although this is not generally correct as the exception vectors should be here; as they are not required by such a trivial program it will behave correctly using the simulator. Program E.4 does not require a global label or and ENTRY directive in order to run on the simulator. To run it on a target development system download tools are required; these are usually provided with the target system and tend to be unique for each manufacturer.

In general the .ORG directive is not used in the absolute form of Program E.4 except for some embedded applications. Most programs are divided into text (code) and data sections as in Program F.1 which is Program E.4 modified with the origin directive replaced by the directive .TEXT. The .DATA directive shows how to create a data section; although not used in the example it is necessary when *startup.s* is included to prevent a link error. The text section has label *_start* before the first instruction and label *_data* before the first data item. These are exported so that *startup.s* links correctly. In most cases the file *startup.s* will not require any modifications if the program file is prepared as in this example.

```
# Simple example program in file demo2.s in project GNU2
# Date:-      16th July 2007
# Revision:-  revised to have more general form
# Author:-    J.R. Gibson
# Performs simple addition to illustrate Keil tools
            .ARM                        /* not essential but a useful reminder */
            .TEXT
            .GLOBAL _start
_start:     MOV     r3, #25      /* load a first value */
            MOV     r7, #204     /* load a second value    */
            ADD     r2, r3, r7   /* form the sum of the two values */
# a never ending loop because the processor continues to fetch instructions
    Stop:   BAL     Stop
            .DATA
            .GLOBAL _data
_data:
            .END
```

Program F.1 Modification of Program E.4 to more general form

References and further reading

This is not a comprehensive review; it is a starting point for further investigation of many topics and a source of technical information. Unfortunately some technical material is only available from Internet sites and there is a tendency for the owners of internet sites to rebuild them; the modifications may alter references to particular items. Internet links are correct at the time of writing.

References in the text

1. S. Furber S. *ARM System-on-chip Architecture (2nd ed)* Addison-Wesley 2000 ISBN 0-201-67519-6

2. A.W. Burks, H.H. Goldstein and J von Neuman *Preliminary description of the logic design of an electronic computing instrument.* US Army Ordinance Report 1946
    This is reproduced in Volume V pages 34-79 of
    Taub, A. H. (ed) *John von Neumann: Collected Works*, 1903-1957
    UK publisher Pergamon Press, Oxford 1961-63; USA publisher Macmillan, New York 1963

3. Royal Academy of Engineering and the British Computer Society *The Challenges of Complex IT Projects*
    The Royal Academy of Engineering 2004 ISBN 1-903496-15-2
    Available at http://www.raeng.org.uk/news/publications/list/reports/Complex_IT_Projects.pdf

4. U.S. Department of Commerce *The economic impacts of inadequate structure for software testing* U.S. Department of Commerce RTI Project Number 7007.011 2002
    Available at http://www.nist.gov/director/prog-ofc/report02-3.pdf

5. I. Sommerville *Software Engineering (6th ed)* Addison-Wesley 2000 ISBN 978-0-201-39815-1

6. R.S. Pressman *Software Engineering : A Beginners Guide* McGraw-Hill 1988 ISBN 978-0-0705079-06

7. J. Robinson *Software Design For Engineers And Scientists* Newnes 2004 ISBN: 0-7506-6080-5

8. IEEE 754-1985 Standard for Binary Floating-Point Arithmetic 1985 ISBN 0-7381-1165-1

9. E.W. Djikstra *The E. W. Dijkstra Archive : the manuscripts of Edsger W. Dijkstra* 1930–2002
    http://www.cs.utexas.edu/users/EWD/

10. IEC 61508 *Functional safety of electrical/electronic/programmable electronic safety-related systems* 2005
    An introductory brochure is available at http://www.iec.ch/zone/fsafety/pdf_safe/brochure.pdf

11. B. Wichmann, G.Parkin and R. Barker *Software Support for Metrology Best Practice Guide No. 1: Validation of Software in Measurement Systems* NPL (UK) HMSO 2004 ISSN 1471-4124
    Available from link on http://www.npl.co.uk/ssfm/download/#ssfmbpg1

12. D. Seal *ARM Architecture Reference Manual (2nd ed)* Addison-Wesley 2000 ISBN 978- 0-201-73719-6

13. A.N. Shloss, D. Symes and C. Wright *ARM System Developers Guide: Designing and Optimizing System Software* Morgan Kaufman, 2004 ISBN 978-1-55860-874-0

14. ARM Architecture Procedure Call Standard (see ARM documents, next page)

15. RealView Compilation Tools (v2.2), Assembler Guide (see ARM documents, next page)

ARM documents

Search either http://www.arm.com/documentation/ or at http://www.arm.com/community/academy/university.html if the links fail. The Keil tools and related information are at http://www.keil.com/demo/

ARM Developer Suite version 1.2 Assembler Guide   DUI 0068B
  http://www.arm.com/pdfs/DUI0068B_ADS1_2_Assembler.pdf
RealView Compilation Tools Assembler Guide (v2.2)   DUI 0204F
  http://www.arm.com/pdfs/DUI0204F_rvct_assembler_guide.pdf
ARM7TDMI (Rev 4) Technical Reference Manual   DDI 0210B
  http://www.arm.com/pdfs/DDI0210B_7TDMI_R4.pdf
Procedure Call Standard for the ARM Architecture   GENC-003534 v2.05
  http://www.arm.com/pdfs/aapcs.pdf
A list of error numbers, *etc.*, produced by ADS and RealView tools are at
  http://www.arm.com/support/ADS_Errors_and_Warnings.pdf
  http://www.arm.com/support/RVCT22_Errors_and_Warnings.pdf
ARM Laboratory Exercises For the ARM Evaluator-7T Board and the OKI ML67Q4000   DGI 0011A
  http://www.arm.com/miscPDFs/4718.pdf

Logic circuits

J.R. Gibson   *Electronic Logic Circuits (3rd ed)*   Butterworth 1992   ISBN 978-0-340-54377-1

F.P. Prosser, D.E. Winkle   *The Art of Digital Design (2nd ed)*   Prentice-Hall 1987 ISBN 0-130466735

C.H. Roth   *Fundamentals of Logic Design (5th ed)*   Thomson 2004 ISBN 0-534378048

Computer hardware, arithmetic, *etc.*

A. Clements   *The Principles of Computer Hardware (3rd ed)*   OUP 2000   ISBN 0-198564538

H.C. Cragon   *Computer Architecture and Implementation*   CUP 2000 ISBN 0-521-65168-9

M.D. Ercegovac, T. Lang   *Digital Arithmetic*   Morgan Kaufmann 2003 ISBN 978-1-55860-798-9

M.J. Flynn, S.F. Oberman   *Advanced Computer Arithmetic Design*   Wiley 2001 ISBN 0-471-412090

S. Furber.   *ARM System-on-chip Architecture (2nd ed)*   Addison-Wesley 2000   ISBN 0-201-67519-6

I. Koren   *Computer Arithmetic Algorithms (2nd ed)*   (A.K.Peters 2001)

B. Parhami   *Computer Arithmetic: Algorithms and Hardware Designs*   OUP 2000 ISBN 0-19-512583-5

A.S. Tanenbaum   *Structured Computer Organisation (5th ed)* Prentice-Hall 2006 ISBN 978-0-131485211

Software design/engineering

Also see main text references [5, 6 and 7].

D. Galin   *Software Quality Assurance: From Theory to Implementation*   Addison-Wesley 2004
  ISBN 0-201-70945-7

R.S. Pressman   *Software Engineering : A Practitioners Approach (6th ed)*   McGraw-Hill 2005
  ISBN 978-00730193

N. Storey   *Safety-Critical Computer Systems*   Addison-Wesley 1996 ISBN 0-201-42787-7

Index

Not all mnemonics, directives and similar quantities are included in the index. Only those that have been described in detail are listed; a full list of instruction mnemonics is in the ARM Architecture Reference Manual [12]. Lists of assembler directives are in the manuals for each assembler.

LaVergne, TN USA
28 July 2010
191229LV00002B/5/A